EPORTFOLIOS FOR LIFELONG LEARNING AND ASSESSMENT

EPORTFOLIOS FOR LIFELONG LEARNING AND ASSESSMENT

Darren Cambridge

JOSSEY-BASS
A Wiley Imprint
www.josseybass.com

Published by Jossey-Bass
A Wiley Imprint
989 Market Street, San Francisco, CA 94103-1741—www.josseybass.com

Readers should be aware that Internet Web sites offered as citations and/or sources for further information may have changed or disappeared between the time this was written and when it is read.

Limit of Liability/Disclaimer of Warranty: While the publisher and author have used their best efforts in preparing this book, they make no representations or warranties with respect to the accuracy or completeness of the contents of this book and specifically disclaim any implied warranties of merchantability or fitness for a particular purpose. No warranty may be created or extended by sales representatives or written sales materials. The advice and strategies contained herein may not be suitable for your situation. You should consult with a professional where appropriate. Neither the publisher nor author shall be liable for any loss of profit or any other commercial damages, including but not limited to special, incidental, consequential, or other damages.

Jossey-Bass books and products are available through most bookstores. To contact Jossey-Bass directly call our Customer Care Department within the U.S. at 800-956-7739, outside the U.S. at 317-572-3986, or fax 317-572-4002.

Jossey-Bass also publishes its books in a variety of electronic formats. Some content that appears in print may not be available in electronic books.

Library of Congress Cataloging-in-Publication Data

Cambridge, Darren, 1974-
  Eportfolios for lifelong learning and assessment / Darren Cambridge.
    p. cm.
  Includes bibliographical references and index.
  ISBN 978-0-470-50376-8; ISBN 978-0-470-90127-4 (ebk); ISBN 978-0-470-90128-1 (ebk);
ISBN 978-0-470-90129-8 (ebk)
    1. Electronic portfolios in education.   2. College students—Rating of—United States.   3. Education, Higher—United States—Evaluation.   I. Title.
  LB1029.P67C36   2010
  378.1'66—dc22

                                                                    2010025092

Printed in the United States of America

FIRST EDITION

HB Printing   10 9 8 7 6 5 4 3 2 1

The Jossey-Bass
Higher and Adult Education Series

To my mother, Barbara Cambridge, consummate lifelong learner, collaborator, teacher, and friend

CONTENTS

PART THREE: EPORTFOLIOS FOR LIFELONG LEARNING

PREFACE

Lifelong learning is an ongoing process of developing knowledge, skills, and strategies; putting capabilities and self-understanding into action over time; and thereby establishing an identity. To support lifelong learning, higher education needs to look beyond the content knowledge, practical techniques, and professional capabilities that have been its primary focus. Colleges and universities need to commit to helping students craft identities that reflect their own values and equip students to put that self-understanding to work in their communities and the rest of the world. To be meaningful lifelong learners, individuals need to take ownership of their thought and let it guide their action. A major purpose of education is enabling individuals to have agency in the world through their evolving understanding of themselves, their capabilities, and their connections to others.

Addressing this broader conception of the goal of education means considering questions such as: What kinds of people should we be, and how do we find out? How are agency and power to be balanced between individuals and institutions in making decisions in a democratic society? Eportfolios provide a lens for examining these questions and a means to put the answers into practice. As a way to reflect on and articulate identity, eportfolios can guide and reinforce cultural ideals about identity and social participation. As a way to communicate self-understanding in order to make an argument to institutional authorities—for example, "I'm ready to graduate from high school," "Here's what I think it means to be an excellent teacher," "You should hire me as your graphic designer"—eportfolios reflect dynamics of power. The negotiations of which this communication is a part may in turn shape how that balance of power operates in the future in colleges and universities and in the other institutions in which individuals participate throughout their personal, professional, and civic lives.

This books shows that eportfolios are of increasing importance to higher education and that they are proving valuable to individuals outside formal educational contexts as well. Because eportfolios are only one element in a larger set of identity-shaping experiences and interactions with institutions, however, it is important to examine them in a larger framework of cultural ideals that underlie existing practice and might guide practice into the future.

This book's first three chapters consider three such ideals: authenticity, integrity, and deliberation. The argument for these ideals engages in what philosopher Charles Taylor (1991) calls a "work of retrieval" (p. 22). According to Taylor, a promising strategy for addressing pressing ethical challenges is to look for the cultural ideals that underlie the ways people already act and try to articulate them more clearly: "Articulacy here has a moral point, not just in correcting what may be wrong views but also in making the force of the ideal that people are already living be more palpable, more vivid for them; and by making it more vivid, empowering them to live up to it in a fuller and more integral fashion" (p. 22).

The opening chapters examine model learners and educators who are "already living" through how they compose, facilitate the composition of, respond to, and assess eportfolios and suggest ways they might live up to those ideals more fully.

One serious consequence of failing to understand the ideals in practice is a misguided bifurcation of individual learning, advancement, and self-actualization, on the one hand, and, on the other hand, programmatic and institutional assessment and the systemic definition of educational and professional competencies. A fuller understanding suggests that the two types of activity can have a symbiotic relationship.

Overview of the Book

Eportfolios for Lifelong Learning and Assessment has three parts. Part One offers an aspirational view of eportfolios' promise, drawing on exemplary practices. Parts Two and Three chart the challenges of realizing this promise within less ideal contexts and suggest resources for bridging the gap between current practice and future potential. The book's introduction tells the story of my own introduction to and evolving understanding of eportfolios as it parallels the growth of the contemporary eportfolio movement. The book's conclusion draws connections between the transformation needed to realize the potential of eportfolios and consonant movements for change in higher education in the service of learning.

Part One argues that the first two of the three cultural ideals that underlie eportfolio practice, while conventionally assumed to be solely personal, are simultaneously social in nature. This dual nature suggests a necessary interrelationship between personalized learning and institutional assessment and decision making, challenging the widely held view that these processes must necessarily conflict in eportfolio practice. Chapter One introduces the ideal of authenticity through closely examining two eportfolios, which exemplify two common types: the personalized and the standardized. This examination shows that the ideal of authenticity may explain the motivations behind both types, not just the personalized, as often assumed. The standardized model, however, reflects a misunderstanding of what it means to be truly authentic. Chapter Two looks carefully at a professional eportfolio to introduce the ideal of integrity, showing how this ideal reflects the changing nature of careers and professions. Both adults and traditional-age college students increasingly need to articulate their identities as committed and coherent across contexts and over time, and eportfolios show promise in helping them achieve this goal. Such articulation also has the potential to contribute to the definition and evolution of professions.

The chapters in Part Two look at how eportfolios can be used to promote institutional innovation in colleges and universities that capitalizes on both the personal and social potential introduced in Part One. Chapter Three examines how the ideal of deliberation, which derives from deliberative democracy theory, can be used in programmatic and institutional assessment with eportfolios. It details how deliberative assessment works in the practice of an exemplary program and compares it with the more common standardized model of assessment. Drawing on results from the Inter/National Coalition for Electronic Portfolio Research and an analysis of the Association of American Colleges and Universities' Valid Assessment of Learning in Undergraduate Education project, Chapter Four argues for the importance of taking advantage of the distinctive characteristics of the eportfolio genre, which combines reflection with diverse evidence, as opposed to more limited forms of authentic assessment that consider individual samples of work in isolation from their context. Chapter Five suggests that some educational outcomes that have traditionally been considered ineffable—impossible to assess—can be incorporated into deliberative eportfolio assessment if they are treated as essentially contested concepts—outcomes whose development benefits from putting multiple perspectives into dialogue. The broadened dimensions of learning that can be assessed require a similarly broadened understanding of how evidence functions in eportfolios and require rethinking the relationship between individual eportfolios and online social context.

Part Three examines how eportfolios are being used beyond the academy and how emerging genres and technologies can be used to support the eportfolio process. Chapter Six provides an overview of how individuals, companies, government agencies, and professional bodies are using eportfolios for developing individual and collective knowledge and managing transitions between levels of education, education and the workplace, and places of employment. It argues that the character of the eportfolio genre is often compromised to accommodate existing institutional processes, and that a better balance is needed for eportfolios to maximize their impact. Chapter Seven compares the eportfolio with two other genres that have recently become prominent tools through which individuals articulate their identities: blogs and social network site profiles. It suggests that there are two styles of self-representation and learning—the networked and the symphonic. Although research shows that social software corresponds with the networked and eportfolios corresponds with the symphonic, lifelong learning may be best supported by a combination of the two styles. Chapter Eight examines technology that has the potential to support eportfolio processes. Rather than considering the current generation of eportfolio tools, it surveys a wide range of technologies that could be used to capture and manage eportfolio evidence, reflection on it, analysis of eportfolios, and deliberations about them.

The book's companion website includes video guided tours, narrated by me, of several of the eportfolios discussed in the book. It provides a more detailed look at the design and content of the portfolios than is possible within the text. The website is located at www.josseybass.com/go/darrencambridge; password josseybasshighereducation.

Intended Audiences and Ways of Using This Book

This book is intended for a broad audience of people involved in, researching, or contemplating the use of eportfolios for lifelong learning and assessment. Readers might include:

- Faculty and staff from a variety of disciplines, including such fields as rhetoric and composition, engineering, history, education, psychology, social work, and medicine
- Learning support staff, such as directors of centers for teaching and learning and instructional designers
- Academic and student affairs administrators, such as deans and heads of personal development planning

- Learning technologists, such as directors of academic technology and learning technology developers
- Leaders of lifelong learning and workforce development agencies
- Policymakers guiding and funding eportfolio projects in compulsory, higher, and adult education and in workforce development.

Teams composed of individuals from several of these categories often lead the strongest eportfolio initiatives. With this in mind, the questions for practice at the end of each chapter are designed for discussion within such teams. While some questions, such as those dealing with curriculum design, may most often inform decisions traditionally made by faculty members, eportfolio research suggests that learning support staff, academic technologists, and student affairs professionals can make valuable contributions to working through them. Similarly, while technology choices have traditionally been in the hands of technologists and workforce development policies in the hands of government employees and policymakers, faculty members and those in other roles within and beyond higher education can also speak to these decisions. While most of this book is not written to be particularly accessible to undergraduate students, it does argue that they have a central role to play in assessment and in shaping initiatives that support lifelong learning. They too ought to be invited to help think through questions for practice.

Nevertheless, readers with different interests may wish to employ different strategies for reading the book. While Part One may be more theoretical than that to which some readers are accustomed, the ideas and examples introduced within it are foundational to the arguments advanced throughout the book; all readers should start here. Like the rest of the book, it does not presuppose any particular discipline or role-specific background knowledge and avoids overly specialized terminology whenever possible. Readers with a particular interest in assessment or higher education will likely want to continue on to Part Two, while those primarily interested in the use of eportfolios beyond the academy may wish to skip to Part Three. In the second two parts, readers who are interested in learning about the current state of research and practice will be particularly interested in Chapters Four and Six, while those more focused on the future potential will probably find Chapters Three, Five, Seven, and Eight most engaging. The opening section of Chapter Eight presents a general perspective on the relationship between eportfolios and technology that is likely to be helpful to all readers, while the remainder of the chapter may be more appealing to readers with a technological bent. The conclusion returns focus to higher education and is therefore most salient to readers concerned with the use of eportfolios in colleges and universities.

What the Book Does Not Do

While *Eportfolios for Lifelong Learning and Assessment* presents the most wide-ranging account of eportfolio practice and potential to date, it does not address many important topics and questions. It is not a guide to implementing and managing eportfolio technology or programs, although it does raise issues that implementers need to address. Similarly, it is not a guide to eportfolio pegagogy, although eportfolio teachers will benefit from considering concepts and research it presents. Finally, it does not address in detail the current and potential role of eportfolios in learning and decision making that is independent of institutions such as schools, colleges, universities, companies, nonprofit organizations, unions, and governments. Learning and knowledge creation that is achieved through participation in social networks not sanctioned or initiated by institutions is of great and growing importance, as demonstrated by research on such topics as distributed cognition, emergence, crowdsourcing, long-tail communities of practice, and connectivist and networked learning. The connections between these topics and eportfolios are ripe for exploration. By identifying and exploring the key cultural ideals that are embodied by the eportfolio genre and its best current use—use that is primarily situated within institutions—this book lays conceptual groundwork for such future scholarship.

ACKNOWLEDGMENTS

Because this book synthesizes work over the past decade that drew in a multitude of individuals from around the globe, from each of whom I learned something reflected in the pages that follow, this may very well be the hardest section to write. This being said, I especially thank those who were directly involved in the production of this book: my research collaborators, my students and teachers, and my family.

I thank my editor, David Brightman, and the excellent staff at Jossey-Bass for their support for the project and their guidance throughout its completion. I deeply appreciate the thoughtful suggestions of all the external reviewers, as well as the less formal feedback I received on the ideas expressed here through the comments and questions of audience members at presentations I have given, participants in workshops I have facilitated, and educators at institutions with whom I have consulted. Perhaps most significant, I am grateful to the authors of the portfolios and leaders of the programs featured in this book for allowing me to learn from their work.

While the flaws in this book are mine alone, many of its strengths are the result of highly collaborative scholarly work in which I have had the privilege of participating. Coleading the Inter/National Coalition for Electronic Portfolio Research has profoundly influenced my thinking, and I thank all of its participants, in particular, coleaders such as Kathi Yancey, Rob Ward, Janice Strivens, and Steve Outram, and members of the George Mason University Cohort III team, including Kim Eby, Leslie Smith, Kara Danner, Juliet Blank-Godlove, and Julie Owen. My understanding of eportfolios has been indispensably enriched through working closely with members of the Open Source Portfolio/Sakai, IMS Global Learning Consortium, and Learning Recording Online development communities. In particular, I appreciate the conceptual and technical conversations I have shared with Simon Grant and Bill Holloway.

Although I have learned through all of these collaborative contexts, I also treasure the powerful experiences I have had in the classroom as both a teacher and a student. Thanks go out to all of my students at George Mason University and the University of Texas and to my professors across the university from my years in Austin, who seeded the interdisciplinary breadth of my work, and to my teachers at Wabash College, who grounded it in rigorous analysis and a rich ideal of intellectual community.

It is within this group that I turn to the people without whom this book would never have been written. Peg Syverson and the late, great John Slatin at the University of Texas at Austin were not only responsible for my first experience with eportfolio learning that I describe at the beginning of this book but they also provided resources—both intellectual and material and far beyond what I could reasonably expect over the next six years—that launched my career.

I am profoundly grateful to my family for the inspiration, support, and tolerance without which writing this book would not have been possible. In particular, I thank my incredible wife, Kara Gotsch, who was with me from the genesis of this book to its completion, and my miraculous son, Oliver Angelo Cambridge, who came into the world alongside it.

I thank my mother, Barbara Cambridge, most of all and dedicate this book to her. She alone has played a role in each of the categories I have listed here. Her responses to the manuscript shaped each chapter of the book, adding clarity and concision. Serving together with her as a coleader of the Inter/National Coalition for Electronic Portfolio Research, a coworker at the American Association for Higher Education, and a copresenter and facilitator at events over the years, I hope that I have absorbed some of her intuitive grasp of how to help people understand their strengths and how they connect to those of others in the service of change that promotes learning. Throughout my education, the efforts of my teachers have been multiplied through her influence, and one of my greatest satisfactions has been to see how she too has learned from my experiences as I have developed my own professional identity. Besides all this, she is a loving and attentive mother, grandmother, and friend. I have a lot to live up to.

Darren Cambridge
Washington, DC
May 2010

ABOUT THE AUTHOR

Darren Cambridge is assistant professor of Internet studies and information literacy in New Century College and affiliated faculty in the Higher Education Program at George Mason University. Previously he was a director at the American Association for Higher Education, a fellow with the EDUCAUSE National Learning Infrastructure Initiative, and assistant director of the Computer Writing and Research Lab at the University of Texas at Austin. A frequent speaker and facilitator, he consults with colleges, universities, software companies, publishers, nonprofit organizations, and governmental bodies worldwide.

He coleads the Inter/National Coalition for Electronic Portfolio Research, through which sixty teams at institutions of higher education in six countries are investigating the impact of eportfolio use on teaching, learning, and assessment. He also serves as chair of the board of directors of the Association for Authentic, Experiential, and Evidence-Based Learning. He headed the IMS Global Learning Consortium work on eportfolio technical standards and George Mason's participation in the Association of American Colleges and Universities' Valid Assessment of Learning in Undergraduate Education project. Lead developer of the award-winning Learning Record Online, he has been active in the Sakai open source community.

His work appears in such journals as *Campus-Wide Information Systems, Computers and Education*, the *Journal of General Education*, and *Metropolitan Universities*. He is coeditor of *Electronic Portfolios 2.0: Emergent Research on Implementation and Impact* (Stylus, 2009) and is currently completing an edited volume on the global diffusion of eportfolios and leading development of the Augusta Community Portfolio.

More information about Cambridge's work can be found on his website at ncepr.org/darren.

EPORTFOLIOS FOR LIFELONG LEARNING AND ASSESSMENT

INTRODUCTION

My first experience with eportfolios was as a learner. In the fall of 1996, I began work on a Ph.D. in English with a concentration in computers and English studies at the University of Texas at Austin. It was an important time in my life, during which I was trying both to make sense of the sea of knowledge into which I had plunged and to find the shape of my life as I progressed further into adulthood. One class that fall asked me to compose an eportfolio that documented and reflected on my learning and development, not just in terms of specific goals of that class but also in relationship to my learning and development as a whole. Through the eportfolio, I was able to validate the academic concepts and ideas I encountered in the course by connecting them to my distinctive passions, interests, and ways of seeing, as well as to concepts and ideas from other courses and to experiences from my life both within and beyond the university. Over time, through capturing critical moments of my development and collecting samples of my work, both formal and informal, I began to accumulate the materials for understanding and communicating what I was coming to know, be able to do, and be committed to. Although I abstractly valued such reflection before I entered the program, it became concretely powerful for me because the class offered me an audience. As I read and responded to my colleagues' eportfolios and considered their and my teachers' responses to my own, I began to see my learning and development as part of a process of both becoming and being a member of a professional community. While my understanding of myself and my understanding of the discipline had up to that point felt like largely private matters, through composing an eportfolio I began to see articulating them as part of my participation in a social world to which I very much wanted to contribute.

I am opening with the story of my own evolving understanding of eportfolios in part because I hope it will help you understand the distinctive perspective from which I write, which is shaped by the experiences I describe. Perhaps more important, the evolution of my understanding largely parallels the development of the eportfolio movement between the mid-1990s and today, offering a historical background for the discussion of the current state of the field that comprises the body of this book.

Eportfolios are the offspring of print portfolios. Although portfolios have a long history in arts and design disciplines, the tradition on which the portfolio pedagogy I experienced drew, and on which the contemporary eportfolio movement is built, originated in the field of rhetoric and composition in the early 1980s. Portfolios were introduced as a means of assessing writing that supported learning through asking students to reflect on and make judgments about their own work. Such assessments could account for writing in multiple genres and contexts and for the development of writing ability over time. The contribution of composing a portfolio to learning proved significant enough that emphasis in the field shifted from the use of portfolios primarily as assessments to using them primarily as assignments that promote learning. As both an assessment and a means for supporting learning, portfolios soon were taken up by faculty in a wide range of other disciplines, particularly education. Around the time I was composing my own first portfolio, educators were beginning to ask students to publish their portfolios, now beginning to be called electronic portfolios, on the Web. While I had created websites for campus groups as an undergraduate as early as 1994, my eportfolio that first semester at Texas was the first piece of my own writing I published online, and the sense of a public audience contributed to the connection between my own experience and the social world it brought into focus for me.

Given how powerfully eportfolios had supported my own learning and developing identity, I naturally incorporated them into my syllabi when I began to teach writing courses at Texas. While serving as assistant director of the Computer Writing and Research Lab (now called the Digital Writing and Research Lab), I led the development of a Web application to support the eportfolio pedagogy I had experienced as a student and embraced as a teacher: the Learning Record Online. While this software won awards and proved highly effective in supporting this particular course-based process, it proved difficult to adapt it to other ways in which people might want to compose and use electronic portfolios. In my later work cultivating technology to support eportfolio practice—through writing functional requirements for the Open Source Portfolio (now a part of Sakai) and leading the development of the IMS ePortfolio interoperability specification—I endeavored to give eportfolio authors and audiences increased flexibility, the importance of which would soon come into focus.

After graduate school I worked for two national higher education associations, the American Association for Higher Education (AAHE) and EDUCAUSE, through its National Learning Infrastructure Initiative (now the EDUCAUSE Learning Initiative). Part of my job was to engage educators at scores of institutions across the United States in conversations about the use of eportfolios to support learning through the organizations' conferences and a virtual community of practice dedicated to the topic, EPAC. It was through this work that I began to see why such flexibility was essential. One reason was the diversity of educational practices and priorities in place at these institutions, which ranged from tiny community colleges to huge research-focused universities. No single eportfolio format, process, or tool could accommodate all of them. Through working with and visiting numerous campuses using eportfolios in innovative ways, I came to see the value of a wider range of approaches.

My time at AAHE and EDUCAUSE coincided with a rapid expansion of interest in and use of eportfolios in higher education. This growth was a product of new software that made creating, sharing, and evaluating eportfolios easier, combined with increased systematic attention to student learning at an institutional level. Institutions were beginning to embrace the capabilities of technology to support learning across campus, launch initiatives that promoted integrative and reflective learning, and take more seriously the imperative to measure learning outcomes. Eportfolios seemed relevant to each of these ends and had the potential to join them up. While eportfolios took off most quickly in the United States, their adoption as a strategy for supporting learning and assessment was also becoming international in scope. At the first international conference on eportfolios in 2003, hosted by the European Institute for E-Learning in France, where I had the honor of being a keynote speaker, colleges and universities from Canada, the United Kingdom, Australia, China, and several continental European countries were represented. Conferences in subsequent years would see South American and African participation as well.

At the same time that I was facilitating conversations about eportfolio use in higher education, I was also beginning to investigate their potential to support lifelong learning. As I read research about adult learning, the changing nature of careers, and the psychological and social demands of adult life, it became clear to me that the needs that composing an eportfolio helped me meet as a student were needs that many people were negotiating throughout life. Many individuals want to engage with knowledge and with other people in a way that embraces and puts into use their own distinctive capabilities and sensibilities. They seek authenticity. Many people, too, want to think about their lives as a whole—to be able to tell stories of commitment and coherence that link their roles across multiple spheres of modern life, personal, professional, and civic. They seek a kind of integrity. Many also want to participate in the process of making decisions in the institutions with which they interact—schools, universities, religious institutions, businesses, professional bodies—and want to bring their distinctiveness to bear on shared problems. They seek to participate in deliberation. Considered in this way, lifelong learning means more than just acquiring a set of skills needed for employment. It means developing the means to deal with fundamental challenges that adults face throughout their lives, across roles and over time. While the composition and use of eportfolios surely does not eliminate these challenges, it seemed to me a promising means for grappling with them.

During this period, the use of eportfolios to support lifelong learning beyond the academy was taking off. In Minnesota and Wales, all residents gained access to eportfolio software. In the Netherlands, companies were developing eportfolio programs to help laid-off workers inventory their skills and find new employment. In England, unions were supporting their members' professional development with eportfolios; coalitions of universities, schools, and employers were exploring the use of eportfolios to help individuals negotiate transitions between different levels of education and between the academy and the workplace. Many projects were supported by funding from regional and national governments and the European Commission. Through empirical research on the eFolio Minnesota project in the United States and critical analysis of the European policy discourse that was guiding government investment into eportfolio projects, I began to see both the correspondence between what individual eportfolio authors valued and my own understanding of lifelong learning and the limitations of lifelong learning policy focused on a narrowly defined idea of employability.

In the conversations about eportfolios I was facilitating with educators, I also saw enthusiasm for the lifelong learning potential of eportfolios. In countless conference presentations, workshops, online chats, and hallway conversations, people advocating the use of eportfolios in higher education spoke of ways that they could help develop the habits of mind needed for learning throughout life, how they could enable workers to document and present their capabilities, and how they could assist people in exploring and articulating their identities. What seemed to get people excited about eportfolios, I thought, was not just that they provided a more efficient, or even more accurate, means for assessment of student learning; it was not just that they added to the depth of understanding of standard subject matter through reflection and not just that they helped students find high-paying jobs after graduation. Rather, I felt that the enthusiasm was rooted in a desire to think about how higher education could better support lifelong learning in the broad sense I had experienced. Eportfolios were exciting because they could help us think about key issues in supporting student learning and development: What kinds of people do we want to help students become? How does academic knowledge relate to knowledge gained from experience beyond the classroom? What role should students play in making decisions about how colleges and universities support their development, and how does that relate to the roles they will play in shaping other institutions in which they will play a part?

Yet there was a mismatch between this desire to consider fundamental questions and the concrete work of implementing eportfolio programs. While lifelong learning was often part of the introduction, the body of most discussions of eportfolios at conferences and in the literature focused on the pragmatics of choosing technology, training faculty and students, determining reflective writing prompts, deciding what should be included in students' curricula vitae, or managing assessment data in order to be accountable to accreditation agencies, professional bodies, or governments. These are real and pressing issues for educators tasked with putting eportfolios into practice, and excellent work has been done to address them. I have collaborated over several years with teams undertaking such work through the Inter/National Coalition for Electronic Portfolio Research, which I colead with Kathleen Yancey and Barbara Cambridge, and with a wide range of similarly engaged colleges, universities, companies, and nonprofit and governmental organizations through my consulting practice. I have learned a great deal from their experiences. However, in the race to put programs in place and develop promising new software, few of these practitioners have had the opportunity for sustained inquiry into the underlying issues about the aims of higher education and its relationship to learning throughout life. Without a grounding in a careful examination of such issues, I worry that the potential of eportfolios to support significant innovation may remain unrealized or, worse, that eportfolios may be co-opted to serve institutional or governmental objectives that actually work against supporting individual learning, development, and participation in the fuller sense that I see as the source of excitement about eportfolios. The situation is much the same with eportfolio initiatives beyond the academy.

While the aims of eportfolio use have not yet received the attention I think they merit, in recent years there has been a great deal of strong research on its outcomes. Many of the nearly fifty teams from five countries that make up the coalition have published their findings, including in an edited collection, *Electronic Portfolios 2.0: Emergent Research on Implementation and Impact* (Cambridge, Cambridge, & Yancey, 2009). Building on the longstanding work in rhetoric and composition and education, other scholars in a wide range of disciplines and professions have documented and analyzed the use of eportfolios for supporting learning and assessment in their domains. While early research focused mostly on explaining the design of programs, more recent work has systematically examined its impact on such factors as professional competency development, student engagement, retention, self-efficacy, and success in finding employment. However, the research is fragmented: the connections between research in different fields, and between the outcomes and the vision of education implicit in how eportfolios are used, are still difficult to discern.

I have written this book as a first step toward filling these gaps. It begins by examining possible aims of eportfolios by looking carefully at examples of practice, from higher education and beyond it, that I find particularly compelling in their support for lifelong learning broadly defined, focusing particularly on academic assessment and professional identity development. Making connections between the exemplary practices and theoretical perspectives from multiple disciplines—philosophy, education, psychology, sociology, anthropology, political science, and rhetoric and composition—I identify three cultural ideals implicit in eportfolios—authenticity, integrity, and deliberation—each of which can also be found in the broader research literature. I then examine this research in relationship to the potential of lifelong learning with eportfolios I have outlined, using the ideals to connect work from multiple fields and tracking points of connection and dissonance. I look particularly at what we know so far about how eportfolios support assessment, how eportfolios are being used beyond the academy, and how the use of blogs, social network sites, emerging digital technologies, and genres relate to eportfolios. I conclude by examining how the eportfolio movement might join with other movements for change in higher education to enact the transformational change needed for teaching, learning, and assessment that better contributes to students' success throughout their lives.

My hope is that this book will help people interested in eportfolios think more generously and critically about their possibilities and the larger issues about learning, education, and work they can help bring into focus. This is not a book that tells which software to buy, what specific strategies to use to motivate learners, how to develop assessment rubrics, or what specific kinds of evidence of competency employers value. The optimal answers to these kinds of questions are deeply dependent on having a situated knowledge of the contexts in which eportfolios are going to be used. Given the diversity of the contexts in which readers are likely to be working, I think it would be presumptuous to offer specific mandates. However, I do believe that thinking about the larger questions that underlie the logistics of using eportfolios in higher education and the workplace can help readers who are putting eportfolios into practice make better choices. Each chapter in this book concludes with a set of questions for practice that are written to help spur thinking about how the ideas and themes from the chapter can inform current and future work.

Today I teach at New Century College, an integrative studies program at George Mason University that has integrated eportfolios throughout its curriculum. While my colleagues come from a wide variety of disciplinary backgrounds, they are united by their commitment to support student learning that, as the college's tagline puts it, connects the classroom to the world. It has proved a fruitful setting for the integrative, interdisciplinary work that was needed for completing this book. Our faculty's collective experience advocating for an integrative studies approach to teaching and learning shows that we need to be particularly careful to ground our claims about practice in recognized research that draws on disciplinary insights from multiple fields to ensure the credibility that more traditional work gains from its situation in a particular discipline. In this book, whenever possible, I have supported my conclusions through reference to systematic, published research, including more informal descriptions of practice only when I determined that their exclusion would offer a substantially incomplete account.

While this book is essentially interdisciplinary, like my colleagues I remain connected to the discipline in which I was trained, and that connection has shaped my approach. From English Studies, I have drawn the method of close reading and the concept of genre. For readers with different professional backgrounds, these may need some explanation.

On one level, the meaning of close reading is straightforward: it means paying close attention to the features of specific texts. In rhetoric and composition scholarship about learning, this attention is often focused on examples of student writing. In this tradition, the first four chapters of this book offer extended, careful analyses of the content and form of specific eportfolios. However, close reading is also theory driven: texts are chosen that can shed light on theoretical issues, and the process of reading them attempts to elucidate those issues. As Randy Bass and Sherry Linkon (2008) put it, "A dialog between theory and textual evidence lies at the heart of the enterprise" (p. 251). The eportfolios I have chosen to analyze are not intended to be representative of all eportfolios; instead, they help explore the cultural ideals underlying lifelong learning and the potential of the eportfolio genre to support their development. By looking carefully at specific eportfolios, I hope that these ideals become less abstract and my claims about them more contestable.

Close reading of specific eportfolios helps me to explore the eportfolio as a genre. A genre is a type of composition. The genre of a text might be poem or memo. The genre of a musical piece might be a show tune or a symphony. Genres are defined by a loose set of conventions, which often are about form. A poem is a poem in part because it uses figurative language and the breaks between lines have significance, while a memo has particular kinds of headings that identify the author, audience, and topic. While the eportfolio is sometimes discussed as a type of technology or a placeholder for certain kinds of learning, I see the eportfolio as fundamentally a type of composition, an emerging genre. As I discuss throughout this book, formal conventions are solidifying that define this genre. Eportfolios usually include a reflective rationale for the choice of documents they contain, for example. At the same time, the genre is still being defined. As I learned from my earlier experiences developing software and convening eportfolio educators from a wide range of organizations, there is wide variation in the form of things the people refer to as eportfolios.

In this book, I deal with this variation by taking the rhetorical perspective on genre most clearly articulated by Carolyn Miller (1984): genres take their shape and come to be used because they help people negotiate particular types of challenges that members of a culture share. The form of a genre matters because it helps people act within the social networks on which they are a part. Analyzing genres is important because they "serve as keys to understanding how to partici-pate in the actions of a community" (Miller, 1984, p. 165). The way to understand the eportfolio as a genre, then, is to look for correspondence between the key cultural challenges it helps people negotiate and the characteristics of its form and the social processes it mediates. This is the approach I have taken in this book. Like the back and forth between theory and text of close reading, so too there is a back and forth between examining the challenges of lifelong learning and assess-ment that define the three cultural ideals and the characteristics of eportfolios that indicate and cultivate them.

This is an exciting time. The eportfolio movement continues to gain strength, both within and beyond higher education. This growth has been fueled by the ability to group together an expansive variety of digital information and activity under the term *eportfolio*. The concept's flexibility, and the growing ability of tech-nology to support it, has been key to the educational and professional innovation it has fostered. Out of this innovation have emerged promising practices that can help us think about and begin to address some of the challenges of identity and participation at the heart of lifelong learning. Successfully bringing these practices to maturity, however, requires more clearly defining characteristics of the eportfolio genre that are integral to such applications. While surveying the richness of varied eportfolio practice, this book argues for core principles that can best put these practices in the service of both individual and institutional growth.

PART ONE

THE POTENTIAL OF EPORTFOLIOS FOR INDIVIDUAL AND SOCIAL TRANSFORMATION

CHAPTER ONE

EPORTFOLIOS AND IDENTITY

Composing the Ethics of Authenticity

An education is truly "fitted for freedom" only if it is such as to produce free citizens, citizens who are free not because of wealth or birth, but because they can call their minds their own. Male or female, rich and poor, they have looked into themselves and developed the ability to separate habit and convention from what they can defend by argument. They have ownership of their own thought and speech, and this imparts to them a dignity that is far beyond the outer dignity of class and rank.

—Martha Nussbaum, *Cultivating Humanity*

The chapters in Part One examine two cultural ideals that underlie eportfolio practice: authenticity and integrity. Certainly these ideals are implicit in the structure of many eportfolio programs and processes, but they are often either invisible to the people designing the programs and supporting the processes or understood in oversimplified ways. A failure to examine the ideals rigorously and chart the implications of such examination has led to a misguided opposition between eportfolios in service of individual lifelong learning and eportfolios as contributions to institutional assessment. (*Assessment* here includes both processes within the academy so labeled and the more general processes of evaluation that occur in other settings, such as the workplace.) In both cases, the ideals are mistakenly assumed to be purely personal, serving only the interests of the individual. In fact, both are at once individual and social ideals, and fully embracing them requires finding ways to make eportfolios simultaneously serve individual self-actualization and institutional transformation. Excellence in lifelong learning and assessment are inextricably linked.

This chapter introduces authenticity in the context of the use of eportfolios in higher education. It begins by describing authenticity as generally understood in contemporary Western culture and traces its roots in the philosophical tradition. Description of an example of one of the two most common types of eportfolios in higher education, the personalized portfolio, illustrates the ideal in practice. This portfolio contrasts with a second example, which is illustrative of the second common type, the standardized portfolio. While personalized portfolios are often considered to be effective in helping eportfolio authors articulate their authenticity, standardized portfolios are generally seen as working against this ideal.

The influence of authenticity on educational practice extends beyond just the particular eportfolio used to exemplify it here, even beyond eportfolios in general. Many of the currently popular concepts in higher education pedagogy and learning theory correspond with the ideal. A closer look at standardized portfolios yields a finding that is surprising in light of the consensus about conflicting goals between the two types of eportfolios but more understandable given the ubiquity of the ideal in educational thought: if authenticity is conceived of in the traditional way, standardized eportfolios may in fact support authenticity by enacting a social process, procedural justice, that is designed to protect individuals' freedom to pursue the ideal. The same ideal actually underlies both types of eportfolio, but it does so in way that still suggests they should be kept separate.

This traditional conception of authenticity has been critiqued from a range of political perspectives, rendering it problematic as a cultural ideal and a focus of educational practice. These criticisms can be addressed by reconceptualizing authenticity. The conventional way of thinking about authenticity neglects the necessary role of the social, which enables individuals to develop, express, and enact it in the public sphere. A closer look at the personalized portfolio example shows that it actually embodies this social version of the ideal. The standardized model, in contrast, precludes the opportunity to enact authenticity through social participation through influencing institutional decision making. Higher education institutions have a responsibility to provide opportunities for such participation, and programmatic and institutional assessment could be done in a way that makes that possible.

The Origins of Authenticity

The cultural ideal of authenticity, deeply rooted in modern Western culture, constitutes the basis of the most common understanding of the self. To be authentic requires understanding and being true to oneself. Examining and articulating one's nature is key to being truly human, to living a full and productive life. In addition to being ends in themselves, self-understanding and self-articulation are also key to truth and moral action. Every person's nature is unique, and it is important to express this uniqueness and let it guide actions.

Whether or not one agrees philosophically with this ideal, it emerges from a strong intellectual tradition and underlies much Western thought and culture. Practices of examining the self to connect with the grace of God trace back at least as far as Augustine's *Confessions* and the reflective practices of the Puritans. The modern version of authenticity began in the eighteenth century with Jean Jacques Rousseau, who believed that each of us embodies nature, which is the source of the moral order, but also that each of us is unique. Each of us has our own unique nature, and this individualized nature is the source that we must access in order to know what is right for us. Later, romanticism added an emphasis on participation, expression, and depth. By engaging with the world and interpreting it through the lens of our own unique natures, we come to understand ourselves, the key to understanding the world. We learn how to live through participation in life.

Important in relation to eportfolios, however, is the principle that we do not really understand our unique selves or participate fully in life until we express our natures. Because the true nature of the self is complex and inchoate, it does not reach its full power until it is made clear through representation. Taylor (1989) makes the point that expression gives life "a definitive shape. A human life is seen as manifesting a potential which is also being shaped by this manifestation; it is not just a matter of copying an external model or carrying out an already determinate formulation" (pp. 374–375). In other words, by expressing who we are, we are defining ourselves, calling ourselves into being. Thus, creativity becomes essential to understanding how we should live.

This calling into being through representation continues throughout our lifetime. The self has depth: there is always some part of ourselves that we don't yet fully understand. As we articulate ourselves through our creativity, our inner depths are transformed in ways that call for further expression. The process of coming to know through articulating the unique nature of ourselves is a lifelong undertaking. The educational goal of lifelong learning is based in this understanding of the continually emergent self, understood through self-representation.

In our contemporary culture, the aspect of authenticity that valorizes the centrality of the self has often been interpreted as the autonomy of self. Genuine authenticity, however, requires shared cultural touch points beyond the self in order for meaningful self-definition to be possible. Social science research shows that forming an identity and rendering it relatively steady over time depends on connections beyond the autonomous self. Understanding authenticity this way, as a social as well as an individual ideal, suggests an essential role for institutions such as colleges and universities. It also calls into question the supposed opposition between lifelong learning and institutional assessment that cripples the potential of eportfolios in higher education and beyond. In examining two kinds of eportfolios,

I highlight the ways in which identity formation and connectedness are enacted through these eportfolio types and practices.

Authenticity in Two Capstone Portfolios

The personalized and the standardized are two models common in eportfolio practice that are often thought to serve irreconcilable purposes. In fact, both are connected to the conventional understanding of the ideal of authenticity. This connection can be seen clearly through examination of an example of each type.

Both examples originate within higher education in a capstone course, a common curricular component designed as a culminating experience in an undergraduate major (Henscheid, 2000; Smith, 1997). Generally taken during the final year of undergraduate school to provide a culminating experience in the major, capstones focus on students' integration of their learning over time and across contexts to demonstrate their accomplishments and plans for their future. In research and policy discussions about eportfolios for lifelong learning, authors often identify the transitions between stages of education and professional practice as key sites where portfolios can be powerful (Hartnell-Young, Smallwood, Kingston, & Harley, 2006; Treuer & Jenson, 2003). In U.S. higher education, capstone courses are an increasingly common site for composing portfolios designed to address the transition from undergraduate education into the workforce or on to graduate school (Henscheid, 2000; Smith, 1997). The following two examples originate in two capstone courses, one that I taught at George Mason University in Fairfax, Virginia, and a second taught by a professor in teacher education at Great Lakes State (a pseudonym).

Personalized Eportfolio

The first portfolio, "Spiritual Communities," was composed by Sean Moore (2007) during a fall 2006 capstone course for integrative studies majors in New Century College and then was revised and expanded in spring 2007. It fulfills a graduation requirement for the integrative studies major. Students are asked to compose a portfolio that communicates their understanding of what they have learned, how they have learned it, why they chose to learn what they did, and what they hope to learn and achieve after leaving George Mason, drawing on a common conceptual framework supplied by the program for talking about the multiple dimensions of a liberal education. The assignment is intended as a learning experience that helps students integrate and take ownership of their undergraduate learning careers, not as an assessment of whether they have mastered a prespecified body of knowledge or set of skills.

Moore's portfolio is designed to communicate his understanding of his field of study, community studies. Published as a website with approximately thirty-five hyperlinked pages, Moore's portfolio includes examples of his course work, blog entries, photographs, and extensive written reflection. Two sections of the portfolio explicitly address competencies that run throughout the New Century College curriculum, including global understanding and effective citizenship, but much of its organization is of his own creation, interweaving materials elicited by the graduation portfolio assignment from the capstone class with those motivated by his own purposes for the portfolio, detailing his travels in India and presenting his understanding of spiritual community as a concept.

While the portfolio focuses on concepts of community and discourses that surround it, Moore is careful to disavow affiliation for any particular spiritual community or tradition. In his introduction to the portfolio, he writes: "Essentially, I do not have a religion to cling on to; I'm left with the experience of my life and I try to relate it to my own understanding of truth. That, I suppose, is the essence of spirituality—maybe this is all a blessing in disguise. Echoing so many theorists on minorities and social repression, the struggle to simply be what I am is edifying."

For Moore, genuine truth must be arrived at through his own experience of the world. Consequently, the contents of his portfolio document through writings, photographs, and projects experience in a range of social settings, from an ashram in Quebec and an urban marketplace in India to a demonstration outside the student center and a group project in the classroom at George Mason. Reflecting on this material has an ethical purpose: to edify is to instruct or to improve morally. By articulating who he is through reflection on his documented experience, Moore will be more likely to act in accord with his own nature. He is solidly in the tradition of self-examination. The truth that should guide his life cannot be found in the outside world; it must come through the self.

In reflective writings in Moore's portfolio, particularly those composed during the capstone course, the movement toward this experiential truth comes through a series of engagements and rejections. After high school, Moore first finds a sense of connection in the "party scene" but then comes to believe that the scene is shallow and unfulfilling; he moves on to art school to explore creative expression as a means to spiritual understanding, but finds other reflective practices more powerful; entering communities organized around these practices, he finds a lack of openness and intellectual rigor that he returns to college to seek out; and so forth. While interactions within these contexts are helpful to the extent that they advance his project of self-definition, they are subservient to his own feelings of what is meaningful and good. These feelings are firmed up through making clear how he is different from those in each context and not fully aligned with any of the communities' beliefs or practices.

Similarly, while Moore adeptly uses an impressive range of academic abstractions to work through his experience, drawn from sociology, theology, history, and cultural studies, these theories and facts are not valued for their own sake. Rather, they are valid and significant to the extent that they help him articulate and define himself. The portfolio provides strong evidence that Moore is well versed in perspectives on community and spirituality from the several disciplines that intersect in his concentration of community studies. In both his reflective writings in the portfolio and the samples of his work composed prior to the capstone course, he applies ideas agilely from prominent scholars in each field, integrates the words of these other authors, and cites his sources. However, the portfolio's primary purpose seems more to be understanding and articulating Moore's identity than it does demonstrating his knowledge of and ability to apply academic concepts. What is most important is how his own emerging theories align with his life experiences and his intuitions.

Because the portfolio includes samples of Moore's writing and other creative expression collected over a period of several years, the degree to which these personal theories are emergent becomes clear. Through the process of reflective writing, Moore articulates more than a preexisting identity. He is in an ongoing process of writing an identity into being. The reflective writing in the portfolio also includes detailed examination of how his postgraduation plans, which include graduate school in sociology, are informed by what he is articulating about himself and how he anticipates his understanding to continue to evolve.

While Moore is an insightful writer with a strong voice, his portfolio also conveys meaning through its creative visual design. The portfolio is framed through a clean and attractive layout that connects together themes from the rest of the portfolio (see Figure 1.1). The color palette of earth tones suggests a grounding in the organic and elemental. Repeating scriptlike icons and religious symbols evoke the spiritual communities the portfolio explores, while the varied and idiosyncratic kerning and line spacing of the portfolio banner text and page title suggest the individuality and complexity of the author's self-understanding. Photographs that depict or give a feeling of the ideas and places being discussed are integrated throughout. Here too, the composition of the portfolio matches Moore's understanding of how he interprets the world. He writes that he learns not just through text but also through other modalities, though multimedia: "Each semester, I surf the internet and find downloads of lectures, films, documentaries and audiobooks on relevant subjects to supplement my curricular learning."

FIGURE 1.1. SEAN MOORE'S EPORTFOLIO

SEAN MOORE

spiritual communities
electronic portfolio

Community **studies**

BLOG|PHOTOS|PORTFOLIO

Welcome to my electronic portfolio for Spiritual Communities. I have attempted to collect here a few images and stories to accompany my electronic portfolio; and this has been a great learning experience. This portfolio is also the **creative project for my New Century Graduation Portfolio.**

Otherwise, the navigation is divided into three parts-- my **blog** from India (**originally located here**), my **photos and naratives,** collected for my **draft electronic portfolio** last semester, and my **written portfolio** for my Spiritual Communities study, including competency essays.

Moore has clearly learned something about how he thinks, learns, and makes ethical choices through the reflective writing and visual design that went into his portfolio. His portfolio tells a story of his evolving understanding of himself and his field, drawing on materials not only from academic work but also from a wide variety of life experiences during his college years. While the portfolio does fulfill the set of requirements imposed by the class and program, it is not constrained by them, and also engages in a thoroughgoing moral reflection that is clearly more than an academic exercise.

In a personalized portfolio like Moore's, a primary purpose is to support learning directly, with learning being defined primarily by the individual learner. Authors learn something important through the process of reflecting on their work and communicating it to others in the form of a portfolio. The portfolio often communicates the author's understanding of his or her learning through narrative. The author feels in control of the experience; he or she has a range of choices to make about what to include, how it fits together, who reads it, and what conclusions ought to be drawn from the assembled materials. It is therefore well suited to the varied purposes portfolios might serve in supporting learning over the course of a lifetime. Along with the focus on the individual often comes the assumption that such personalized eportfolios are not suited to play a role in institutional assessment and that so employing them would retard or even negate the learning they are designed to support, necessarily imposing the constraints of the standardized portfolio on them to deleterious effect. A deeper examination of the nature of authenticity will call this assumption into question.

Standardized Eportfolio

Helen Barrett and her collaborators call personalized portfolios "portfolio as story" and standardized portfolios "portfolio as test" (Barrett & Carney, 2005; Barrett & Wilkerson, 2004). The purpose of a standardized portfolio is to support learning more indirectly by providing data about the achievement of learning outcomes that can be used to measure the effectiveness of an experience (such as a class or seminar), a program (such as a major course of study or professional development fellowship program), or an institution (such as a university or government agency). Portfolios may also take the place of standardized tests in the process of assessing their author's competence to enter or progress in a profession. The format of standardized portfolios is often tightly controlled by the program or institution eliciting it to make comparisons possible across multiple portfolios. Since standardized tests are increasingly being used this way in higher education in the United States and are the portal to entry into many professions, Barrett's metaphor is apt.

Mary Moss's portfolio is a standardized one. (Because this portfolio is part of a high-stakes assessment and has not been published, as Moore's has, I am using pseudonyms to refer to both the author and institution.) Moss, a student at Great Lakes State studying to become a high school biology teacher, composed her portfolio in a capstone class using LiveText, an online portfolio assessment management application. The portfolio is organized around a set of standards for what a secondary school teacher in the United States should know and be able to do, as defined by the National Council for Accreditation of Teacher Education (NCATE). In order to maintain their accreditation, teacher education programs need to demonstrate that their graduates can meet the full set of NCATE standards that focus on aspects of classroom performance and content knowledge. For example, teachers are expected to demonstrate their knowledge of the key facts and theories from the subject they teach through "inquiry, critical analysis, and synthesis" and to be able to "accurately assess and analyze student learning" in that area (National Council for Accreditation of Teacher Education, 2001).

The portfolio consists primarily of samples of Mary's work and evaluations of it by instructors in the teacher education program, linked together using the predefined structures within the software. Moss includes electronic documents, such as lesson plans she has written and videos of her teaching a first-grade class, for each of the externally defined standards. The process of uploading and arranging this evidence is controlled by LiveText. (See Figure 1.2 for a screenshot of an eportfolio similar to Moss's.) Also for each standard, Moss explains what the standard means and why the evidence is appropriate and sufficient to show competency as defined in the rubrics used to evaluate it.

The portfolio also includes numerical ratings for each standard, using a Likert scale ranging from 1 (Unsatisfactory) to 5 (Excellent). Instructors rate the portfolios with the aid of an evaluation rubric that describes the characteristics of evidence and explanation that match each of the possible ratings. Raters receive training before evaluating portfolios so that their judgments are normed in order to establish interrater reliability. The goal of the evaluation process is for the ratings to be the same no matter who is doing the rating. Each candidate for teacher certification is to be treated the same, regardless of demographics, personality, values, aspirations, affiliations, and past history with the evaluators.

The primary purposes of Mary's portfolio are two-fold. First, her successful completion of it ensures that she has an externally defined set of knowledge, skills, and abilities needed for her future profession. This success is verified through a process of evaluation that strives for objectivity. Second, when its numerical ratings are analyzed as part of a collection of all the portfolios completed by teacher candidates in the program, the institution can demonstrate that its educational program is successful in adequately preparing future teachers. If some standards are not met consistently at a sufficiently high level, then the data can help the program adjust curriculum to better address the relevant standard. In this way, Moss's portfolio contributes to the future learning of other students in the program, although it is unclear how much it contributes to her own or how much control she feels over her portfolio. Aside from deciding which works to include, she is offered few choices about the portfolio structure, look, purposes, audience, or evaluation. The portfolio does enable her to receive a degree and could provide compelling evidence of her capabilities for potential employers.

Barrett and her colleagues advocate keeping the processes of composing personalized and standardized portfolios separate because they arise from different paradigms, a view echoed in much of the eportfolio literature. (See, for example, Batson, 2007.) The lack of reflection and the external locus of control of standardized portfolios, for example, can negate the potential of portfolio composition to help learners understand and plan their own learning over time. People introduced to portfolios this way are unlikely to use them for lifelong learning.

FIGURE 1.2. AN EXAMPLE OF A LIVETEXT EPORTFOLIO

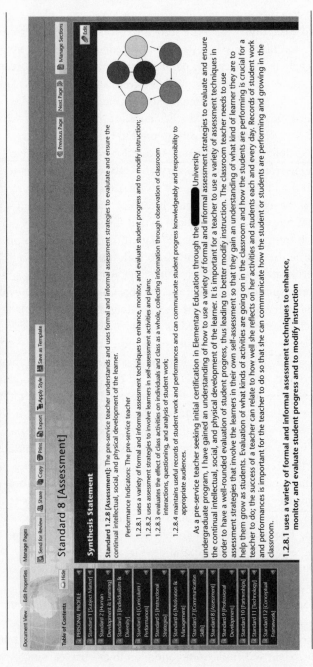

Image courtesy of LiveText, Inc.

Although the two models are in tension, more binds them together than just the fact that people call both "portfolios" in practice.

Using the two examples I have just discussed, I will argue that the cultural ideal of authenticity underlies both models. While undergirding congruence does not resolve the tension, it reframes it in a way that opens a possibility for synthesis. Rightly understood, the shared commitment to authenticity makes it possible to see how the impact on both individual self-development and institutional innovation can be multiplied when linked.

Authenticity and Learning with Eportfolios

Moore's eportfolio demonstrates the ways in which his purpose for it exemplifies characteristics of authenticity, which also resonate with popular contemporary notions about education, including vocation, creativity, diversity, reflection, participation, and self-authorship. The portfolio's purpose is an articulation of Moore's self in order to understand how he should live his life. Moore wishes to "be what I am"—to make clear what his true nature is so that he can determine what enterprises to undertake after his graduation and how he should relate to other people and ideas. This knowledge comes through participation in the world filtered through his feelings, intuitions, and reasoning. Examining the depths of his personality as reflected in how he makes sense of his experiences, he uses the insight gained to make plans for the future. A central theme of the portfolio is that as his articulation of his authentic self becomes more sophisticated, his life becomes happier and more productive. This articulation is achieved through the exercise of considerable creativity in reflective and expository writing, hypertextual organization, photography, and visual design. These are all modes he associates with his ways of acquiring knowledge. Through expressing himself in the way most natural for him, he becomes more himself, and thus more fully human.

The purpose of the portfolio is not to show how he matches up to some external tradition or institution's standards. He takes pains to qualify his associations with the spiritual and intellectual communities with which he engages as contingent to his emerging self-understanding. This understanding is often discussed by showing how it conflicts with or exceeds the limitations of these social entities and the other individuals he encounters through them. Uniquely himself, he is ultimately "left with the experience of [his] life" and his "own understanding of truth" as the ultimate test for different possible notions of the good.

Authenticity and Educational Theory

A possible objection to the argument so far is that the character of the chosen example of a personalized portfolio may be the result of the idiosyncrasies of an individual author or the atypical dynamics of a distinctive program. This is right up to a point. Part One of this book presents archetypal rather than typical eportfolios and eportfolio practices. Moore's portfolio, like Samantha Slade's in the following chapter, exemplifies an ideal fully realized that is more often more imperfectly and unconsciously engaged in other personalized eportfolios and eportfolio programs. One of the sources of the problematic maxim that the use of portfolios for learning should be insulated from their use for institutional assessment is the fact that many, perhaps even most, eportfolio initiatives in higher education that have attempted to combine the two have allowed the standardized model to overpower the personalized model. In order to envision an alternative that skirts this danger, it makes sense to set aside these failed experiments and begin with examples of what is possible if the ideals are more intentionally and fully embraced. In Parts Two and Three, I examine in more detail the practical contingencies and challenges of developing programs that support the realization of the ideals, drawing on a large body of empirical research on both exemplary and more problematic eportfolio initiatives.

Another objection might be that the philosophical sources on which this chapter draws are unfamiliar to many in higher education, and therefore they are unlikely to have had a direct impact on practice. Here again, this is correct—up to a point. However, many of the concepts in contemporary educational theory that are most familiar to and popular with the kinds of faculty and staff likely to lead eportfolio initiatives have at least some connection to authenticity. By identifying its distinguishing features, philosophical analysis of authenticity helps make those connections apparent. The idea that we need to seek guidance for the future through examining the true nature of our selves is not uncommon in the educational philosophies that inform many proponents of the kind of learning in which eportfolio authors such as Moore engage. Progressive educators frequently seek to help students discover their *vocations*, exercise their *creativity*, embrace *diversity*, *personalize* their educational experiences, engage in *reflection*, and take *ownership* of their learning, becoming *self-directed* learners who develop *self-efficacy* in relationship to tasks in their fields and *self-authorship* over their whole lives. Each of these concepts connects to one or more defining features of authenticity.

One example is the emphasis on vocation in the work of Parker Palmer. A frequent speaker at education conferences and a widely read author, he has made a significant impact on many school teachers' and college professors' understanding of the purposes of education. Palmer is a leading proponent of the ideal of authenticity, which is reflected in his writing about teaching and his several works about how to learn throughout life, such as *Let Your Life Speak* (Palmer, 2000). In this book, Palmer explores the idea of vocation—that is, of each person having a calling he or she needs to discover in order to achieve happiness. A person finds what he or she ought to do in the world through adhering to an external moral code and looking within to determine the moral principles that are part of one's unique natures: "Before you tell your life what you intend to do with it, listen for what it intends to do with you. Before you tell your life what truths and values you have decided to live up to, let your life tell you what truths you embody, what values you represent" (Palmer, 2000, p. 3). Rather than trying to transform themselves to fit career paths to which they believe they ought to aspire, people should instead try to articulate their true selves and, from this expression, determine what they are best equipped to do. Growing out of Palmer's Quaker background, these ideas are echoed in contributions to recent discussions of the role of spirituality in higher education and its relationship to authenticity (Chickering, Dalton, & Stamm, 2006). The popularity of this work speaks to the widespread appeal of the ideal of authenticity.

Discussions of the value of eportfolios and of a liberal education more generally often emphasize creativity, a key to the expressive self that is an essential component of authenticity. Proponents argue that portfolios allow learners to tell their own story, expressing who they are through how the portfolio is designed and what materials are included. The degree to which students can put their unique stamp on their portfolio is indicative of how powerfully it is able to capture their learning. For example, Miles Kimball (2005) argues that "creating a portfolio should be an imaginative, creative" act of communicating the "rich process of considering one's self and one's learning experiences" (p. 452). Indeed, many consider creativity a valuable outcome in its own right—a central component of the liberal education needed for a successful career and life as a citizen in democratic society (Association of American Colleges and Universities, 2007) and as the key to such other essential capabilities as integrative thinking (Sill, 2001).

In addition to helping students discover their vocation and exercise their creativity, eportfolios are also seen as valuable because they help take into account and celebrate students' individual differences. At the heart of authenticity is this conviction that individual differences in identity are of paramount importance. Embracing individual and group-based difference is also at the heart of the embrace of diversity that is ubiquitous in higher education. The flexibility of eportfolios to include a wide range of types of evidence of learning and performance allows each student to make his or her own unique capabilities visible in his or her own way. For example, eportfolios can be used to allow primary school children to express their multiple intelligences (Stefanakis, 2002) and for community college students who are recent immigrants to show connections between their newly acquired academic knowledge and their native cultural traditions (Eynon, 2009). While other ways of supporting and assessing learning focus only on institutionally defined outcomes and particular styles of learning, portfolios allow students to present a more individualized picture of their learning, which is better able to take into account the ways they are distinctive. A prime example is the Learning Record portfolio assessment system developed in London and Los Angeles for use in the public schools and adapted for higher education as the Online Learning Record (Syverson, 2000). The Learning Record was a response to the need to systematically capture the development in reading, writing, and mathematics that teachers knew was occurring in their classrooms. However, this development was missed by more traditional assessments because of the staggering, and ever growing, diversity of students' backgrounds, interests, and learning styles. Portfolios have proved successful in accounting for these differences (Hallam, 2000).

One response to the need to support diversity is personalization. In the United Kingdom and Australia, in particular, the potential role of eportfolios in personalizing educational opportunities available to students throughout their lives is a key rationale for policies that are supporting the use of eportfolios to support lifelong learning (Beetham, 2006; Department for Education and Skills, 2005; Wills, 2008). Portfolios may speak to the diversity of life paths in a way that facilitates connecting individuals with resources for learning that match diverse needs. Governments may assume responsibility to the citizens they serve through providing funding to institutions such as schools, universities, professional bodies, and workforce development agencies and through providing guidance and infrastructure to enable eportfolios to be used across them over time.

Many broader educational theories influential in eportfolio circles share with authenticity an emphasis on participation. The central premise of the push for authentic assessment is that knowledge and skills should be measured through assessment that mirrors the activities and contexts that students will encounter through participation in actual practice (Maki, 2003; Wiggins & McTiche, 1998). The movement toward experiential learning suggests that students best understand a domain of knowledge and practice through direct experience (Kolb, 1983; Moon, 2004). Students may learn most powerfully through "legitimate peripheral participation" in a genuine community of practice (Lave & Wenger, 1991; Wenger, 1998). This conviction has led to new interest in traditional, participatory models of education such as apprenticeship (Ainley & Rainbird, 1999). Eportfolios are increasingly being used to support experiential learning activities such as internships, service-learning projects, and study abroad. Scholars point to the potential of eportfolios to capture evidence of learning from diverse participatory contexts—both those facilitated by educational institutions and less formal sites of everyday learning, and to integrate that learning with curricular work to present a fuller picture of an individual's development (Tosh, Werdmuller, Chen, Light, & Haywood, 2006). Grounding learning in individual experience rather than codified academic content is consonant with the ideal of authenticity.

Although the impact of these experiences depends on a growing understanding and adoption of shared ways of acting and knowing, the common emphasis on reflection in eportfolio pedagogy suggests that this engagement must be expressed through the self for it to result in deep learning. Currently popular in higher education pedagogy, reflection has also been at the heart of the pursuit of authenticity throughout the philosophical and literary tradition surveyed earlier. Traditionally reflection has been a key component of portfolios (Hamp-Lyons & Condon, 2000; Yancey & Weiser, 1997). Through reflection, students analyze their documented experiences and emotional reactions in light of their values, goals, and past experiences in order to decide how to act in the future (Boud, Keogh, & Walker, 1985; Kolb, 1983; Schön, 1983). Students come to see how their experiences of practice align with an understanding of their unique identities and to express that relationship so that they truly own what they are learning.

In so processing their learning through thought and feeling, students establish a sense of ownership of their learning, as Nussbaum (1997) suggests in the passage that opens this chapter. The idea of autonomous ownership of one's own identity and action is at the core of the conventional conception of authenticity. Barrett and her collaborators argue that ownership is essential to motivation and to learning through eportfolio composition. Ownership entails a sense of alignment between knowledge and experience and one's identity but also taking control of the process of learning. To establish ownership, students need to become "self-directed learners" (Brookfield, 1986; Taylor & Burgess, 1995). People also need "self-efficacy," the justified belief that they can shape the course of their lives in particular domains (Bandura, 1997). According to Baxter Magolda (2001), having the ability to examine the world and interpret it through reflection on one's beliefs constitutes "self-authorship" and is necessary for a rich and meaningful adult life. Self-authorship requires not just skills but access to one's authentic identity. A person's sense of what is important and what is valuable needs to come from within, not through reliance on received codes or institutional authority. Eportfolios can be powerful because they provide a context to develop attitudes and abilities that provide a stronger sense of ownership, self-efficacy, and self-authorship than students typically experience. In giving students a place to reflect on their experiences through the artifacts of those experiences and the ability to creatively express their understanding of who they are and what they have accomplished, eportfolios take into account the importance of authenticity to deep learning.

Authenticity and Procedural Justice

Given the wealth of connections between key concepts on contemporary discussions of learning and the ideal of authenticity, it is worth considering whether the ideal might be present where it is not expected. While the standardized model of the eportfolio is generally thought to work against the interests of authenticity, a closer looked at Moss's standardized portfolio and the assessment process of which it is a part may reveal that authenticity may underlie them as well. The way in which the second example portfolio relates to the ideal, however, is more complicated than with the first. Showing how authenticity also underlies this second model requires returning to considering the implications of the ideal for organization of society. This discussion will describe procedural justice and how this perspective may actually contribute to authenticity, at least as it is understood so far.

The opening section of this chapter suggested that one way of interpreting authenticity common in our culture is defining oneself without reference or in opposition to shared sources of morality. If a social system favors a single under-standing of a good life, then the ability for each person to live well in his or her own special way is threatened. The social system therefore must not endorse a common conception of the good, but protect a set of rights that enables individuals to live out their unique natures. Michael Sandal (1984) calls this kind of social system a procedural republic: "What makes a just society is . . . its refusal to choose in advance among competing purposes and ends. In its constitution and laws, the just society seeks to provide a framework within which its citizens can pursue their own values and ends, consistent with a similar liberty for others" (p. 82).

The danger of overemphasizing individual values and ends, of course, is what is sometimes called the "liberalism of neutrality" that limits the role of public life to protecting our individual rights. This uncritical embrace of choice leads to what Taylor (1991, pp. 11–12) calls a "soft relativism" where "everybody has his or her own 'values,' and about these it is impossible to argue. . . . That is their concern, their life choice, and it ought to be respected." To obviate this relativism, some people insist that the social world needs to be governed according to what Bellah and his coauthors (Bellah, Madsen, Sullivan, Swindler, & Tipton, 1996) term "procedural justice," a clearly defined, consistent set of principles and processes for distributing resources and settling disputes that is independent of the individual identities of the society's members.

This principle of procedural justice applies to Mary Moss's eportfolio. The process of which her standardized portfolio is a part is designed to measure the knowledge, skills, and abilities that the teaching profession has agreed are necessary for competent performance in the classroom. These standards are public and clearly defined, as is the required structure and contents of a portfolio and the procedure by which faculty will determine whether the assembled evidence and explanations are sufficient. The process is calibrated so that any given evaluator is likely to make the same judgment of the portfolio regardless of his or her knowledge of the student beyond what is in the portfolio. The portfolio is designed explicitly to factor out the kinds of evidence and explanations that were valued in Moore's personalized portfolio. There is no place for moral reflection or creative expression of identity. To the greatest extent possible, Moss's unique identity has been excluded from representation in the portfolio. What traces there are of her distinctiveness, evaluators are trained to ignore.

However, this does not necessarily mean that the Great Lakes State education program does not value authenticity. In fact, it may mean the opposite: the program might believe that because each student has a unique and valid vision of the good life based on her understanding of her own nature, it is not the place of the program or the university to endorse one vision and not others. Rather, the purpose of the institution should be to judge according to value-free standards, using objective methods, that are attainable by any student, regardless of the student's authentic identity. In this way, the process is fair to everyone and does not interfere with individuals' living their lives according to their own understanding of the good. (Although it is not possible to tell from her portfolio, Moss herself also may not wish for her self-understanding to factor into the university's judgment of her professional ability.) By holding to the principles of procedural justice, the standardized portfolio process tries to make space for authenticity.

The differences of form and purpose that Barrett and other scholars identify between the personalized and standardized portfolios remain. Rather than conflicting, however, the underlying philosophies behind the models may in fact align. The personalized portfolio provides an opportunity to express the authentic self in order to develop a more sophisticated understanding that guides future decisions. The standardized portfolio ensures that institutional values do not impinge on this process. The former supports authenticity directly; the latter supports it indirectly.

At least that is how it appears given the way of understanding authenticity discussed so far. From this take on authenticity, the personalized and standardized portfolios could be two sides of the same coin. By this logic, Barrett's admonition to keep the two models separate still makes sense. The personalized portfolio author needs choices; the standardized portfolio author needs rules. The personalized portfolio reader needs to see creativity; for the standardized portfolio reader, creativity would muddy the water. And so on. However, this understanding of authenticity has serious limitations, both philosophically and for the desired impact of eportfolios on both lifelong and learning and assessment.

Critiques of Authenticity

The ideal of authenticity, and the contemporary cultural changes and educational practices to which it is linked, faces criticism from both the right and the left. From a conservative perspective, the pursuit of authenticity leads to narcissism and atomism because it creates a culture of self-absorption. Relationships that ought to be enduring, such as allegiances to family, country, and religious faith, are treated as provisional. Instead of honoring these institutions, people see them as contingent on their contribution to self-fulfillment (Bloom, 1987; Himmelfarb, 1996; Lasch, 1991). Instead of feeling bonds of mutual obligation and looking to shared tradition as sources of meaning, people fail to look beyond their own interests. Procedural justice is an insufficient mechanism for coordinating society because it abdicates society's role in cultivating and maintaining shared values based on enduring commitments. A shared vision of the good life ought to be at the heart of a civilized society.

From this conservative perspective, education has a responsibility to instill an understanding of and loyalty to shared values, so an educational program that encourages learners to focus on themselves is fundamentally misguided. Personalized portfolios are therefore not just a waste of time but counterproductive. From this perspective, a more productive portfolio practice would take as its inspiration not Rousseau's pursuit of his unique, natural self but the autobiographical practice of another key eighteenth-century figure, Benjamin Franklin. He sought self-invention rather than self-discovery. Franklin (1985) aimed to "achieve moral perfection" by shaping himself to the values and virtues handed down to him by the society in which he hoped to establish his place.

At the other end of the continuum, theorists on the left question the very possibility of the objective processes of procedural justice and the autonomous authority of the true self posited by authenticity. Knowledge, moral or otherwise, is socially constructed; therefore, it is deeply intertwined with the subjectivity of the people doing the constructing and the relationships of power that shape how they do it. Work in the philosophy and sociology of science suggests that even the most seemingly empirical and objective information is the result of complex social processes of negotiation (Harding, 1991; Kuhn, 1970; Latour, 1991; Rorty, 1982). From this perspective, the idea is naive that educators or professional leaders could develop professional standards of performance that do not carry the traces of the identities and institutions that created them and could be applied in a manner free from subjective judgments shaped by the identities of both evaluator and the evaluated (Moss, 1994, 2004). Not only do standardized portfolios not protect difference; they make matters worse by attempting to hide the ideologies they enact.

Similarly this perspective holds that the idea that individuals have a true nature that they can express and can provide moral insight is mistaken. In reality, little about the self is fixed: it is social through and through. Jacques Derrida suggests that subjectivities are brought into being by, and are inextricable from, language. Linguistic meaning is impossible to pin down definitively, so the self ultimately has no grounding. Michel Foucault points to the social functions of the idea that the self has depth, which he sees as illusory. Social institutions instill this illusion through engaging individuals in practices of self-examination and self-scrutiny that produce the kinds of compliance the institutions need to function. Both Derrida and Foucault look toward a practice of radical freedom of self-definition that calls into the question the ways we typically think about the self and that destabilizes the linguistic relationships of power they trace. Derrida (1980) sees a liberating potential in the "free play" of language, while in his late work, Foucault (1984) suggests that we practice an "aesthetics of the self."

Most often, when the personalized model of eportfolio is critiqued, the critics point to the difficulty of establishing psychometric rigor when it is used in the context of high-stakes assessment (Wilkerson & Lang, 2003; Shavelson, Klein, & Benjamin, 2009). However, critics not focused on assessment sometimes use the ideas of these theorists. Invoking Foucault, Mhari MacAlpine (2005), in her analysis of the privacy risks of support for personalized portfolios by educational institutions and governments, warns that eportfolios may become mechanisms for "internalizing social control." In their place, she suggests that educators might elicit expressions of self that emphasize play and rhetorical invention rather than trying to articulate some underlying truth about one's nature. One example of such an assignment is the "mystory" or "widesite" proposed by Gregory Ulmer (1989, 2003), which encourages interplay and juxtaposition between images, texts, and symbols from popular culture, academic and professional writing, and personal and community memory to create new self-representations that may be "directed against the institutions of one's own formation" (Ulmer, 1989, p. viii).

The critiques from both the right and the left call into question the idea that the self has a fixed nature. The former would have individuals mold themselves to fit moral obligations that originate beyond the self, while the latter would have individuals shape their lives in ways that frustrate the power of institutions over our identities. These arguments for the malleability of the self are also supported by recent work in neurology that shows that the very structure of the brain evolves throughout life (Eakin, 1999). However, both perspectives suggest that we might define ourselves distinctively primarily in opposition to social relationships. From the first perspective, such opposition is a threat to social harmony, while for the latter, it is our hope for some kind of freedom.

Selfhood defined only in opposition to social relationships, however, is as intellectually problematic as autonomous selfhood. It is also a poor basis for a practical theory of authenticity that can inform mutually supportive individual and institutional development. The argument for the necessary role of the social in articulation of the self is supported by analysis of language in literary theory and feminist reinterpretation of how individual identity comes into being and changes over time. According to the literary theorist Michael Bakhtin (1982), language is fundamentally dialogical. The meaning of any expression depends on the social history of the words being used. When we speak or write, we evoke the web of meanings into which others have woven those words through their use over time. Truly unique, individual meaning, unconnected to this social background, is impossible.

Relationships within a social context are also central in the critique of autonomous selfhood by feminist theorists from a variety of disciplines. For example, Carole Gilligan's (1982) work in psychology suggests that children's moral decisions become more sophisticated not only by appealing to abstract reasoning but also through taking into account concrete relationships and commitments. Jessica Benjamin's (1988) psychoanalytical theory suggests that children's development of a sense of autonomy itself depends on the recognition of another. The autonomous and relational aspects of our identities are fundamentally intertwined. Feminist critics of autobiography from Mary Mason (1980) to Sidonie Smith (1993) have shown how the critical preference for narratives of autonomy has caused female life stories, and stories from non-Western cultures, which may be more relational, to be undervalued. Although much of this feminist scholarship originally associated the relational and the female, more recent work has shown that both men and women's identities are formed in relationship. This broader conception of the self opens up a much broader set of models of self-representation, from both men and women, than had previously been examined by autobiography critics (Eakin, 1999). These new models may have the potential to better capture the complexity of the contemporary lives individuals need to articulate through their eportfolios. In Chapter Six, I examine this idea in more detail through the work of the anthropologist Mary Catherine Bateson (1989).

Authenticity as Manner Rather than Content

Accepting the validity of these accounts of the self as articulated in dialogue with a shared cultural background and defined through relationships over time does not mean that authenticity needs to be abandoned. Rather, they suggest that dialogue and relationships are an essential element of the ideal. Insisting that the self be defined solely in isolation from or opposition to what is beyond the self is a misinterpretation of the ideal. This correction opens up new ways to think about eportfolio practice that can bridge the lifelong learning-assessment divide. The path to understanding the good life can still pass through the self; it just cannot stop there. Taylor (1991) makes the distinction between manner and the content of the pursuit of authenticity: "On one level, it clearly concerns the manner of espousing any end or form of life. Authenticity is clearly self-referential: this has to be my orientation. But this doesn't mean that on another level the content must be self-referential: that my goals must express or fulfill my desires or aspirations, as against something that stands beyond these" (p. 82).

Knowledge of the way we ought to live may come through examining how we make sense of our participation in the world through our emotions, intuitions, and reason. But this process of interpretation and expression is fundamentally in relationship to shared linguistic and cultural background, and the result of the examination may be a fuller commitment to goods that have their origin in the kinds of enduring institutions that some critics of authenticity worry are being abandoned in our contemporary culture.

Because the self is not given but shaped through interactions with those with whom one comes into contact over time, the process of articulating authenticity fundamentally is social as a process as well as in its content. Interactions with others help us come to understand which of our feelings and ideas are significant and valuable enough to become part of whom we believe ourselves and present ourselves to be. As Bernard Williams (2004) puts it, "We are all together in the social activity of mutually stabilizing our declarations and moods and impulses into becoming things such as beliefs and relatively steady attitudes" (p. 193), the components of a genuinely authentic identity. For this reason, "We need each other in order to be anybody" (p. 200).

Authenticity is also a social ideal in a stronger sense. Charles Guigon (2004) suggests that we often see those who choose not to cultivate their own authenticity not just as failing themselves but also as betraying a collective interest. He argues that we make this judgment because a successful democratic society must be "made up of people who use their best judgment and discernment to identify what to them is truly worth pursuing and are willing to stand for what they believe in" (p. 159). Achieving authenticity entails not just the freedom to shape a distinctive identity but also a responsibility to contribute to building social institutions and establishing cultural norms that protect and enhance that freedom. Being truly authentic ought to mean "to be constantly vigilant in one's society, to be engaged in political action aimed at preserving and reinforcing a way of life that allows for such worthy personal life projects as that of authenticity" (p. 162). One key means for engaging in this action is through participation in democratic decision making with institutions, holding them accountable for providing opportunities to participate and capitalizing on those opportunities.

Ensuring that the dialogue between individual and institution is more than one way also answers criticism from the other end of the political spectrum. Here there are worries that the process of self-articulation in relationship to moral sources beyond the self is simply a way to ensure participation in our own social control. Through institutional practices, such as the composition of eportfolios, we learn to think of ourselves as people who embody the values that help reproduce the power of those institutions. But Foucault's own work suggests that power is constitutive, not just oppressive, and that we participate in its function throughout our lives. Through expression in eportfolios, we may be able not just to reproduce shared and institutionally embedded values but to shape them. Drawing on Anthony Gidden's theory of structuration, Melissa Peet (2005) shows how students enact the social structures of which they are a part through their own actions and the way they represent themselves. Peet also demonstrates the impact of portfolio composition on students' understanding of the ways they can transform institutions through their participation in them. In order for individual self-expression to have a more powerful impact on institutional values in practice, the relationship between individuals and the institutions in which they participate needs to be governed by the cultural ideal of deliberation. The potential role of deliberative democracy in assessment in higher education is the focus on Chapter Three.

Peet's work is an example of how the conception of authenticity as both a personal and a social ideal is beginning to emerge in some of the most promising scholarship on eportfolios and on teaching and learning in higher education more generally. Indeed, most of the concepts surveyed in the section on authenticity and educational theory earlier in this chapter have a social component. Being successful in discovering a vocation, for example, may not just mean listening for an inner voice in isolation but also discerning "what is genuinely worth pursuing with the social context in which [one] is situated" through reflection in dialogue with others (Guignon, 2004, p. 155). Developing true self-authorship requires establishing and being nurtured by rich and meaningful relationships, not just the ability to achieve a critical distance from them (Baxter Magdola, 2001; Kegan, 1994). Pedagogies of engagement, such as service-learning, explicitly situate individual learning and identity development within the context of social action.

Authenticity Through Social Dialogue and the Multiple Curricula

Returning to Moore's portfolio, we can see both the relational background of his quest for an autonomous spiritual identity and the ways in which his representations of those social connections offer new possibilities for institutional growth. While Moore stresses that he does not affiliate himself solely with any specific religion or discipline, his self-representation does depend on a central commitment to "service to others" in pursuit of "social justice." Both concepts are deeply rooted in Eastern and Western religious traditions and the humanist and scientific academic fields he encounters through his studies and travel. In addition, they were present in the environment in which he was raised. His understanding of service to others is expressed through reflection on his engagement with these spiritual and intellectual communities, and his commitment to service is strengthened by the ways he is able to articulate it as a common theme across them. For Moore, service transcends any specific tradition. This identification of a common theme speaks to another shared principle that underlies Moore's self-examination: a quest for the universal. His critical examination of specific institutions is in pursuit of what is shared between the visions that attracted him to them as much as it is in search of what is unique about himself.

Similarly, in his discussion of globalization and India's relationship to the West, Moore laments what he sees as the unidirectionality of the cultural exchange. This observation, which he first develops in relationship to the picture of economic development in Thomas Friedman's *The World Is Flat* and the immigrant experience as depicted in Jhumpa Lahiri's *The Namesake*, is further validated by Moore's reflections on his own interactions with others as a Westerner studying in an Indian city. Like the supposedly level cultural exchange in Friedman that Moore concludes is actually unbalanced, he determines that his own conversations with merchants and strangers, outside of the context of the spiritual communities into which he has made a commitment to integrate himself, are similarly one-directional. He does not feel the need to make an argument for the importance of the cultural exchange being more mutual. He makes the assumption that his reader shares his conviction, clarified and strengthened through reflection on direct experience and academic knowledge, that mutuality is important. The principle is part of shared cultural background that unites author and audience. What the portfolio demonstrates, to both the reader and Moore himself, is that his sense of himself and sense of this principle align. He has taken ownership of the shared principle.

Moore's understanding of each of these central ethical principles—service, universality, and mutuality—is validated by how they resonate with his own sensibilities and reasoning processes. His path to ownership of the principles is through himself. The portfolio demonstrates that they work for him, that they match up with experiences as interpreted by his distinctive emotions, intuitions, and ways of thinking. However, each suggests not a turning inward and a focus on self-fulfillment but a need to engage in community in pursuit of a common good. While the manner of Moore's establishing his connection to these moral principles is through the self, the content of the resulting vision of how he should live his life focuses beyond the self.

Indeed, his expression of identity in his eportfolio leads him to reaffirm the centrality of community to the type of society in which he wishes to live and dedicates himself to helping such community prosper. Achieving authenticity entails working toward social change. He writes, "Wherever the source of the inspiration, raising a sense of community in my surroundings and in the world at large is my highest hope." These principles are accessible only through commitment to others facilitated by institutions that support the kinds of community that sustain them, be they ashrams or sociology departments. While the institutions may have flaws, his goal is to help them improve rather than to demonstrate their unimportance. Thus, he titles the introduction to the portfolio, "Spiritual Communities, Backward." Through examination of himself, he finds a commitment to what he sees as universal values that underlie the multiple traditions to which he has a connection. These lead him back into community in support of those values in a manner informed by how he believes himself to be distinctive. His eportfolio thus illustrates a version of authenticity more in line with the retrieval of the ideal as both personal and social than the less sophisticated popular understanding it appeared to embody on first reading.

Technology plays an important role in Moore's articulation of his authenticity. From his use of photos, visual design elements, and a multilinear organization, we glimpsed the potential of the digital medium to support creativity. It provides more options for the constitutive articulation of identity than print does, enabling portfolio authors to express their selves in ways that align with their distinctive ways of knowing (Hull & Katz, 2006). In light of the social, as well as personal, nature of authenticity, a second dimension of how technology supports this fuller version of authenticity is important to note. The networked medium also enables new kinds of connections to the social world that shape identity and in which they participate. Moore is able to make links to websites representing the communities he explores. Through publishing his portfolio on the Web, he makes it accessible to readers in these social contexts. The portfolio could then serve as a way for him to introduce his identity into a community dialogue about values and priorities.

Part Three of this book examines these social capabilities of Internet technology in much greater detail.

Moore takes a similar approach in his treatment of the New Century College competencies, which need to be well represented in his eportfolio to fulfill the requirements of the capstone course and for graduation. As will become clearer in Chapter Three, Moore's relationship to the competencies, prompted by the academic context in which he writes, suggests an alternative model of assessment that better matches the dialogical model of authenticity than the standardized model examined in this chapter. Moore does not uncritically accept the competencies as they are officially defined by the college and try to shape himself to them, as Benjamin Franklin did to his list of received virtues. But neither does he define himself through a wholesale rejection of them. Rather, he uses them as an interpretive framework for articulating himself in connection with the academic community of which he is a part. He uses the competencies to arrange and discuss both his formal course work and his less formal learning as represented in his blog writing and photography. Through this process, he determines what they mean for him and presents a distinctive take on each. He establishes his ownership of the competencies.

Learner self-representations in eportfolios like those of Moore and Moss provide differing degrees of illumination for institutions about the full complexity of learning. Learner self-representations in eportfolios like Moore's, tied to their distinctive understandings of institutionally embedded conceptions of what it means to be an educated person, can be of tremendous value in improving the performance of institutions themselves. They can make visible the multiple curriculums—delivered, experienced, and lived—that Kathleen Yancey (1998, 2004b) argues are always present. Most conventional assessments concentrate on how well student performance of assigned tasks matches the goals of the delivered curriculum, the set of educational materials and the experiences designed by faculty. Through their ability to accommodate diverse evidence as interpreted through student reflection, however, eportfolios also capture the experienced and lived curriculums. The delivered curriculum has an impact on the experience of learners only through how it is experienced—how learners make sense of the curriculum in relationship to their knowledge, expertise, and values. This experience is shaped by and shapes the lived curriculum composed of both formal and informal learning throughout life. Personalized portfolios help to capture the experienced and lived curriculums.

This capability points to the limitations of standardized portfolios in serving the first of their two purposes: providing information to improve institutional performance. While the standardized model of eportfolios is able to say something about the match between the delivered curriculum and student performance, it does not provide a window into the other two curriculums, which we need to understand to create educational environments that support learning throughout life. In excluding this richer picture of learning, standardized portfolios provide less powerful guidance for improving institutional performance than they might if personalized elements were included.

Mary Moss is limited to demonstrating her ability to "accurately assess and analyze student learning" through a set number of formal assignments or recordings of herself in the classroom and showing how they match up with a rubric that defines what constitutes accuracy in assessment and effectiveness in analysis. Although scoring this portfolio may help show if Mary meets this specified requirement, it does not speak to key questions such as these:

- Is her analysis of student learning in the classroom informed by her observations of teaching and learning in other settings and her own learning experiences?
- Do the processes of assessment about which she has learned resonate with her own sense of what is important to measure about teaching and learning?
- Do they match her values about fairness, difference, and privacy? How do assessment and analysis fit into her larger understanding of what it means to be a teacher, and how does she see this role connecting to her life as citizen, partner, and parent?

These last questions about values and the interrelationships between social roles point to limitations of the standardized model in fulfilling its second purpose as well: measuring preparation to enter a profession. The standardized model assumes that factors such as personal values and nonprofessional commitments are irrelevant to professional practice. The next chapter will show that they are in fact integral elements of a fuller account of professional practice that Howard Gardner and his colleagues (Gardner, Csikszentmihalyi, & Damon, 2001) term "good work." The future of teaching may in fact depend on having teachers who are able to bring their full authenticity to how they shape the profession through their practice.

Toward a Dialogical Authenticity in the Use of Eportfolios

The primary limitation of the standardized model, then, may not be that it precludes creative expression of a vision of the good rooted in individual uniqueness. As we have seen, it may support such expression indirectly by placing it outside the gaze of formal evaluative processes. If both are supported but kept separate, the personalized and standardized models could support this popular conception of authenticity. The problem may be that isolating the process of self-articulation and the process of institutional evaluation from each other distorts both. The problem may be that this separation does not recognize that shared values are necessary for effective self-expression and that such personalized self-representations are essential to determining what institutions should value. The reformed conception of the ideal of authenticity suggests that the processes of individual and institution definition and decision making are inextricable. Both unfold in dialogue; both are linked. Our choice is not between keeping them separate or not. It is between trying to pretend they do not exist or intentionally embracing the connections and shaping them to better support both processes.

The attempt to keep them separate reflects not only a misunderstanding of authenticity but also failure to imagine alternative relationships between self and society, between individuals and institutions. As Alistair MacIntyre (2007) points out, there is a widespread belief in Western culture that "there are only two alternative modes of social life open to us, one in which the free and arbitrary choices of individuals are sovereign and one in which the bureaucracy is sovereign, precisely so that it may limit the free and arbitrary choices of individuals. . . . Thus the society in which we live is one in which bureaucracy and individualism are partners as well as antagonists" (p. 267).

Barrett critiques the use of standardized portfolios as a mechanism of bureaucracy that threatens the expression of authentic selfhood. This chapter has shown that it can be seen instead as an effort to protect individual choice. Either way, however, maintaining a dichotomy between the personalized and the standardized models accepts the idea of no middle road between radical independence and deadening conformity. Chapter Three shows that the model of deliberative democracy provides an alternative. Through deliberation mediated by authentic and integral eportfolios, programmatic and institutional assessment can become processes that support both personalized learning and organizational innovation. The deliberative model capitalizes on the reality of dialogue between the self and society and adds to it the spaces and rules needed to make those exchanges inclusive and directed toward the common good. As Nussbaum suggests, individuals can gain ownership of themselves through the guiding rules of argument. Through a similar process of deliberation, our institutions too may be better "fitted for freedom."

Questions for Practice

The role of authenticity in both personalized and standardized eportfolio models and the potential that a new understanding of that ideal as grounded in relationship has to bridge those models raise several questions for practice:

- To what extent does the cultural ideal of authenticity underlie your understanding of learning and education? Does it inform the understanding of identity held by the learners with whom you work? If authenticity is not central, then what alternative understandings of identity and personal development stand in its place, and what are their implications for how you use eportfolios?

- How might your eportfolio model better support creative expression of learners' identities? How do learners develop a sense of ownership over their eportfolios? What role might multimedia evidence and visual design play?

- How can you ensure that evaluation procedures are fair to everyone being evaluated without excluding consideration of individual values, experiences, and relationships that are integral to fully understanding learning and performance?

- How might you help learners articulate their identity and development in their eportfolios in dialogue with shared interpretive standards? How well do the standards you use support interpretation in light of individual values, experiences, and relationships? Could they be adapted or framed so that they do so more effectively?

CHAPTER TWO

EPORTFOLIOS AND VOCATION

Integrity for Good Work

Close reading of Sean Moore's personalized eportfolio and Mary Moss's standardized one in Chapter One demonstrated that authenticity is an ideal underlying both dominant models of eportfolios in higher education. The common perception of a necessary conflict between eportfolios for self-directed learning and eportfolios for programmatic and institutional assessment was shown to be in error if authenticity is seen not solely as an individual ideal but also as a social one. Authentic self-representation can contribute not only to the intrinsically motivated learning of individual eportfolio authors but also to the collective project of making colleges and universities more conducive to supporting such learning. Genuine authenticity requires students to participate in such projects, and higher education institutions serious about cultivating authenticity ought to provide opportunities for them to do so.

This chapter makes a similar argument in a significantly different context about a closely related ideal, integrity. The philosopher Cheshire Calhoun (1995) suggests that integrity—defined as having and acting on relatively consistent and deep commitments—has generally been considered a solely personal virtue. The true value of integrity, she suggests, may not be just to the individual but also to the society in which that individual lives because acting with integrity is likely to yield more just and fulfilling relationships and institutions.

This chapter examines the changing nature of careers and professions and looks closely at one professional's eportfolio. This example shows that eportfolios can empower individuals to articulate their integrity, helping them build professional identities that are integrated with their values and commitments as enacted in their personal and civic lives. Not only are such integral self-representations beneficial to the individuals who compose them, but they also contribute to the development of the professions of which those authors are a part. In this way, integrity is an ideal that benefits both individuals and the larger society.

Institutions and Careers

While professions were once pursued primarily through single institutions over extended periods of time, the nature of relationships between individuals and institutions in all spheres of life has changed significantly in recent decades. In the past, most people pursuing higher education attended a single institution full time for each level of schooling in a relatively continuous sequence from childhood into late adolescence or early adulthood. Now, almost a third of students take courses from multiple institutions en route to an undergraduate degree (American Association of Colleges and Universities, 2002). A majority of higher education students are now adults, and many study part time. While there was once an expectation that many careers would be defined by long-term employment within a single organization, such relationships are becoming increasingly rare. Changes in employment are even more dramatic. Over the course of their working lives, most Americans entering the job market today can expect to have at least ten employers (Bureau of Labor Statistics, 2008). Even in European countries like the Netherlands, companies are beginning to find the lifetime employment model unsustainable in the new global economy in which they compete. (See the discussion of the Nedcar company in Chapter Seven.) People are increasingly being asked to take personal responsibility for their employability and the shape of their careers as they interact with multiple employers, at once and over time. Single institutions seem to be less and less suited to provide the frame in which academic and professional identities can be defined.

In the changed environment, many new professional relationships are possible. Even within single organizations, individuals are increasingly engaged to perform services related to specific projects rather than to serve in ongoing roles. Contracts between employers and individuals are increasingly transactional rather than relational (Rousseau, 1990). They specify the performance of time-bounded tasks using specific competencies for monetary compensation rather than establishing ongoing relationships that also include nonmonetary benefits such as mutual loyalty and support. Job search and social networking technology make it easier for individuals and organizations to learn about each other and make connections, facilitating the easy establishment and dissolution of these shorter-term, more narrowly defined relationships (Bridges, 1994). Such an environment may offer increased flexibility in work schedules and sites that present new opportunities for interweaving personal, civic, and professional lives. Such an economy may offer those adept at navigating it what former U.S. Secretary of Labor Robert Reich (2000) calls "the terrific deal"—the ability to constantly negotiate new and better relationships that serve one's interests. While once framed by organizations and jobs, many careers are becoming "boundaryless" (Arthur & Rousseau, 1996). An individual may find the freedom to assemble a "protean" career from multiple and diverse experiences of work, community involvement, and personal pursuits (Mirvis & Hall, 1994).

However, if the institutions for which they work no longer provide boundaries, people seeking to build careers may need to make those boundaries elsewhere. While constraining freedom, boundaries do serve a range of purposes important to individuals. First, rather than necessarily empowering them, the perfect employment market Reich and others envisioned may actually shift the balance of power away from individuals further by making them more continuously subject to the rapidly changing state of the labor market. As Hirsch and Shanley note (1996), "Formal boundaries provide limits within which individuals exercise discretion. Eliminating boundaries will not render individuals free, but, instead may increase the external constraints on individual actions and unpredictability" (p. 227). Without enduring connections between individuals and organizations, individual action also is less likely to be able to influence the organization's values, procedures, and strategic directions. In addition, the bounded, persistent relationships with others in the workplace provided by long-term employment in well-defined roles have traditionally been essential for socialization within a community of practice—for gaining the tacit knowledge needed for expert performance in a domain and influencing the practice of others through one's own activity (Lave & Wenger, 1991; Wenger, 1998). Such contexts for socialization may need to be found elsewhere. Finally, and perhaps most crucial, long-term working relationships, well-defined jobs, stable internal labor markets, and a clear demarcation between work and home have provided clear narrative structures that individuals can use to make meaning of their lives (Sennett, 1998, 2006). Those for whom these models no longer apply now must take on the complex task of figuring out the relationships between the different spheres of their lives—personal, professional, and civic—and craft them into coherent life stories.

To prosper in the midst of these changes, people need new means to achieve integrity, the second cultural ideal central to eportfolio practice explored in this book and the focus of this chapter. I take *integrity* to mean achieving systemic understanding of how one's values, commitments, and actions cohere and interconnect—how they are made consistent to a holistic understanding of one's identity across personal, professional, and civic roles and over time. More so than other forms of self-representation common in professional and academic contexts, the eportfolio genre facilitates the articulation of integrity. Research indicates that successful achievement of integrity is strongly related to the degree of impact of eportfolios on learning and relationships to others. In addition to the means to articulate integrity, people also need social contexts in which to cultivate and defend it. Occupational communities, when organized on the model of professions, may provide such a context, and eportfolios can play a central role in their evolution.

Samantha Slade's Competencies and Employability

To explore the intersection of integrity and the idea of a profession, I begin with an example—an eportfolio composed by Samantha Slade of Montreal, Quebec, Canada. An adult educator and learning designer, Slade began composing an eportfolio at what she saw as a turning point in her life. Entering her forties, she was contemplating leaving her job with the government of Quebec to form her own company so that she could chart the direction of her professional activities. Her job within the boundaries of the government was secure and meaningful, but it did not give her the freedom to choose projects that drew on her vision of the potential of educational technology to transform learning in the workplace and to broaden access to knowledge work for new immigrants (Slade, 2008a). She was considering moving toward a boundaryless career, with all the possibilities and challenges it was likely to entail. Slade needed to take stock of her experiences, values, and commitments in order to choose a path forward and communicate her capabilities to those with whom she hoped to form professional relationships in her new career. On the opening page of her portfolio, Slade explains that its purpose is to "help me reflect upon, understand, and give value to what I've done, what I can do, and where I'm going."

Slade's portfolio consists of an interlinked collection of wiki pages (that only she can edit), written in English, French, or in some cases both. Most pages include either pictures or brief videos, and many link to the websites of organizations with which she has relationships or to educational media and research she has produced. The opening page features a video of Slade walking through a store in her neighborhood in Montreal, interacting with friends in her home, and playing with her children in a park, while a voice-over, alternating between English and French,

lists character traits: "Dependable . . . Flexible . . . Adaptable . . . Samantha."
From this page, readers can choose from three sections: I'm Competent At, My
Learning, and About Me.

The Competencies section is the most extensive. The page lists her competencies across six categories: technical (career specific), organizational, social and
personal, languages, computer and digital, and artistic and other. The introduction to the page explains to what the varied competencies listed add up. Her
varied capabilities enable her to "formalise and instrument learning and work
flows . . . [through] analysing, synthesising and structuring . . . motivating, organ-
ising and animating." The proliferation of verbs suggests a focus on dynamic
processes, capitalizing on change, and learning as an ongoing and emergent
phenomenon that can be supported by the structure offered by technology but
should not be limited by it.

She details her professional competencies by reference to the instructional
design competencies established by the International Board of Standards
for Training, Performance and Instruction and the Professional Teacher
Competencies of the Ministry of Education of Québec. For example, she asserts
her ability to "establish and spearhead an instructional/learning design committee for any type of project" through reference to the collaborative projects she led
while completing an online master's degree program, as well as her use of instructional design support tools in working with collaborating agencies in her previous
job with the government. To the set of competencies established by the board
and the ministry, she adds a collection that corresponds to her own understanding
of what is important in instructional design and pedagogical practice, such as
the ability to "design tools to help make competences visible and to facilitate the
development of competences." Description of this competency links to a detailed
survey of professional literature related to competency-based approaches to lifelong
learning, ongoing work that charts her evolving understanding of cutting-edge
research and practice. In correspondence with the overall vision articulated by
her introductions and the video examples included on many of the pages, her
chosen competencies emphasize skillful guidance of processes, respect for individual differences, and an embrace of the dynamics of rapidly changing contexts
for learning and work.

Each of the competency categories also includes one "competency under
development" in which she is currently improving through undertaking a range
of activities. The detailed account of each of these competencies illustrates
how she puts into practice in her own learning the approach to using competencies to "assist and document non-formal learning" that she grounds in
current research elsewhere in the portfolio. For each chosen competency, she
captures her plans for learning, assessing her own current and desired level

of mastery, her goals for improvement, why she values the competency, and the means toward improvement she intends to capitalize on. Planning is then followed by monitoring and evaluation sections, in which she establishes performance indicators and means to measure them. For example, because she must be "able to organize and manage [her] paperwork for [her] new position" as the leader of a small consultancy, she is currently developing her skills in accounting. She is seeking assistance from professional accountants and reading a book documenting a model of good practice from a similar organization. She recognizes that she has little experience with this kind of activity and needs to acquire sufficient familiarity to manage her enterprise, but does not need or desire to become an expert. Periodically she is keeping a reflective record of her progress that she will evaluate through conversations with more experienced financial record keepers.

Slade's account of her competencies in her eportfolio demonstrates several of the ways eportfolios can be used to enhance an individual's employability. Increasingly employability is a key policy driver behind programs to support eportfolio use in higher and adult education, the workplace, and employment services, particularly in Europe. (Recent projects focused on employability are examined in detail in Chapter Seven.) Many employability eportfolio projects share a common competency-based approach.

First, they help individuals identify and document their competencies. The resulting competency profiles then are compared to profiles established by industry or professional organizations detailing what employers value. Next, eportfolios are used to help individuals plan and carry out learning that helps them fill gaps between what is demanded of them by the job market and the skills they already possess. Finally, the resulting documentation of competencies is used to help portfolio authors locate employment opportunities and demonstrate their qualification to fill them.

Although Slade seeks employment opportunities in the form of projects rather than positions, the approach she takes with her eportfolio parallels this competency-matching process in a number of ways. She documents the competencies she possesses by analyzing and presenting evidence of her education and experience. She draws on formal competency frameworks developed by associations and industry bodies related to her profession to situate her skills within her occupation. By examining what is required of her in her new role as an independent consultant, she identifies knowledge and skills that will make her better able to attract and retain clients and work with them in accordance with her understanding of excellent educational practice. Through inviting potential clients to read her portfolio, she can share examples of her work and reflections on her experiences that document her competencies, demonstrating how she is well suited to help them meet their organizational challenges.

Career Identity and Integrity

When considered within the context of a career rather than just a particular episode of searching for a job or a client, employability entails more than just having a set of well-documented marketable skills and the means to find people who are willing to pay for those skills. Research on employability suggests that successful careers require "know why" as much as they do "know how" or "know who" (DeFillipi & Arthur, 1996). Shaping a meaningful career requires that choices about work and learning be guided by and connected to values, commitments, and other aspects of identity that exceed a person's knowledge, skills, and associations. Fugate, Kinicki, and Ashforth (2004) point to career identity as one of three crucial dimensions of employability that go beyond acquiring and demonstrating a collection of competencies. Elements of career identity "may include goals, hopes, and fears; personality traits; values, beliefs, and norms; interaction styles; and time horizons" (p. 20). In the past, employers have played a significant role in shaping a sense of career identity, an understanding of the purposes of vocational practice. As the relationships between individuals and organizations become more transactional, individuals increasingly must take on personal responsibility for developing this understanding.

Understanding the values, commitments, goals, and relationships one has that are relevant to developing a career identity necessarily extends beyond the professional into the personal. Values are expressed in choices made in both private and public life. Resources of time and attention have to be allocated across sometimes competing commitments to one's profession, family, and community. Exploring how one's values are, or fail to be, consistent across the different roles needed in life becomes an important element of defining one's career identity. Making explicit and reflecting on commitments across the scope of a life are similarly essential. An understanding of a person's character traits that may prove relevant to professional activity is at least as likely to come through examining personal experiences and investments as from analyzing vocational engagement. Indeed, the idea of a career might be broadened to include consideration of such a broader life context in a manner similar to how the field of occupational therapy defines "occupation." Many occupational therapists conceive of a person's occupation not in the colloquial sense of his or her primary job category but as the totality of his or her "self-initiated, self-directed, purposeful, culturally relevant, organized activity" (Yerxa, 1994, p. 587), which includes identity, action, and intention in "a synthesis of doing, being, and becoming" (Wilcock, 1999). The cultural ideal of integrity calls for just such a holistic approach to understanding a career situated within a person's larger identity.

What distinguishes Slade's eportfolio from those often produced through programs that emphasize the competency-matching approach is the integration of the personal. With its images of life beyond the workplace, the opening video suggests that she sees her professional role as intimately connected with the other spheres of her life. Her private life is woven throughout the portfolio through the use of personal experience as evidence and illustration, charting values that guide both her professional choices and her personal interests, planning learning that serves both, and using this picture of the whole to articulate a professional philosophy.

Certain human competencies that contribute to her strength as a learning designer have been developed and demonstrated most clearly in her family life. Her ability to "control emotion . . . to nurture & care for others, [and to take a] positive and optimistic approach to activities, people, events" is evidenced by her success as a parent and partner, weathering illness and faithfully discharging the day-to-day work of maintaining healthy relationships. Similarly, her "ease and enjoyment working with other cultures" is as equally evidenced by living and working in a francophone culture as a native English speaker and in isolated fishing villages as someone raised in an urban environment as it is by the adult learning projects she has led in Central America and Africa. Similarly, her informal learning experiences in her personal life illustrate the approach to learning she seeks to facilitate in her professional work. For example, a video introducing the My Learning section of the portfolio places Slade in her garden examining her tomato plants early in the growing season. Confessing a lack of sophistication as a gardener, she explains how she would go about gaining expertise, moving from making a decision to learn, to planning the learning process, coming up with metrics for assessing success, and finding a way to share and celebrate what she has learned.

Slade's plans for her learning, as articulated in her portfolio, also integrate the private and the public. For example, she seeks to develop her competence at "communicating clearly when communication involves confronting." Reflecting on both her personal and professional experiences, she recognizes that confrontation consistently causes her "stress and anxiety." Recognizing that the cognitive and affective challenges of managing conflict are similar across the roles she plays throughout her life, she plans a process of self-observation, practice, and reflection that includes her full range of experiences. Even for competencies in which she is currently improving that she classifies as primarily personal, she connects her learning to the ongoing development of an integrated identity. While the course she is taking on playing African percussion is motivated by her love of music and dance and a desire to participate in such artistic expression more fully, she also believes that the new practice will "help [her] to take [her] place in the world."

Drumming is a way to connect to the experience of another culture. It helps situate her identity globally and feel connected to the diversity of cultures she encounters through her professional work supporting immigrants in documenting their existing capabilities and developing the new ones they need to prosper in Quebecois society.

In addition to her competencies, Slade's portfolio articulates her values. (See Figure 2.1.) Many of these, such as sustainability, creativity, collaboration and sharing, respect, efficiency, and courage, are just as clearly related to her personal interests and experiences that she chronicles in the portfolio, such as travel, children, design, and ecology, as they are to her career-specific competencies and achievements. Values such as responsibility and motivation, which can be traced throughout the personal and professional elements of the portfolio, are used to explain a professional philosophy that could also be applied to the challenges

FIGURE 2.1. ABOUT ME PAGE OF SAMANTHA SLADE'S EPORTFOLIO

Samantha Slade's ePortfolio: I'm competent at | My learning | **About me**

My values | My interests and hobbies | My resources | What people say about me | People who inspire me | Cultural favorites | Future

I'm positive, enthusiastic and determined for myself, my projects and others. I like to plan and organise, processes, events, trips, projects etc. Creativity and innovation are important and natural for me.

Sir Ove Arup, an engineer who inspires me

- My values
- My resources
- My interests and hobbies
- My personality awareness ⌐
- What people say about me
- Cultural favorites
- Future to do (or be able to do) list

Image courtesy of Samantha Slade.

of family and community life. For example, Slade embraces an ethic of personal responsibility: "Each individual is responsible for his or her learning, career, health, [and] personal happiness. . . . Blaming others, feeling like a victim, waiting for the day—that's not the way. If you want something to happen you got to make it happen." Responsibility is not role bound; it applies to the whole of a person's life. However, "organizations, institutions, [and] experts . . . need to accompany and facilitate each individual in assuming [his or her] responsibilities." Her role as an educator and designer of learning environments is to help individuals take action to improve their lives. Her role as a parent might also entail providing such support to her adolescent children as they begin to take on more of the responsibilities of adulthood.

A similarly integrated perspective is clear in her commitment to taking motivation into account. Effectively channeling motivation requires understanding the "whole individual" because "an individual is more than the sum of [his or her] formal work and educational experiences. If [he or she is] to embark on any kind of 'professional development' or 'continuing education,' the individual needs to be motivated. The whole individual is made of personal interests and activities, values, and stories as well as the competencies and skill set that organizations are interested in." This insight into motivation probably owes as much to reflecting on long-term personal relationships as it does to Slade's personal experience. Turned around, it can help one connect to others' motivation in private life as well. In order to fully understand the values they embrace or the stories they tell, and to help people examine and author them, one needs to get some understanding of their capabilities.

The incorporation of videos and pictures throughout the portfolio reflects and contributes to the interweaving of Slade's personal and professional worlds. The pictures and videos consistently situate her within domestic and community life. Rather than in offices or in classrooms, Slade appears in such spaces as on her couch with her cat, out walking in Montreal, or against a backdrop of paintings in her home. These are comfortable, inviting spaces, organic and a bit gritty, filled with interesting people and things to look at and touch. Viewing these clips and snapshots, the reader feels welcomed into an informal, nourishing space. While the reflections and stories she presents in the videos focus on her understanding of her professional competencies and aspirations, the visual environment she creates situates this professional activity within a larger ecology of her life. In addition, the choice of spaces and their design serves to reinforce Slade's message about supporting learning: learning spaces need to be personalized and welcoming, stitched together from materials from multiple sources, rich in both information and interactions, connecting to the whole of learners' lives.

Perhaps most striking about Slade's portfolio is how well its form embodies its content. Not merely asserting the importance of the whole person to learning, she demonstrates it through chronicling her own learning across her personal and professional roles. Beyond just arguing for the importance of taking personal responsibility for learning, she enacts this responsibility in her portfolio. The very choice of a wiki as the technology in which to compose and publish her portfolio aligns with her emphasis throughout on embracing change and choosing flexible structures that help learners capitalize on it. (In fact, when I was halfway through writing this chapter, the portfolio itself changed: a new page appeared, providing insight into her "personality awareness" using a newly available online analysis service.) In charting the relationships between her personal and professional competencies, values, interests, experiences, and projects through the content and form of her eportfolio, Slade articulates the integrity of her identity.

Career Identity and the Symphonic Self

An interweaving of the personal and professional is one of the crucial elements of developing a career identity. However, in the contemporary workplace, and particularly for those pursuing boundaryless careers, the challenge does not end there. Developing a career identity requires not just chronicling experiences and reflecting on aspirations but determining how they can be synthesized into an understanding of the role of work in one's life that can guide vocational choices (Meijers, 1998). Knowing what one's capabilities, values, dispositions, and relationships are or could be is not enough. Rather, individuals must develop organizing principles to help them prioritize their attention and establish the boundaries between their roles, developing a holistic understanding of their identity as a coherent system. To have successful career identities, people need to create a critical distance that allows them to examine the relationships between their relationships and their relationship to their relationships, that is, to *have* their relationships rather than to be defined *by* them. In Kegan's (1982, 1994) terms, rather than being subject to their traits, values, commitments, and connections with other individuals and organizations, individuals need to make these things the object of their inquiry and design. They need to build a theory or narrative that guides their identity development in order to successfully negotiate a career in the changed workplace in which many find themselves.

This challenge requires moving to what Kegan call the "fourth level of consciousness." Kegan's (1994) analysis of contemporary accounts of effective parenting, successful partnering, personal development through therapy, and adult education suggests that adults are equally challenged to understand their private lives at this advanced level of cognitive complexity as they are to understand their public lives at work over the course of a career or in the classroom as returning students. Parents have to demonstrate leadership, setting boundaries and establishing limits that are no longer clearly dictated by social institutions. When gender roles and living arrangements are more fluid, partners need to transcend similarity as the primary basis for their bonds and develop a mutually supportive and celebratory relationship to their differences. As the diversity of the dynamics of families grows, people in therapy are asked not simply to identify how their histories have shaped them but to decide how to use that understanding to transform their lives for the better. In the classroom, students are asked to be self-directed learners who understand and apply the structure of the disciplines they study not simply as collections of values or facts but as systems of procedures for producing and evaluating them. While in traditional society, the fourth-order functions were often provided by religious traditions, community norms, and guidance from paternalistic institutions, adults today increasingly are called on to provide these functions for themselves. Together these distributed demands amount to a lived curriculum embedded throughout our culture that calls for greater cognitive complexity than was previously needed.

Putting it another way, portfolio authors need to articulate their integrity as "symphonic selves" (Cambridge, 2008b). The symphonic style of self-representation not only demonstrates integrity through documenting personal, professional, and civic life as interlinked but also synthesizes the many connections it catalogues. It provides an explanatory framework that makes clear the overriding principles the author uses to manage his or her relationship to his or her relationships, values, skills, beliefs, and goals. More than a list or a collection, more than an aggregation of discrete reflections on specific experiences, pieces of evidence of isolated competencies, or decontextualized goals, a symphonic eportfolio provides an overall narrative, theory, or map that demonstrates consistency and identifies conflict, showing coherence and surfacing dissonance. The work of making a symphonic self-representation is like that of composers or conductors. Pink (2005) notes that their work involves not just making connections between "a diverse group of notes, instruments, and performers" but also exercising their "ability to marshal these relationships into a whole whose magnificence exceeds the sum of its parts" through controlling "the relationships between relationships" (pp. 136–137).

The close association between integrity and the symphonic style in portfolio practice makes sense given both the softening of boundaries between home and work and the common level of the cognitive demands of the lived curriculum for contemporary adults in both spheres. Portfolio authors need to figure out how to establish authorship of their competencies, values, commitments, and relationships across all the domains of their lives, creating their own boundaries and principles to govern the whole. That cognitive development in both the private and public roles generally occurs in parallel is supported by over twenty years of empirical research. Using a formal interview protocol with thousands of individuals in diverse settings, psychologists at Harvard have shown that most individuals vary only slightly, if at all, in the level of consciousness they use to make sense of their personal and professional lives (Kegan, 1994). Baxter Magdola's (2001) longitudinal studies of individuals from entry into higher education in their late teens and early twenties through their midthirties confirm the close relationship of how people construct knowledge in academic, home, community, and family settings. If cognitive development is consistent across life, then it makes little sense to focus on professional development without also devoting attention to personal development, or vice versa.

Slade's eportfolio demonstrates not only integrity but also the symphonic style. At first glance, this is not obvious. A number of sections of the eportfolio read as simple lists, suggesting aggregation rather than synthesis. For example, her Formal Education page is primarily a list of institutions attended and credentials awarded, with a brief sentence or two describing each, arranged in reverse chronological order, similar to what a reader might expect from a résumé or CV. While personally rather than professionally centered, her Culture Favorites page lists books, movies, and dance companies she enjoys as she might in a social networking profile on sites such as Facebook and MySpace. However, other pages link back to these lists, contextualizing items they contain. How she has used her more recent degree in instructional design to build her capacity for project management and test her ideas about building environments for informal and organizational learning is explicated in her Technical and Organizational competency pages, which also reference other pages within her My Learning section. In her discussion of personal competencies, she explains the contribution of her musical appreciations to her global understanding and her ongoing learning that is enriched by the fuller listing of favorites.

Lists or collections of competencies, values, activities, and preferences play a role in Slade's self-representation in her portfolio, but they are not allowed to stand alone to define her. Rather, they serve as evidence and context with which to construct and convey her self-understanding. That self-understanding, and the process of self-making that it enables and of which it is a result, is governed by the overarching philosophy of learning and development that the portfolio conveys. While this theory is communicated using the languages of education and instructional design with a professional audience in mind, its application to her own learning throughout her life demonstrates its integrity. Given that this theory embraces learning as relevant to the whole person, its integrity helps to demonstrate its validity.

From the portfolio, the reader comes away with an understanding of learning as a lifewide and lifelong process, requiring individual motivation to take personal responsibility for one's holistic development. By embracing their own curiosity, values, and passions, individuals can grow into more effective family members, workers, and community leaders. This learning is best supported in resource-rich environments that are welcoming to diverse people and personalized to each person, inviting connection and collaboration. Rather than being divorced from daily life, these environments should be integrated within them. Learning technology in its broadest sense—composed of both electronic tools such as wikis and conceptual tools such as competency frameworks—is most powerful when it adds flexibility and broadens access, serving as a heuristic that stimulates and guides but never constrains individuals in their efforts to better themselves.

This theory is not articulated on a single page or in a single section of the portfolio. Rather, it is communicated through integrative section introductions, frequent cross-linking between pages and sections, recurring themes, and the incorporation of multimedia that provide a consistent tone, offer narrative illustrations, and, in conjunction with the agile technology into which it is incorporated, evoke a space that embodies Slade's overarching understanding of learning. Both the personal and professional material in the portfolio is essential to and structured by the overall theory. The meaning of the portfolio cannot be grasped by examining its elements in isolation. Understanding the portfolio, and appreciating how it embodies the ideal of integrity and the cognitive sophistication of the symphonic self, requires considering it as a whole.

From Employability to Good Work

As a whole, Slade's portfolio provides a powerful tool for planning, guiding, and evaluating her learning; recognizing and documenting her capabilities; and communicating her expertise and vision to potential clients and partners. However, the theory of learning the portfolio expresses and embodies is not valuable solely to Slade and those with whom she has direct relationships. Rather, it is—or ought to be taken up as—a contribution to defining excellence in her profession. It differs from traditional understandings of instructional design as primarily the development of sequenced content that conveys information in a manner that is easy to understand and remember and the construction of tests to judge how well that information has been absorbed by a learner, a view that still has currency in some organizations (Clarke & Mayer, 2002). It also differs from a conception of learning design as the development of tools and activities that guide learners through a specific set of steps and interactions that promote a deeper sort of learning defined by specific learning outcomes specified by the designer, a more recent way of thinking that enjoys widespread popularity in the profession (Koper & Tattersall, 2005; Weigel, 2001). Slade's view focuses squarely on the individual as the nexus of learning. Materials are valuable if they provide access to knowledge and skills that serve individual needs, as they themselves define them. Learning designers, and the institutions that employ them, should help individuals define what they need to learn; facilitate access to a wide range of content, tools, and services from which learners can select the means best suited to them; and support individuals as they use their networks of resources to learn.

The central ideas of Slade's theory are not unique to her work. Well-known advocates for shifting the focus of learning designers and other educators to supporting self-sponsored learning through cultivating distributed, flexible, content-rich spaces and tools that connect learners include fellow Canadians Steven Downes, of the National Research Council, and George Siemens, of the University of Manitoba (Downes, 2007; Seimens, 2005). However, the authenticity and integrity of Slade's self-representation in her portfolio strengthen the argument for this way of thinking about learning design. Authentic self-representations that provide accounts of the uniqueness of individual learning and identity in relationship to shared ideas and languages provide an essential input of deliberative discussions about collective goals and actions. When collective decisions are emergent from and incorporated into authentic self-representations, their claim to legitimacy is stronger. When these accounts have integrity, examining the whole of the author's life, this claim is stronger still. In demonstrating how this manner of learning permeates both Slade's personal and professional life in a way that is distinctive to her biography and representative of an approach others in her field share, Slade makes an important contribution to defining how learning designers ought to conduct their work. The value of her contribution demonstrates that individual integrity is not only a personal but also a social virtue.

Slade's use of competencies differs from the typical approach in many employability-oriented eportfolio programs; she does more than just identify competencies, match them to the needs of the market, and engage in learning that makes for a stronger alignment of personal skills and organizational needs. She goes further and documents and examines the personal and professional elements of her life using an overarching theory of how she wishes to develop as a person and contribute to the development of others. While her approach places personal choice and personal responsibility front and center, it suggests that other factors need to be taken into account in making good choices beyond just what potential employers or clients say they want. In this way, it differs from the dominant discourse of employability and lifelong learning in most Western societies, which frames the individual role as shaping the self in ways that strengthen the economy.

This economic perspective is pervasive in lifelong learning and workforce development policies and programs, including many of the eportfolio initiatives discussed in Chapter Seven. These policies and programs are part of a larger shift in economic perspective and ideas about the duties of citizenship. Rose (1999, p. 162) charts how promoting national economic success in the West has shifted in recent decades from a responsibility of government and public institutions to a duty of individuals. Rather than ensuring that jobs are available that suit the needs of citizens, the primary role of institutions that support lifelong learning and employment is to motivate people to make choices that align with what potential employers desire:

> Unemployment [is] now conceptualized as a phenomenon to be governed . . . through acting on the conduct of the unemployed person, obliging him or her to improve "employability" by acquiring skills, both substantive skills and skills in acquiring work, and obliging the individual to engage in a constant and active search for employment. . . . Each individual is solicited as a potential ally of economic success. Personal employment and macro-economic health is to be ensured by encouraging individuals to "capitalize" themselves, to invest in the management, presentation, promotion and enhancement of their own economic capital as a capacity of their selves and as a lifelong project.

Aspects of the self count as human capital only to the extent that they match that for which potential employers are willing to pay. In this larger context, the competency-matching approach makes perfect sense. In order to do their social duty of generating wealth, people need to be able to figure out what employers want, how they stack up to those demands, and what they can do to be more appealing. Even for those pursuing boundaryless careers, the key to success is to exercise "market discipline," making choices according to specifications of those who are likely to contract for one's services (Bird, 1996; Bridges, 1994). All people should shape themselves according to the desires of current and potential employers and clients.

The attitude Slade takes toward her work as a learning designer in her eportfolio is significantly different. As documented, her professional practice certainly takes into account the needs and preferences of her clients. However, she asserts her own authority to carry out the work in accordance with her own understanding of learning and the role of learning designers in promoting it, which is informed by and put into action throughout her public and private lives. For Slade, success in learning design is not simply determined by the number and caliber of clients or projects but by the degree to which her practice is consistently guided by her theory of professional excellence. What those with whom she has a current or potential professional relationship with are likely to ask of her is one factor taken into account when choosing which competencies are valuable, but these demands are considered alongside her own beliefs, values, experiences, concepts, and personal relationships: her hard-won sense of how the whole should function determines her professional choices. While the choice to hire her or fire her may belong to her potential clients and employers, in how she conducts her work she is responsible not only to them but more powerfully to her own standards of excellence and the professional community in relationship of which they are situated.

Rather than a particular social status, Kegan (1994) suggests that such an "ability to hold onto two different conceptions of power and authority within one work relationship" may be what defines professionalism. Professionals take ownership of how they carry out their vocational responsibilities even as they depend on others to choose to engage them. In this way, "some lawyers are not professionals and some housecleaners are" (p. 158). Professionalism is a psychological capacity of significant cognitive complexity, requiring the fourth order of consciousness that is supported by the symphonic style of self-representation.

Yet the social dimension also demands attention. The shape of a contractual relationship between an individual and an employer, governed by regulations and societal expectations as well as by specific terms, is a major factor in determining the degree to which individuals can take on this dual relationship to their work successfully. While it may be possible for a housecleaner to exercise professionalism, it is a great deal easier for a lawyer to put himself or herself in a position to do so. One of the reasons for this disparity is that lawyers have been socialized to believe that professionalism is important, and they have had the opportunity to participate in ongoing deliberations within a professional community about excellence in the practice of the law that generally are held as legitimate and authoritative by the state and the public.

Unlike other workers, members of traditional professions, such as the law and medicine, have historically been given considerable autonomy in determining the standards for judging performance in their occupations. This freedom comes with a responsibility to balance individual self-actualization with a concern for the common good. Joining a profession should both expand a person's ability to fulfill goals and commit him or her to a shared project of collective betterment. Sullivan (2005) writes that, on the one hand, "professional occupations create recognized opportunities for individuals to make something of their talents and capacities. On the other hand, this is possible only through personal commitment to the disciplines of a community of practice. At its best, professional life enables individual freedom to find fulfillment as it advances the well-being of the larger society" (p. 284).

While the decisions of leaders of employing organizations are likely to be driven primarily by a concern for the bottom line or for ensuring the stability of the organization, professions offer a social context in which professionals can deliberate about their practice. At the same time, they take into account their own integral, symphonic understandings of the role of work in their lives and how their guiding principles, situated in relationship to the shared virtues and practices of their profession, can help them make a positive difference in the larger society. The autonomy granted to professionals in the practice of their occupations and the opportunities for deliberation offered by professional associations, conferences, publications, and online forums enable the development of "ethical communities of practice" that can serve both individuals' needs and the common good (Nyham, 2006).

Communities of practice can be cultivated not only within institutions but across them. The argument for deliberation in the next chapter assumes that the decision-making process occurs primarily within institutions. However, for those like Slade, whose careers are increasingly boundaryless, involving relationships with multiple institutions, both at once and over time, an employing organization is unlikely to provide a sufficient social context for deliberation about excellence in their fields. Professions themselves may expand to fill the gap. Slade clearly sees value in professional forums through which she can share her understanding of powerful practice in learning design and the realities of her life as a learning designer, influencing the shape of the field and refining her own understandings in dialogue with other members of the profession. Slade is an active participant in professional forums, as evidenced by the presentations she has given and meetings she has organized, which she documents and reflects on in her portfolio, as well as the connections she makes to formalized frameworks for thinking about her professional competencies. Through her new organization's blog, to which her portfolio links, she connects to emerging dialogues about professional practice that may be beginning to have as much influence on her profession's trajectory as those that are institutionally grounded.

Slade's portfolio is a powerful example of how integrity—the linking of private and public life through systems thinking—is important to defining excellence within a profession. The research of Gardner, Csikszentmihalyi, and Damon (2001) on two professional fields, journalism and genetics, confirms that such integrity plays a central role in a profession's function and evolution. The health of a profession should be judged by how well it enables its members to do "good work." The meaning of *good* in *good work* is twofold: good in the sense of expertise (doing work well) and good in the sense of ethics (doing work that serves the good). For members of a profession to do work well, they need certain competencies. There need to be means to define which competencies are important, help people develop them, and document how performance embodies them. However, defining the good that a profession should do and enabling its members to do it requires more than occupation-specific competencies. It also requires taking into consideration the values, beliefs, and commitments held by its members, considering commonalities and conflicts in relationship to the public's expectations of the profession. The good to be done has both private and public dimensions: it includes both the contribution of professional work to personal integrity and meaning and that work's contribution to the larger society. Good work in a profession requires alignment between expertise and these two types of ethically laudable impact. A lack of alignment threatens the health of the profession, and diagnosing how healthy a profession is requires considering not just the technical but also the social and personal dimensions of professional practice.

Higher education generally prepares students for careers within occupations commonly considered "professional," which may provide some space for autonomy of, and deliberation about, practice outside the constraints of institutional priorities and the whims of the market. However, many occupations do not currently offer such support for professionalism. This may be in part because occupations viewed as professional are perceived as more socially important than others: educators contribute to the success of the next generation, doctors help lengthen lives, and so forth. However, welders building bridges also make essential contributions to public safety and economic growth, as do carpenters and electricians. The distinction may have more to do with a perception that such trades require less intelligence and are less cognitively complex than professions as traditionally defined. Rose (2004) suggests that the problem may be that "particular kinds of work can be defined and perceived in ways that mask the range of human abilities that make the work possible" (p. 30). In his study of six traditionally working-class occupations, Rose demonstrates that considerable, multiple intelligences and cognitive sophistication are required to practice them well. Being a waitress, for example, requires not just physical endurance and skills of memory, but also the ability to manage the competing demands of multiple relationships—customers, cooks, managers, fellow servers. It also requires distance from and mastery over one's emotions, organizing relationships and feelings according to the waitress's own understanding of excellent performance, which rarely aligns precisely with those of all her customers and her employer. In Kegan's terms, this is a fourth-order capability on the same level as those called for in more conventionally professional work. Through their ability to capture the complexity of work in the larger context of individual identity and social connectedness, eportfolios might provide one means for helping these underappreciated occupations argue for their right to the means for professional self-definition.

The Impact of Integrity on Eportfolio Authors

Samantha Slade's case illustrates the shape and value of integrity in eportfolios in both shaping an individual life course and defining a profession. The importance to individuals it suggests for integrity is supported by recent research into the impact of eportfolio composition on authors' learning and identity. This research shows that articulating integrity is important not only for preparing to enter a profession or for promoting employability; it also powerfully contributes to the impact of eportfolios on learning and engagement in the early years of undergraduate education and adult learning more generally. For participants in the eFolio Minnesota project, the achievement of integrity across personal and professional roles was one of two primary factors that predicted a high level of perceived impact on learning and institutional relationships (Cambridge, 2008a). At LaGuardia Community College in New York City and Kapi'olani Community College in Honolulu, the capability of portfolios to integrate students' home cultures with the new academic and professional cultures of which they are invited to become a part has had demonstrated impact on retention, course completion, student engagement, and learning skills (Eynon, 2009; Kirkpatrick, Renner, Kanae, & Goya, 2009). The diversity of the contexts in which integrity is being shown to be important suggests that the ideal merits attention from all eportfolio practitioners.

The eFolio Minnesota project makes eportfolio software and services available to all residents of the State of Minnesota, and to date over eighty thousand people have taken advantage of it. (eFolio Minnesota is discussed in detail in Chapter Six.) Although this group includes students, it also includes many Minnesotans working full time, in both established professions and less prestigious occupations, from computer consultants in their twenties to secretaries in their sixties. The age distribution of users parallels that of the state as a whole. About a fifth of the users surveyed in research conducted in 2004–2005 reported that they felt their experience with eFolio Minnesota had had a high impact on their learning and relationships with others within the institutions where they worked or studied (Cambridge, 2008a). Intensive interviews with members of this group pointed to the achievement of integrity as one of two key factors tied to significant impact. When eFolio Minnesota authors felt that their portfolio experience was very important, they often pointed toward its ability to help them articulate the relationship of their professional, academic, and personal lives, to demonstrate how they managed conflicts between competing commitments, acting on values and beliefs that were consistent and coherent across contexts. They valued the ability to represent their "whole human being" through their eportfolios.

Tracy Wright, one of the portfolio authors interviewed in the research, provides a representative example. Her portfolio includes details of her work as a nurse, a nursing educator, and a family member. While hers is clearly labeled a "professional portfolio," she sees her professional life as integrally related to her personal investments and feels that it is important to communicate that interrelatedness to her students and colleagues. In an interview (Cambridge, 2008a) she said:

> I think it'd be difficult to separate completely, you know, who I am and what my immediate family loves are versus just me as a professional educator and nurse. . . . I am not someone who's isolated to the world of professional nursing [or] education. I also have conflicting, or competing maybe, obligations within my life that I need to balance, just as students do and other professionals do, and I think that that's a good thing, to show . . . people that are reading my sites, I have other obligations in my life, and I manage to hopefully balance them all and be able to perform to the best of my ability in all those domains.

Seeking a sense of balance through integrity across domains was a common theme in interviews with almost all of the participants reporting eFolio Minnesota having a high level of impact on them. While others had less success than Wright in showing connections among the various roles they played, they found the experience of composing and reflecting on their portfolios valuable in helping them think through ways that they might place them into better alignment.

The capability of eportfolios to help authors articulate integrity is also proving powerful in academic settings. A large percentage of LaGuardia Community College students are recent immigrants to the United States, and for most, LaGuardia is their introduction to American higher education for themselves, their families, and their friends. Over the course of their studies, many students choose to compose multimedia eportfolios, which they revise multiple times as they progress through the program and become more skilled at expressing themselves with technology. Students find these portfolios meaningful in large part because the portfolios enable them to represent both their existing identity as a member of their home culture and their new identity as a member of an academic community and a profession. Through their portfolios, students can share their cultural heritage and life story in the new environment, while also making sense of their new academic and professional lives to their family and friends at home. Through the portfolio, students show that they need not choose one over the other; they can be integrated. Research conducted by LaGuardia faculty and staff through the Inter/National Coalition for Electronic Portfolio Research (I/NCEPR) demonstrated measurable impact of portfolio composition. As compared with those who had not, students who had composed portfolios showed significantly higher degrees of student engagement as measured by questions from the Community College Survey of Student Engagement (CCSSE). For example, in questions related to critical thinking, eportfolio students scored 9.5 percent higher than their peers at LaGuardia. Students were also more likely to stay enrolled semester-to-semester, with a two-semester mean retention rate of 75.5 percent for eportfolio students as compared with 70 percent for the student body as a whole; and to pass classes, with a 74.9 percent pass rate for eportfolio classes as compared to 69.1 percent for comparison courses (Eynon, 2009).

At Kapi'olani Community College, another member of the I/NCEPR, student compose portfolios using a matrix that allows them to make connections

FIGURE 2.2. KAPI'OLANI MATRIX

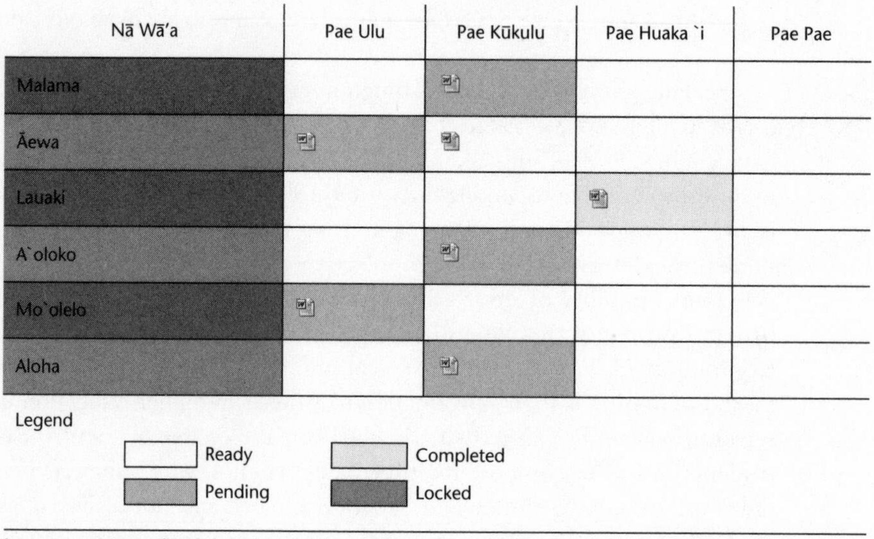

Nā Wā'a	Pae Ulu	Pae Kūkulu	Pae Huaka ʻi	Pae Pae
Mālama		🖼		
Āewa	🖼	🖼		
Lauaki			🖼	
A'oloko		🖼		
Mo'olelo	🖼			
Aloha		🖼		

Legend

☐ Ready	☐ Completed
☐ Pending	☐ Locked

Image courtesy of Judith Kirkpartrick.
Hawaiian Translations:
Mālama: To take care of, tend, attend, care for, preserve, protect, serve, honor.
Āewa: Possessing a family or lineage. We all come from someone and somewhere.
Lauaki: To cooperate, work together, as of experts; to concentrate on the same task; to pool talents.
A'oloko: Innermost teaching, inspiration. We are our innermost teachers, only we can allow ourselves to learn.
Mo'olelo: Story, tale, myth, history, tradition, literature, legend, journal, log, record. We all have a story to tell of our past as well as our present and future.
Aloha: Love, affection, compassion, mercy, sympathy, kindness, grace, charity.
Pae Ulu: Growth stage. Still being inspired. Still tending to the tree.
Pae Kūkulu: Building stage. Foundation is being built; the tree is ready to be carved into a canoe.
Pae Huakài: Canoe has set sail and is traveling on the ocean.
Pae Pae: The canoe has landed, and the individual is ready to be a support to others.

among their academic work, professional aspirations, and native Hawaiian culture. (See Figure 2.2.) The two dimensions of the matrix are defined by six native Hawaiian values and the four stages of the journey of a canoe, an important metaphor for life in native Hawaiian culture. Students select artifacts from their course work and cocurricular learning for each cell of the matrix and write a reflection that examines the connection between their learning as captured in the selected evidence and the Hawaiian value and stage of the canoe's story that intersect in that cell. Faculty guide the process and respond to each reflection. The process enables students, who are often the first in their families to attend college, to make connections between their lives in their communities with their new experiences in the academic environment, weighing the professional commitments into which they are moving alongside their identification with the culture of their homes. As at LaGuardia, students are able to transcend the assumption that the two must be at odds to see how they can be integrated. This experience of integrity also yielded gains in student engagement on six of twelve CCSSE questions for Kapi'olani students who have composed eportfolios when their scores are compared to their peers and to national averages. In addition, Kapi'olani eportfolio students showed significantly larger gains during the period in which they composed their portfolios compared to college and national averages on eight of ten questions from the Learning Strategies and Study Skills assessment (Kirkpatrick et al., 2009).

Implications for Educators

This chapter has shown that the symphonic style of integrity is central to developing a career identity in our increasingly boundaryless society. While developing specific skills and knowledge contributes to employability and professional success, understanding how personal values, beliefs, and aspirations intersect with the social functions of work and asserting the value of one's strategies for weaving them together is at least as important. Such a capability is essential to assuming the critical relationship to institutional and market forces that is needed to ensure that work serves both individual interests and the common good. Like authenticity, integrity proves to be both an individual and a social ideal. Through articulating their symphonic selves in communities of practice, individuals can contribute to the health and growth of the professions of which they are a part.

Eportfolios have proven effective in representing integrity in a symphonic way, helping individuals articulate their identities systematically. As a whole, an eportfolio can integrate the diverse elements of identity needed to present a theory, story, or map that explains the coherence of the whole. The symphonic capabilities of the eportfolio genre are supported by the multiple media that eportfolios can incorporate, the patterns of linking that can structure them, and the dynamism offered by the tools used to compose them. Integrity has proven a central factor in the impact of eportfolios on learning as reported by learners of all ages and as quantified by standardized measures of retention, student engagement, and learning skills. As will become clear in Part Two, students' authentic and integral self-representations can also play a central role in programmatic and institutional assessment in higher education.

Questions for Practice

This analysis suggests that educators supporting the composition and use of eportfolios who are persuaded by this analysis to seek to support integrity and symphony should ask several questions about their practice:

- In what ways might integrity be emphasized as a crucial component of professional and disciplinary identity in the curriculum and cocurriculum? How can eportfolios be used to help synthesize experiences inside and outside the classroom to represent a learner's prior and emerging professional identities?
- More generally, how can your institution's eportfolio processes provide spaces for representing and acknowledging the value of personal, civic, and professional experiences and engagements? How can learners' home cultures be made visible? What space is there for articulating their relationship with academic concepts, experiences, and skills?
- How might learners' eportfolios be connected to audiences within professional communities of practice, such as through alumni mentors, students' current employment, co-ops and internships, and service-learning? In what ways can they use their self-representations to participate peripherally in deliberations about the function and future of their chosen areas of focus?
- In order to model such engagement, how can we support each other in composing our own eportfolios that articulate the integrity of our own professional identities in relationship to our institutional, disciplinary, and professional communities?
- Perhaps most challenging, to what extent are audiences ready to receive the complex and challenging representations of professional identity and capability that eportfolios offer? How do we help audiences beyond the academy, such as employers and professional associations, see the value of integral, symphonic eportfolios and incorporate them into their processes of organizational decision making? Progress toward and obstacles in the way of answering these questions are taken up in Chapter Six.

PART TWO

EPORTFOLIOS AND ASSESSMENT IN HIGHER EDUCATION

CHAPTER THREE

EPORTFOLIOS AND ASSESSMENT

Deliberation for Democratic Decision Making

Compared with the reality which comes from being seen and heard, even the greatest forces of intimate life—the passions of the heart, the thoughts of the mind, the delights of the senses—lead an uncertain, shadowy kind of existence unless and until they are transformed, deprivatized, and deindividualized, as it were, into a shape to fit them for public appearance.

. . .

The reality of the public realm relies on the simultaneous presence of innumerable perspectives and aspects in which the common world presents itself and for which no common measurement or denominator can ever be devised. For though the common world is the common meeting ground of all, those who are present have different locations within it, and the location of one can no more coincide with the location of another than the location of two objects. Being seen and being heard by others derive their significance from the fact that everybody sees and hears from a different position.

—HANNAH ARENDT, *THE HUMAN CONDITION*

In the context of programmatic assessment in higher education, this chapter focuses on a third cultural ideal that underlies eportfolio practice: deliberation. It returns to the example eportfolios introduced in Chapter One to show how personalized eportfolios can realize the potential to contribute to assessment suggested for them in the conclusion of that chapter. Personalized portfolios can both provide otherwise inaccessible information for, and facilitate wider participation in, institutional improvement if the social model of procedural justice that informs standardized eportfolio assessment processes is replaced by the principles and practices of deliberative democracy. While Chapter One showed the need to participate in a social context such as that provided by deliberative assessment for achieving authenticity (an argument now extended to integrity), this chapter argues that all stakeholders in higher education should be invited to engage in dialogue, mediated by authentic and integral representations of student identity and performance in the form of eportfolios, in order to produce institutional innovation.

From Expression to Recognition

In Part One, we saw that the use of eportfolios is often animated by the cultural ideals of authenticity and integrity. Through personalized eportfolios, individuals can articulate their understanding of who they are, to what they are committed, how that identity is held steady across time and multiple contexts, and how that understanding dictates how they might live. Through this process of creative expression of self in dialogue with others, previously inchoate identity and commitment are clarified and put into action. Whether distinctiveness originates from a natural self given at birth, through the intersection of multiple cultural influences and social structures, or from a combination of both, each of us participates in and understands the world uniquely. Powerful knowledge and moral commitments are validated through connecting to this uniqueness through expression. For this expression to be both possible and meaningful, however, it must be made in relationship to horizons of significance beyond the self, such as cultural traditions, political affiliations, and professional practices (Taylor, 1991). In eportfolio use, authenticity and integrity operate through a common emphasis on critical reflection, ownership, and creative synthesis. While a standardized process of eportfolio assessment might make space for individual self-definition and moral diversity by attempting to be neutral through following impartial procedures, this process fails to take into account institutional power that underlies its seeming objectivity and the organizational value of authentic and integral representations of individual experience.

Although eportfolios serve both individual and institutional needs, placing these two in opposition has deemphasized both the shared cultural influences that guide individuals and the diversity of individuals that can inform institutions. This divide reflects a misunderstanding of authenticity and integrity as solely personal, rather than simultaneously personal and social, ideals. This misperception is evidenced both within higher education assessment, as demonstrated in Chapter One, and in professional discourse and practice, as shown in Chapter Two. What is needed instead is to align individual self-articulation with institutional decision, making both more effective. This chapter suggests that a final widely held cultural ideal, deliberation, can help create such an alternative arrangement in the context of programmatic academic assessment in higher education.

Eportfolio practice guided by this ideal can lead to more effective and more just institutional judgments through fuller self-articulation and deliberative institutional practices. In the passage that opens this chapter, Arendt (1958) suggests that our unique experiences become fully real to us when we express them not just to ourselves but to others in a public forum. As argued in Part One, we need our authenticity and integrity to be seen and heard, not just imagined and said. Both authenticity and integrity are at once individual and social ideals and require social participation to be realized.

As Charles Taylor (1995) demonstrates, this need emerges in the demand for external recognition—the social affirmation of the worth of what we find valuable. Recognition of meaningful individual differences requires us to look beyond ourselves, to what Taylor calls "horizons of significance." To be useful in affirming value, these horizons of significance themselves need public recognition. While some versions of multiculturalism insist that any horizon is valuable, Taylor suggests that to claim to recognize the value of cultural and social standards beyond the dominant culture without critically evaluating and making judgments is patronizing. Respect for multiple traditions requires real understanding and reasoned evaluation of multiple standards of value, both current commitments and alternative perspectives that could enable improvement. This process yields a fusion of horizons. Ideally, the process of assessment in higher education programs and institutions would contribute to such a fusion.

This fusion does not necessarily come easily or look the same for everyone. As the second Arendt passage makes clear, the power of recognition in public space comes precisely from the inherent differences of those assembled within it. Although some conflicts about what is good and right may not be resolvable in a definitive way, they may allow multiple reasonable judgments (Gutmann & Thompson, 1996). For the possibility of multiple reasonable judgments, in public spaces conclusions must be held as provisional, new perspectives must be taken seriously, and diverse voices must be welcomed to the table. The social perspective of deliberative democracy affirms the advantages of the authenticity and integrity captured through eportfolios more than either liberalism or soft pluralism, more than either standardized assessment or an outright rejection of assessment beyond the individual classroom.

The ideal of deliberative democracy also provides an alternative to the vague, organic conceptions of community that are often invoked in discussions of eportfolios. For example, in eportfolio policy discussions, the idea of the learning organization is frequently used to suggest that individual learning and organizational learning will support each other (Ketcheson, 2009; Ravet, 2005). This idea relies on a conception of community as a natural state that minimizes difference. Like the deliberative perspective explored in this chapter, the learning organization suggests that capitalizing on individuals' range of knowledge and experience can contribute to the ongoing improvement of the institutions in which they take part. However, the conflicts in interests and differences in commitments between different groups of individuals and between each individual and the organization are often glossed over (Elmholdt & Brinkmann, 2006). Individuals are assumed to naturally want to learn in ways that organically correspond with how the institution needs to learn to make it more effective. The individual desire of self-development and the organizational mandate are assumed to be the same.

Peter Senge, originator of the term *learning organization*, defines it as a space "where people continually expand their capacity to create the results they truly desire, where new and expansive patterns of thinking are nurtured, where collective aspiration is set free, and where people are continually learning how to learn together" (quoted in Elmholdt & Brinkman, 2005, p. 173). Senge wants to see the organization serve individuals' desire for self-actualization and for those processes to lead to a more effective organization. Although this is very much in line with the deliberative model advocated here, Senge's definition harbors the mistaken assumption that the "results" that individual members of an organization desire and the goals of their individual self-development will align with each other and with the goals of the organization, as defined by existing relations of power. This assumption is as problematic as the converse belief that individual interests and collective priorities are necessarily in conflict, challenged in Part One. A better model of the learning organization would reframe the alignment of individual and institutional growth as a hard-won, necessarily partial achievement, always provisional, not a stable and inevitable outcome.

This chapter explores how the ideal of deliberation can be applied to organizational decision making to provide such an alternative conception of the learning organization. Examining the deliberative use of eportfolios for programmatic assessment in one higher education program as a model, this chapter shows that deliberative democracy can profitably serve as a source of governing principles for processes of assessment. Returning to Mary Moss's portfolio from Chapter One clarifies some of the limitations of the standardized model to which the deliberative is offered as an alternative. In an examination of the assessment process at New Century College of George Mason University, the context of Sean Moore's portfolio (also from Chapter One) demonstrates ways in which the genre of the eportfolio contributes to fulfillment of deliberative principles. This example also illustrates how the capabilities of eportfolios can help address limitations to the effectiveness and inclusiveness of some models of deliberation.

Principles of Deliberative Democracy

Before analyzing examples, however, it is important to briefly define *deliberative democracy*, including its purposes and principles. Deliberation is a cultural ideal in the same sense that authenticity and integrity are: an understanding of how things work—or ought to—held by many people in Western cultures and influencing how they organize their lives. Although people may not have thought carefully about deliberative principles, they generally believe that public decisions should be made through discussion that is governed by reason and publicly accessible to everyone affected by the decisions and that leaders ought to be accountable for acting in accordance with them. When these conditions hold, we think of an institution as being democratic, and we think of democracy as a way of relating to each other that we should extend as widely as possible.

Deliberation serves two key purposes. First, it is a process of solving problems. Part of accepting the ideal means believing that deliberation will yield better solutions to shared challenges than alternative processes and that it is a just way of settling conflicts. In the same way that authenticity leads to a richer understanding of how we each should live, deliberation leads to a better collective life. Second, deliberation is a way of legitimating decisions. Judgments emanating from deliberation have a more meaningful kind of social authority than those made without it. As authenticity lends additional force to understanding through connecting it to the self, so deliberation strengthens decisions by legitimating them as the product of the community. Deliberation is thus both instrumental and expressive (Gutmann & Thompson, 2004).

A wealth of political theory develops norms for deliberative democracy. While the idea of deliberation in Western thought extends back to ancient Greece, the modern connection to democracy begins with John Dewey and his contemporaries and has been most strongly established in contemporary discussions through the work of Jürgen Habermas. A reading of the helpful contemporary work of Amy Gutmann and Dennis Thompson (Gutmann & Thompson, 1996, 2004) and of Iris Young (1996, 2002) identifies four key principles applicable to consideration of deliberation in eportfolio processes: publicity, inclusiveness, reasonableness, and provisionality.

These four principles focus on process, people affected, diversity, and further consideration. First, although meaningful deliberation happens in public forums and in closed forums, transparency of process is essential for deliberative democracy. Decision makers must provide rationales for decisions and accessible venues for discussing them, with outcomes of public discussions taken into account in subsequent decisions. Second, everyone affected by collective decisions needs to be able to understand the reasoning behind them and to be able to accept the decisions as not unreasonably excluding them by limiting participation. Third, while it is not always possible to achieve consensus, individuals must try to understand one another's perspectives sufficiently to locate both common interests and irreconcilable differences. Gutmann and Thompson (2004) call this the "economy of moral objections." Even if we hold views passionately, we should be open to being convinced that our views are incomplete or even wrong. And, fourth, just as individuals must hold open their own convictions, we must hold open that decisions and the roles and norms of making them are also up for reconsideration.

Unlike some theories of participatory democracy, in deliberative democracy some decisions are made through executive authority or on the basis of expert judgment. Such decisions, however, like all others, need to include the right of those affected to reconsider through discussion the resulting judgments or the decision-making process itself. All decision-making processes should be informed by and accountable to the whole of the deliberative system of which they are a part. Deliberative democracy is achieved when multiple sites of deliberation by members of an institution or a community, with differing levels of formality and authority, together form a system that as a whole ensures that the four principles hold. A college or university that wishes to undertake deliberative assessment must become a deliberative system; eportfolios can help them achieve that goal.

Limits on Deliberation in the Process of Standardized Eportfolio Assessment

Eportfolios can support deliberation in two ways: the processes of assessment for which they are composed and read can be made deliberative, and the characteristics of the eportfolio as a genre that align with deliberative principles can be emphasized. This chapter considers these two dimensions in turn. Although the standardized process of eportfolio assessment described in Chapter One for Mary Moss's portfolio does not fully live up to the principles of the ideal, the assessment process for Sean Moore's portfolio suggests an alternative, genuinely deliberative model of assessment. The characteristics of this portfolio itself illustrate how the eportfolio genre is well suited to contributing to such a deliberative assessment process.

In the standardized example from Great Lakes State, Mary Moss's eportfolio is tightly structured according to standards defined by a national professional organization. Faculty evaluators judge by rubrics available on the departmental website how well evidence in the portfolio demonstrates Moss's competence in relationship to each standard. If the process works as planned, the judgment should not depend on who is doing the judging or who is being judged. The process does not require deliberation to reach the intended result because everyone involved shares a common understanding of the standards and their validity in representing the competent teacher. The standards are unambiguously and universally defined and are applied objectively.

Despite this intention to be neutral and universal, the process necessarily involves some deliberation. The standards themselves were set through the deliberation of national experts. The rubrics were developed through discussions among faculty members in the program. Because the national standards remain at a fairly high level of abstraction, they have to be further specified in the departmental rubrics to deal with the specifics of the institutional context in which they are situated. The ways in which faculty members apply the rubrics were likely made consistent through norming, in which multiple faculty members score portfolios individually and, if their ratings differ, discuss the evidence and the rubric descriptions to come to consensus on the correct judgment. Only through deliberation can the results be made "objective." While this deliberation largely occurs behind the scenes in order to foreground the seeming neutrality of the process, it is integral to the assessment's success.

The standardized portfolio assessment process, however, fails to live up to the core principles of deliberative democracy. For one, the process is not fully transparent. Although the standards, rubrics, and portfolio requirements are made public, the debates that determined them occur behind closed doors. The forums in which these decisions are made are closed to parties who are affected by the assessment process, such as the students being evaluated and the public schools that might employ them. The process of assessment also does not include venues for these various affected parties to question and respond to the specifications once they are set. While students might have such discussions in classrooms and dorm rooms, they are not connected to public deliberation in a way that would enable their substance to influence subsequent institutional decisions.

Second, the reasoning behind how the standards are defined is similarly private, and therefore not inclusive. The documents defining the National Council for Accreditation of Teacher Education (NCATE) standards describe rather than argue. They do not fully explain why the standards are appropriate for judging teaching competence. The rubrics that define how the standards are to be applied in the local context are similarly descriptive and are not accompanied by a rationale that others might critically examine. Without access to the reasons, it is more difficult for all the affected parties to determine whether the standards are likely to be accurate and fair to everyone.

A central drawback to this standardized process is that only those in positions of power are invited to participate. The national standards are determined by experts alone, and the local rubrics are defined by faculty. Although students at the local level influence assessment through arguments that the evidence they include in their portfolios meets the requirements, differences in writing skills and cultural backgrounds may make these means more accessible for some students than for others. As discussed in Chapter One, the highly prescriptive structure of the eportfolios at Moss's institution excludes ways students might represent themselves that could be relevant to determining how they should be judged. For example, the structure might limit students' reflections on their personal values, which Chapter Two argues are important to understanding professional practice. Students also have little access to visual means of arranging and delivering evidence that might capture some professional capabilities more effectively than written language does.

Reasonableness and provisionality are also limited. Because the processes by which standards are set are largely invisible and inaccessible, the standardized assessment process suggests that there is a single, permanent, and universal conception of what it means to be a competent member of the profession. In suggesting only one defensible way to be a teacher, the assessment makes reasonable deliberation more difficult. It does not create space for reasonable disagreement about how to teach and learn. One must either accept the standards or reject them. In presenting the standards as fixed and offering few venues for critiquing them, the process does not acknowledge that judgments ought to be provisional.

The "subjectivist and intuitivist" model Gray (2002) identified as the other perspective on assessment prominent in the history of higher education, like the standardized model, does not qualify as democratic deliberation. This alternative model is embraced by many educators who advocate for personalized eportfolios and also by those who resist systematic programmatic and institutional assessment by any means. The subjectivist model rejects the idea that learning and human performance can be captured in a universal, objective way because they are highly complex and socially situated. The model contends that only professional teachers with direct knowledge of the students being evaluated and the context of the evaluation can make meaningful judgments. Criteria for judgment depend on the tacit knowledge of the teachers. This view often limits the scope of assessment to the individual classroom and rejects standards imposed from beyond it. Aggregating such local judgments in the form of a grade point average or narrative transcript may make it possible to determine the overall competence of a student, but such an overall determination cannot be made through a process divorced from the original contexts of teaching and learning and the expert judgments of teachers.

This alternative perspective, the subjectivist model, may seem to meet the principles of deliberative decision making. It is appealing in that it suggests that judgments are necessarily partial and situated and depend on the distinctive capabilities and commitments of both learners and evaluators. Judgments arrived at in this way may better acknowledge difference and disagreement and are perhaps more likely to be taken as provisional. However, in many respects, this means of assessment also fails to embrace the principles of deliberative democracy. Even more than in the standardized model, the process is private and exclusive, restricted to the context of a closed classroom and acknowledging only the authority of a singular expert judge. Faculty may or may not feel the need to provide reasons for their decisions, and students may or may not be given some opportunity to present a case based on their own understanding of what is important. The power as to which way the decisions goes rests firmly and exclusively in the hands of faculty.

Deliberative Assessment with Eportfolios in New Century College

An alternative to both the standardized and the subjectivist methods of assessment is deliberative assessment, a process that more clearly embodies the principles of deliberative democracy. Sean Moore's personalized portfolio and its programmatic context, introduced in Chapter One, exemplify deliberative assessment. The earlier chapter examined the ways Moore's portfolio expresses his authentic understanding of what it means to be educated and what he is called on to do with his life, a unique perspective developed in relationship to multiple cultural backgrounds, such as the Indian spiritual traditions he studied. However, the portfolio was composed not as a purely individual exercise in self-articulation but as part of a portfolio assessment process required for graduation for all New Century College students. An example of deliberative assessment, this process differs in critical ways from the standardized process in use at Great Lakes State. Rather than having a primary goal of determining whether learners moving into the workforce possess a specific set of skills, it focuses on evaluating and enacting their participation in a deliberative process of determining what it means to be an educated person in the twenty-first century. (For a more extensive account of the use of eportfolios in New Century College, see Cambridge, 2008c, in press-b.)

In accordance with the guidelines for graduation portfolios, Moore's portfolio articulates his learning in relationship to a selection of the nine competencies that run throughout the New Century College curriculum: communication, critical thinking, strategic problem solving, valuing, group interaction, global understanding, effective citizenship, aesthetic awareness, and information technology. Many institutions have developed similar ways of talking about the valued dimensions of general education and evaluative frameworks used in standardized assessment processes. Rubrics specifying what a student should know and be able to do as a competent communicator or user of information technology can be developed, and portfolios can be rated similarly to NCATE portfolios at Great Lakes State. (Chapters Four and Five examine the use of rubrics in eportfolio assessment in more detail.)

However, in New Century College graduation portfolios, the competencies play a different role: they join the students' authentic representations of themselves to an institutional deliberation about what is important in a university education. There are no set criteria for judging what graduate-level communication, for example, looks like. In fact, rendering such a judgment is not the primary purpose of the portfolio assessment. Throughout their course work and experiential learning, students have been exposed to and evaluated using a range of disciplinary and organizational perspectives of each of the competencies. Through their authentic self-articulation in their portfolios, students synthesize these perspectives to present their own understandings of the competencies on which they choose to focus their portfolios. They show how these understandings have changed over the course of their learning careers and examine how their relationship to the competencies may be transformed as they move on to new challenges after graduation. In so presenting the competencies, they articulate a fusion of the horizons of significance with which they are engaged. They take ownership of the competencies, demonstrating that they understand how their learning has progressed, are articulate about their capabilities, and are equipped to continue to develop in relationship to these competencies after graduation. Their unique perspectives on the competencies represent their distinctive goals, priorities, and backgrounds.

These individualized representations of the competencies also serve an institutional purpose. They provide a conceptual framework that enables students' representations to be compared and connected back to the goals of the curriculum and the experiences of other members of the New Century College community. The competencies make a coherent shared conversation about the outcomes of a George Mason University education possible. The competencies are both defined in a broad enough way that they can accommodate a wide range of interpretations and defined clearly enough that they make multiple interpretations mutually intelligible. In this sense, they work as what Susan Lee Star and James Griesemer (1989) have termed *boundary objects:* "Boundary objects are objects that are both plastic enough to adapt to local needs and constraints of the several parties employing them, yet robust enough to maintain a common identity across sites. They are weakly structured in common use, and become strongly structured in individual-site use" (p. 393). Boundary objects make it possible for individuals and groups with different experiences and priorities to collaborate in shared enterprises while acknowledging those differences. The New Century College competencies make possible both supporting students' diverse authenticity and connecting it to the institutional objective of providing a powerful liberal education.

Deliberation about the competencies happens in a variety of forums, involving a wide range of people affected by decisions about how New Century College supports student learning. Together these forums constitute a deliberative assessment system. In the capstone course, students share their portfolios with each other as they develop them, comparing evidence of learning in relationship to the competencies and discussing their meaning in the classroom and through online conversations in blogs and discussion forums. Some students work with alumni mentors, who reflect back on what was important about their own educational experiences while in college and how their understandings of the competencies have evolved as they have moved forward in their careers and civic lives. These private and proto-public dialogues set the stage for deliberation in more public venues.

In Capstone Conversations, students lead discussions of each competency on a panel open to any member of the university community. Panelists include students, alumni, potential employers, leaders of community nonprofit organizations, and faculty and administrators from both within New Century College and elsewhere in the university. The meaning of the competencies and how they should guide New Century College's curriculum and programs is also debated through brown-bag lunches, retreats, and portfolio readings throughout the year. In each case, composing and reading eportfolios organized around the competencies helps to prepare individuals to contribute to the conversation. The eportfolios provide conversation pieces that concretize the discussion, grounding it in evidence and individual experience, while the competencies help make connections across the differences between portfolios and the range of disciplinary and professional styles embodied by the college's curriculum and programs.

This broad range of forums helps to ensure the publicity of the deliberative process of which the portfolio assessment is a part. Both structured and informal, decision making and exploratory, these varied sites of discussion help all affected by decisions about how the college goes about its work at once understand the reasoning behind the decisions and have a voice in how they are made in the future. While many binding decisions are made through more exclusive deliberations, such as in faculty meetings, in curriculum committees, and by the dean, decision makers are committed to taking into account the varied interests and ideas shared in the broader forums throughout the system and being accountable for their decisions through participation in the larger, ongoing discussions. The multiple forums that make up this and other deliberative systems can be expanded through the incorporation of technology for online deliberation (the technology is discussed in Chapters Seven and Eight).

Students' ability to take ownership of the competencies in their portfolios is a test of the inclusiveness of the process. To the extent that students are successful in expressing their experiences and beliefs in an authentic way within the shared framework of the competencies, they demonstrate that the college has been successful in creating an educational vision that accommodates individual and group differences while providing enough of a shared educational vision to link up learning across them. If students are unable to document their experiences through the competencies or if the students' experiences of the competencies as expressed in their portfolios are out of alignment with how they are cultivated through the curriculum, this outcome suggests opportunities for institutional improvement. As explored below, the characteristics of the eportfolio genre and the capabilities of the networked medium help make these diverse perspectives more visible than might be possible in other forms of assessment.

This embrace of plural definitions of the competencies fosters an attitude of reasonableness. Rather than insisting that there is one correct set of skills and core of knowledge that students should possess, the process acknowledges that the many interests being served in the process of education may diverge and conflict. The focus of this deliberative process of assessment is not to determine whether a specific set of outcomes is being met in a particular way but to ensure that everyone involved can justify to one another how they are making their educational choices and determining their progress and ways in which they can learn from the paths of others.

During this process of public deliberation about educational decision making, both individual and institutional perspectives are likely to be transformed. Indeed, most portfolios present a narrative of how the students' understanding of each competency has evolved over the course of their undergraduate careers as they are exposed to new arguments and experiences. Similarly, in the multiple venues for discussion of the competencies discussed above, faculty, alumni, and other participants often share how their own understandings have grown and shifted direction over time. On a regular basis, through retreats and the work of faculty committees, the choice of competencies and their official definitions—and even the importance of having them at all—is considered in light of the varied public conversations. This ongoing process of iterative redefinition reinforces the provisionality of the competencies and the educational experiences that support them.

Communication as Lived and Experienced

Deliberative assessment values learning that changes, through analysis and dialogue, the understanding and practice of students and the institution. For example, two students who arrived at a similar understanding about the competency of communication from very different perspectives influenced their college's definition of communication and its pedagogy and assessment regarding that competency.

Sean Moore focuses on the competency of communication in his graduate portfolio. Using concepts from his course work and his own inquiries beyond the classroom in conjunction with evidence from class assignments and his reflections on his experiences, Moore justifies his current understanding of communication and thereby commits himself to continued development. The New Century College shared description of the competency defines *communication* as "the process of creating and sharing meaning through human interaction." For Moore, what counts as meaning, and the ways in which it can be shared, expanded during his undergraduate years in ways that may have implications for how the college supports growth in communication.

Moore's understanding of communication initially focused on his ability to convey information or persuade others to agree with him. His portfolio presents examples of his writing and accounts of his improvement as a public speaker from several courses that document his marked improvements in these important abilities. The curriculum is rich with opportunities to improve these skills, and Moore shows he took advantage of them. However, as he begins to consider communication in the context of a conflict analysis and resolution course and through his experiences with Buddhist spiritual practices, sharing meaning in communication becomes not just a process of conveying content but also a quality of relationship. He learns from his conflict analysis readings and his efforts to apply them that effectively engaging in difficult conversations requires active listening that affirms an authentic relationship between speaker and listener, where "you are listening because you are curious and because you care, not just because you are supposed to" (Stone, Patton, & Heen, 1999, p. 163, quoted in Moore). While the conflict analysis literature sees this relationship as a means to the end of greater understanding, Moore's experience of what Thich Nhat Hanh, a Vietnamese Zen Buddhist monk, calls deep listening convinces him that the relationship formed by authentic listening can be meaningful in itself. In deep listening, the sole purpose is to "give the other person the chance to speak out and suffer less." Any analysis or resolution is secondary. The felt presence of a listener who cares is itself a source of healing, and this is a new kind of shared meaning. In his experience, subtle, nonverbal markers of connection that might be lost in the exchange of messages that are typically seen as the heart of communication are essential: periods of "silence," the sharing of physical space, or "a glance or a small gesture." Moore's own experiences of learning to listen more powerfully, as documented in reflective writing from his course work and spiritual practice, point to dimensions of creating and sharing meaning that may merit more emphasis in New Century College's curriculum.

In his portfolio, Wayne Lin, another New Century College student graduating in the same semester as Moore, also writes about communication. (See Figure 3.1.) Lin and Moore differ significantly in their interests and dispositions. Compared to Moore's love of open-ended exploration, Lin is more focused on clarity and problem solving. While he shares an appealing curiosity for the world and willingness to engage with academic concepts and apply them to his experiences beyond the classroom, ideas and skills are most compelling for him when they help him maintain focus and produce results. Lin is unlikely to value the more contemplative aspects of communication that intrigue Moore. However, his analysis of communication uncovers some shared concerns.

For Lin, Stuart Hall's (1999) insight that both the speaker and listener in communication have their own theories of how the world works and how it should be interpreted, which comes from their social background and experiences, is of central importance. Successful communication requires translation of the message from one "framework of meaning" to another. In his experience as manager of a campus computer lab, Lin has served as a mentor to students who are learning

FIGURE 3.1. THE COMMUNICATION SECTION OF WAYNE LIN'S EPORTFOLIO

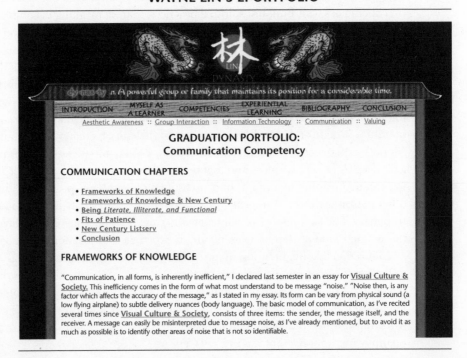

to use computers. Reflection on his experiences in this role, as documented in his portfolio through self-observations and correspondence with other students collected over time, has shown him that the conventional distinction between being "computer literate" and being "computer illiterate" oversimplifies the frameworks of meaning that underlie how the people he serves learn to use computers. In his experience, most students come to the lab as neither literate nor illiterate in computers but as what he calls "computer functional." Students know how to perform basic tasks like saving a document in Word or opening an e-mail message in Explorer. What they have not yet learned to do, and what Lin sees as a key component of genuine computer literacy, is to transfer their understanding of these operations to the learning of new ones. Computer-functional people are not yet able or willing to explore new features and programs of their own, using their sense of how the features and programs they already have mastered work to guide their experimentation.

Lin's teaching practice has convinced him that supporting the shift from functional to literate is significantly different from supporting the shift from illiterate to functional. While people can become functional through memorizing sets of instructions, the most direct way for computer-functional people to complete tasks, such directed assistance does not help learners develop the confidence they need to continue to learn on their own. Effectively communicating to his clients how to act as truly computer-literate learners is more challenging. An essential part of the process is not immediately providing information when students are struggling, but instead serving as a reassuring presence to allow them to explore and experiment, reinforcing their successes and stepping in only when they truly get stuck. This holding back requires "fits of patience," which Lin enacts through nonverbal clues such as keeping his hands away from the mouse and sitting back calmly in his chair. As in the deep communication that Moore values, silence and presence may be as important to powerful communication as exchanging information. Establishing the right relationship is key to stimulating learning, just as it is to encouraging healing.

The importance of the nonverbal aspects of listening in communications was a central theme in the capstone conversations panel on communication the fall of both portfolio authors' senior year. Led by two capstone students, the panel also included a New Century College graduate in a successful career as a management consultant, a New Century College faculty member, and two leaders of the university's institutional research unit. Sharing experiences from contexts such as facilitating business meetings, advising new students, acting on the stage, and conducting interviews for the student newspaper, the participants agreed that nonverbal cues such as maintaining an "active body state" were centrally important to effective communication. Drawing on examples from the sections of their portfolios focused on communication, students noted that beyond some attention to posture and gestures in public speaking courses, their course work put little emphasis on these aspects of communication. Reflecting back on the absence of attention to this dimension in her own graduation portfolio and how she has begun to capture it in her ongoing practice of documenting her professional performance for annual review, the alumna on the panel suggested that most of her learning about the nonverbal elements of listening in facilitating business collaboration had come from her experiences on the job after graduation. The institutional researchers noted that this aspect of communication is difficult not only to teach but also to measure, and as a consequence, there are few data on how well it is supported across the university.

Taken together, the accounts of communication in the two portfolios and in the capstone panel discussion provide important information for those making decisions about how to support this competency. Might writing and speaking be overemphasized in the curriculum at the expense of nonverbal communication? While we may pay lip-service to the importance of listening, are students more often rewarded based on how frequently they speak or the quantity of texts they produce? How might we assess class participation and contributions to group work to better take into account the role of listening and presence? Do we see the value of silence in communication, or do we tend to think about it as a lack of engagement or an inefficiency? How might we better prompt and reinforce the reflections on listening, embodiment, and silence that were important to the port-folio authors' and conversation participants' growth as communicators? Should New Century College expand experiential learning opportunities for students in contexts that have yielded such reflective insight, such as peer teaching and meditative practice?

The intersections of students' portfolios and public forums for deliberation do not provide the answers to these questions. They must be taken up through further deliberation in the formal process of making curricular and programmatic decisions, and the perspectives of each individual may not align fully with the collective interest. For example, while the faculty considering a redesign of the New Century College first-year curriculum may recognize the authors' and participants' embrace of the nonverbal as important, if compelled to choose one over the other, they may conclude that the strong impact of expository writing skills for success in subsequent academic and professional work may make writing instruction more of a priority than helping students develop listening skills. Such a decision, however, would be more likely to be both accurate and accepted as legitimate by students, faculty, community members, and employ-ers because of the full range of alternative perspectives the portfolios made visible. The portfolio assessment process helps to ensure that fuller information about learning is available for deliberative decision making and recognizes the reasonableness of multiple perspectives.

The extent to which this model can be extended to programs in all disciplines and professions is open to question. Certainly in some fields, there is a significant enough level of consensus about a core of knowledge and skills that individual student experience, at least at the undergraduate level, is unlikely to uncover the kinds of gaps and opportunities found in the contexts of integrative studies and general education. Nevertheless, there are surely aspects of practice in almost all fields where such a strong consensus has not yet been, and may never be, achieved. Issues of leadership and ethics, for example, are certainly as relevant to the natural sciences and the health professions as to the humanities and the arts. As the surgeon Atul Gawande (2002) demonstrates, while many of the necessary skills for diagnosing a patient and conducting surgery have been well established through research and experience (we surely do not want novice surgeons going with what feels right to them, scalpel in hand!), questions about how doctors should learn, who makes decisions about the course of a patient's care, and how the consequences of mistakes should be managed are a good deal more contested. While the ability of new doctors to negotiate these issues is of undeniable importance, and consequently ought to be assessed, such assessment may require a deliberative rather than standardized process. Chapter Five takes up this argument.

Challenges in Deliberative Problem Solving

An assumption behind the belief that deliberation yields better decisions is that it enables consideration of issues from multiple perspectives, drawing on the information possessed by each member of a group. The ideals of authenticity and integrity suggest that each individual has a distinct understanding of how her life should be lived based on her distinctive nature, unique social affiliations and life experiences, and lasting commitments as enacted through social participation in multiple spheres of life. One promise of the ideal of deliberation is that it offers a means for groups and institutions to capitalize on the wealth of diverse knowledge provided by these unique identities. As argued in Chapter One, one of the advantages of personalized eportfolios in higher education is that they can represent not just the delivered curriculum but also how that curriculum is experienced by each student and how it interacts with the larger lived curriculum of their learning throughout their lives (Yancey, 1998, 2004b). If we accept that these larger curricula are relevant to making decisions about a university's goals and performance, then an inclusive deliberative forum in which students are invited to participate would enable the unique understanding of the outcomes of educational experiences that each possesses to inform collective judgment. The potential value of such richer representations of learning, as exemplified by Moore's and Lin's portfolios and the public dialogue they informed, should now be clear.

However, the extensive empirical work surveyed by Cass Sunstein (2006) suggests that the assumption that deliberation leads to better decisions may not withstand closer examination. Many studies of deliberating groups trying to solve problems with known correct answers suggest that the process of deliberation may not always improve the performance of the group in solving the kind of problem that has a correct answer compared to simply looking at the aggregate of individual solutions. If deliberation is not as effective in these situations, Sunstein argues, why should we assume that it will be more effective at addressing more ambiguous and morally charged problems? Deliberation may provide democratic legitimacy to the answers, but it may not ensure they are the best possible answers.

Empirical studies point to a number of thorny problems that plague deliberation. One source of problems is that people involved in the discussion do not offer information they hold that might be relevant to the problem. These omissions result in "hidden profiles": better solutions that are missed because the group's full knowledge is not brought to bear (Sunstein, 2006). One reason for this phenomenon is the common knowledge effect: information held by many or most participants in a deliberation is likely to be much more influential than that held by one or a few, for the simple reason that it is more likely to be repeated in the course of discussion. Even when the less common knowledge might be more important, the shared knowledge tends to take center stage.

Another cause of problems is that individual errors tend to be amplified during the process of deliberation through "information cascades" (Sunstein, 2006). Participants in a deliberation have a tendency to say they agree with the judgments others have already expressed, especially when they are uncertain about the correctness of their own views. However, the early speakers may have just as much reason to doubt their positions. As subsequent speakers concur out of their own uncertainty, it seems more and more likely that the position expressed by multiple speakers must be the right one, even though it is in reality no more likely to be a better choice than those the other speakers might have made on their own but chose not to express. This effect is compounded by social pressure to not get in the way of making a decision in a timely fashion. People are likely to agree with an emerging consensus despite holding information that might call it into question out of a desire to be liked by the group or to avoid making trouble. Deliberators also tend to defer to the views of people in positions of power or social prestige, and these people's views also tend to be amplified.

Eportfolios as Conversation Pieces

Eportfolios have the potential to help mitigate the possible distortions of both the common knowledge effect and information cascades in deliberative assessment. First, eportfolios can be used to broaden common knowledge. Without portfolios, it would certainly still be possible to create inclusive forums for deliberation about educational decision making that are accessible to students. However, their success in capitalizing on the unique, authentic information each student holds about the impact of curricular and programmatic choices would require each student to participate actively in the deliberations. While some students might embrace the opportunity, others would likely lack interest, would not see such engagement as their responsibility, or would not trust that their contribution would be taken seriously. (Students from marginalized groups have good reasons for this skepticism. Empirical studies of jury deliberations show that the reasoning of members from disadvantaged groups is often discounted, despite its objective merit. Saunders, 1997.) Others may simply not be able to make participation a priority because of competing responsibilities or commitments. Even if unique perspectives were offered by students in the process of deliberation, the common knowledge effect suggests that the distinctiveness of these perspectives would make them less likely to influence the conversation. The situation changes, however, if students express their authentic positions in eportfolios that participants in deliberation are asked to read prior to engaging in discussion. The portfolios can then serve as shared conversation pieces. Knowledge about learning that was previously private to the individual, and which could enter the conversation only through their direct participation, is now held in common and can be invoked by any member of the group. The individual perspectives become common knowledge, making it more likely that what is significant about them is taken into consideration in the process of deliberative assessment.

When portfolio authors do choose to participate in deliberative forums, having composed a portfolio is also likely to help mitigate the inclination to join information cascades. Analysis of the ideal of authenticity in the previous chapter showed that individuals' previously inchoate understanding of how they are distinctive becomes clearer and more manifest through the process of creative expression supported by eportfolios. Students who have expressed and justified their perspectives in their portfolios are more likely to have a command of them, making it more likely they will be confident sharing them in public forums. Portfolios are also conversation pieces for their authors, offering well-thought-out examples of their work, stories about their experiences, and arguments about their capabilities to share in the process of discussion.

When portfolios are recognized as shared texts in the norms of the conversation, authors will more likely be willing to share their perspectives. The organizational validation of multiple perspectives and the importance of individual distinctiveness, as captured in multiple portfolios as shared texts, may mitigate the impact of social pressures toward conformity with already expressed opinions and the dominant positions. When an individual's priorities are not, in the end, reflected fully in the decisions of an institution, that partial rejection may be less painful because the process simultaneously recognizes the reasonableness and importance of each individual's position. This recognition may also encourage engagement.

Deliberation in Eportfolio Practice Elsewhere in Higher Education

New Century College is unusual in the scope of its commitment to deliberation and embrace of this approach to using competencies in assessment. However, some aspects of deliberation can be observed in how eportfolios are used in other institutions. While in Chapter One we saw that the ideal of authenticity underlies much of the educational theory that commonly informs the use of eportfolios, deliberation is more evident in practice itself. For example, many portfolio assessment processes include "read-arounds" in which faculty—and sometimes students, alumni, and others—come together to read and discuss portfolios. While part of the purpose of these conversations can be norming for standardized assessment, often they move beyond the application of existing standards to critically evaluate them in light of the window into the experienced and lived curriculums offered by the portfolios. These deliberations about what is significant in teaching and learning can happen through electronic media, as well as face-to-face, and can extend beyond a single institution. (Chapters Seven and Eight examine this potential.) A strong example of such multi-institution deliberations is the Portnet project, in which writing teachers from multiple universities across the United States discussed portfolios online over a period of several months, leading to changes in assessment practices (Allen et al., 1997). Assessment standards can be developed through a deliberative process of analyzing actual portfolios rather than beginning from aspirations or theoretical constructs. The developmental scales for ranking primary and secondary school students that have proved highly successful in the Learning Record portfolio assessment system were developed this way, and results of these judgments are regularly critically examined and either reaffirmed or revised through yearly read-arounds, called moderations, at the school, regional, and national levels (Barr, 1995; Barr & Cheong, 1995).

Portfolio assessment processes can also be made more deliberative through involving parties affected by decisions about the institution's curriculum and programs. For example, institutions such as Indiana University Purdue University Indianapolis (IUPUI) and Portland State University (PSU) invite alumni and community partners to serve as eportfolio evaluators. These broader publics are also engaged as the audience for institutional portfolios that contain evidence from student portfolios. IUPUI and PSU were part of the Urban Universities Portfolio Project, through which ten universities developed portfolios that documented their institutional vision and performance (Kahn, 2001; Ketcheson, 2001). Like individual portfolios, institutional portfolios explain values and commitments, demonstrate how the authors' actions have aligned with them, and judge the effectiveness of those actions and what future directions they recommend through presenting and reflecting on evidence collected over time. The process of composing the portfolios required intensive internal deliberation within the institution, which continues as the portfolios are regularly revised. The portfolios also serve as conversation pieces for dialogue with the broader communities of which these institutions are a part about what the universities should do and how well they are doing it. Such institutional portfolios are increasingly being encouraged as part of the self-study process that accompanies accreditation by regional agencies such as the Western Association for Schools and Colleges (Wexler, 2001).

While this section focuses on assessment in higher education, the use of eportfolios encompassing large organizations is beginning to spread beyond higher education. As will be discussed in depth in Chapter Six, other types of organizations are developing eportfolios in order to guide goal setting and track progress. Through the deliberative process of composing these portfolios and making decisions informed by them, organizations become better aligned with the needs of the individuals who compose them, which may ultimately lead to stronger performance. Such organizational portfolios, especially if used in concert with individual portfolios, can lead to a broader understanding of good work than can be captured by standardized processes that track competencies and accomplishments as conventionally defined. That deepened understanding can guide future organizational practices and progress.

Deliberative assessment posits that competencies and skills needed in higher education and in the workplace are more accurately determined through an eportfolio process that is transparent, inclusive, reasonable, and transparent. The process reveals tacit and explicit knowledge and understanding, the continuing evolution of that knowledge and understanding, and the interrelationship of the individual and the institutional and organizational contexts of the learner. Through deliberating with eportfolios as conversation pieces, individuals can chart their own learning, advocating for the organization to support them in achieving their personal and career goals. In adapting to and capitalizing on a richer understanding of individual capabilities, commitments, and differences, the organization, through individuals' portfolios and perhaps the organization's own, becomes itself a learning organization. Eportfolios are the occasion for the kind of assessment process that honors all learners through helping them know and understand more about themselves and others.

Questions for Practice

The model for reflective assessment that embraces the ideal of deliberative decision making discussed in this chapter raises several questions for educators supporting the use of eportfolios:

- How visible is the process of setting standards for assessment to learners and other stakeholders? Are the reasoning behind the standards and the deliberations that produced them documented and available for discussion?
- How inclusive is the process of setting standards and evaluating eportfolios? How might you create opportunities for learners and other stakeholders to participate?
- To what extent can your outcomes and standards serve as boundary objects, helping eportfolio authors and other participants in deliberative assessment connect their distinctive perspective to shared values and judgments?
- How might the various venues in which eportfolios are discussed for the purpose of assessment add up to a deliberative system? Can eportfolios serve as conversation pieces in private, protopublic, and public spaces that enable learners to develop their deliberative skills?
- To what extent do the conversations eportfolios mediate influence programmatic and institutional decisions? How can the link between deliberation and institutional innovation be strengthened and make more visible?

CHAPTER FOUR

FROM AUTHENTIC ASSESSMENT TO EPORTFOLIO ASSESSMENT

Drilling Down and Linking Up

The previous chapter focused primarily on practice within one program to introduce an alternative perspective on how eportfolios can be used in assessment in higher education. This chapter broadens the perspective to consider the use of eportfolios for programmatic and institutional assessment conducted through national and international projects based in the United States: the Inter/National Coalition for Electronic Portfolio Research (I/NCEPR) and the Valid Assessment of Learning in Undergraduate Education (VALUE) project. Insights from the process of developing assessment methodologies and making sense of the evidence of student learning they generate raise important issues for institutions wishing to place assessment in the service of lifelong learning, issues that are informed by the broadened understanding of what it means to be a member of a discipline or a profession presented in Chapter Two. Genuine eportfolio assessment goes beyond the minimal requirements of authentic assessment to capitalize on the full range of affordances of the eportfolio genre, that is, the ways in which its distinctive characteristics, capabilities, and tradition of use suggest it can most profitably be used.

Research on academic assessment in higher education and compulsory education over the past two decades in fields such as rhetoric and composition, teacher education, medicine, and engineering has demonstrated that portfolios (both print and electronic) can be used to assess a variety of learning outcomes. In a manner that has been proved psychometrically rigorous enough to satisfy regional and professional accreditation agencies, portfolios and eportfolios have been used to assess everything from expository writing, to adverse event reporting, to team-based design (Driessen, Overeen, van Tartwijk, van der Vleuten, & Muijtjens, 2006; Haswell, 2001; Williams, 2002). At the primary and secondary levels, portfolio assessments have produced data about students' development in reading, writing, and mathematics that has proved valid and reliable at school, regional, and national levels (Hallam, 2000). Portfolios are also beginning to be used successfully to measure learning in relationship to general education outcomes that are not the province of a particular discipline, such as critical thinking or quantitative reasoning (Cambridge, Fernandez, Kahn, Kirkpatrick, & Smith, 2008; Lorenzo & Ittelson, 2005).

Advocates for these assessments point to two primary factors that distinguish them from more conventional assessments, such as standardized tests. First, portfolio assessment is a subset of authentic assessment (Huba & Freed, 2000). The evidence in portfolios is drawn from authentic performances rather than produced through activities in which students participate solely for the purpose of generating assessment data. The products of these performances more fully reflect students' capabilities because they are produced in contexts similar to those they will work within throughout their lives. Second, portfolio assessment is a kind of learning through assessment (Maki, 2003). The process of composing and presenting an eportfolio to an audience is in itself a powerful learning experience likely to bolster development of the very abilities it can help measure. If students see the direct learning benefit of an assessment, they are more likely to put forth their best effort in engaging with it. Both authentic assessment and learning through assessment are likely to yield a more accurate account of how well learners can apply their knowledge and skills in the academic and professional settings for which educational institutions seek to prepare them.

Achieving these results requires significantly more investment than do alternative means of assessment. Before it produces the kinds of numerical data called for by some accreditors and policymakers, portfolio assessment requires students, faculty, and staff to understand the portfolio genre, learn to use and support the technology that facilitates the process, compose and respond to complex texts, and engage in deliberations about shared standards for evaluating them. If the assessment is to have high stakes, meticulous care must be taken in planning and executing these activities in order to meet legal and scientific standards for responsible practice and ensure accuracy, fairness, and privacy (Wilkerson & Lang, 2003). Because portfolio assessment processes need to be attuned to the specific goals and culture of the institution implementing them in order to fully realize the benefits their advocates attribute to them, the careful design work must be performed locally.

Given these not insignificant challenges, the temptation to fall back on standardized assessments that promise sufficient, if less compelling, results is substantial. For example, while regional accreditation agencies such as the Higher Learning Commission and the Western Association for Schools and Colleges have endorsed portfolios as means for generating evidence of student learning, they also are willing to consider data from tests such as the Collegiate Learning Assessment (CLA) and measurements of activity associated with student learning, such as the National Survey of Student Engagement (NSSE). These measures have serious limitations. The CLA has a problematic sampling procedure, and 81 percent of variance in scores can be predicted by students' SAT or ACT scores (Banta, 2010). The NSSE is an indirect and self-reported measure never intended for use as a summative assessment. However, compared to a rigorous eportfolio assessment, these tests and surveys are quick and inexpensive. If the audiences for assessment data will be satisfied with their results, does the added value offered by eportfolios justify the additional cost? Similarly, if an exam can test technical knowledge and skills in a professional field, such as teaching or clinical psychology, to the desired audience of its results' satisfaction, why go to the added trouble of trying to measure these things using eportfolios? Even if the argument for authentic assessment is made successfully, some institutions may choose to implement less complicated forms, such as collecting and evaluating individual samples of work. While institutions may see eportfolio assessment as valuable in an absolute sense, the learning experience of composing a genuine eportfolio may not appear worth the added effort and expense or may appear to be peripheral to the task of producing the needed type of assessment data.

Implicit in many such decision-making processes is the assumption that the various forms of assessment are each a means to the same ends: producing comparable quantitative data about student learning outcomes. In contrast, research on the use of eportfolios for assessment points to the importance of more complex forms of evidence in making meaning from and taking action on the patterns that quantitative data can uncover. The research also makes clear that how the student learning outcomes themselves are defined may need to change if we choose to value the aspects of student learning and development invisible to assessments other than eportfolios.

Part One of this book examined the broader dimensions of identity and learning that eportfolios articulate, and the previous chapter identified the processes that might be put in place to capitalize on them. Looking at two models of assessment using eportfolios, Chapters One and Three go further to argue that the importance of helping students articulate their authenticity, combined with a commitment to the principles of deliberative democracy in institutional decision making, calls for assessment processes more complex than testing and best supported by genuine eportfolios. What distinguishes the discussion of authenticity and deliberation from the more general arguments in favor of eportfolio assessment is that it points not only to what eportfolios can do better than conventional assessments but also to what they make visible that the other assessment methods cannot. Similarly, the discussion of integrity in Chapter Two presented an understanding of what it means to be a member of a discipline or profession that cannot be boiled down to the isolated collections of concepts and skills on which many nonportfolio means of articulating capability focus, an argument continued in Part Three.

The argument for genuine eportfolios is most likely to be effective if it appeals to important aspects of work that are otherwise invisible to organizations. This chapter examines how the use of eportfolios for assessment of professional competence in higher education shifts attention from a narrow set of skills and behaviors to embrace a broader vision of professional identity and ability. Even for less specialized learning outcomes, such as those of general education or those that run throughout multiple fields, an eportfolio approach makes available for analysis dimensions of these abilities that are otherwise inaccessible. If these aspects are to be taken into account, institutions must broaden their definitions of what counts as meaningful student learning. This broadened perspective is essential because it aligns with the demands of the social world in which graduates will live and work, setting the foundation for lifelong and lifewide learning.

Translating this argument into policy is likely to be challenging because it requires changes in the understanding of learning outcomes, the process of assessment, and the use of faculty, staff, and student time and energy. The next chapter suggests that those advocating for the use of eportfolios for assessment in higher education are likely to be more successful if they first focus on the important aspects of learning and development that are difficult or impossible to measure using more conventional methods. While eportfolios can powerfully support and document a wide range of types of learning, they are most compelling in their ability to track progress toward learning outcomes that, while widely valued, are often considered ineffable because of the inability of conventional assessment methods to shed light on them. By focusing on such outcomes, eportfolio advocates are likely to produce compelling results that could not have been produced otherwise. Armed with such results, educators may then be better able to make a case for expanded use of eportfolios to document a broader range of dimensions of learning, including those that have been the traditional domain of standardized assessments.

Drilling Down: From Numbers to Context

Even when used in processes that are designed to measure conventional outcomes and generate numerical ratings of competence, the composition and evaluation of eportfolios produce a more comprehensive and flexible collection of data than standardized assessments do. Collected and stored electronically during an assessment process, eportfolios can be archived for further study at minimal additional cost. Over time, such archives provide expansive collections of data about student learning, combining authentic evidence and students' reflection on it. The content of this evidence and these reflections can be analyzed to shed light on the meaning of patterns of performance that are suggested by numerical data.

The first-year writing assessment portfolio at the University of Georgia provides an example. Every student who takes the first-year composition course offered by the English Department at Georgia completes a portfolio that consists of a selection of essays written during the class; two are revised prior to inclusion in the portfolio, and a cover letter is added in which the student reflects on his or her development as a writer over the course of the class as it is reflected in the essays he or she chooses to include (Desmet, Griffin, Miller, Balthazor, & Cummings, 2009). Using a rubric developed by the program, faculty assess these portfolios holistically.

In its general structure, this portfolio writing assessment process is similar to many others used at institutions across the United States, such as the writing portfolio completed by all rising juniors at Washington State University (Hamp-Lyons & Condon, 2000; Haswell, 2001; Yancey & Weiser, 1997). While Washington State collects print portfolios from its students, Georgia has students upload their work into <emma>, a custom-developed Web application that facilitates the process of composing and evaluating the portfolios. While the portfolio assessment process supported by <emma> produces numerical scores that provide a snapshot of how well students are meeting first-year writing standards in aggregate, it also archives the essays and reflective cover letters themselves. As of June 2007, the archive contained almost 550,000 documents (Desmet et al., 2009). Faculty examine student work in depth, considering it in relationship to students' reflections and multiple examples of the products of their composition, to understand the dynamics of learning behind the patterns that the numbers reveal. As members of Georgia's I/NCEPR team put it, "The collection of class documents in a single electronic 'place' also allows us to 'drill down' through the collected documents and portfolios of any given student and to examine in some detail both the changes in individual documents and the rhetoric of reflection that provides a context for the students' revised essays" (p. 158). The quantitative assessment data remain connected to the authentic evidence and its reflective framing within the portfolio as a whole, both of which are needed to understand it and take action in response to it.

The University of Georgia faculty used this process of drilling down from broad, quantitative assessment data to the writing and reflections of individual writers to investigate the role of revision in learning to write during the first-year course. By comparing the original scores on versions of essays turned in as class assignments and the scores of the revised versions submitted for evaluation, faculty members were able to determine that revision typically led to an improvement in scores of between a quarter and a half point on a twelve-point scale. This finding confirms that revision does indeed lead to stronger writing for many students at the University of Georgia, suggesting that it is appropriate to include it as part of the first-year writing curriculum. In providing evidence for program or accreditation reviews that this aspect of the program is producing results, this assessment result is helpful and representative of the kind of data these audiences value.

However, to yield information that would help faculty understand how to support more effective revision by student writers, they needed to drill down further. A first step was to identify two groups of essays that represented successful and unsuccessful revision, as determined by the score the essay received, choosing essays where the revised version received a score significantly higher or lower than the original. The kinds of revisions made in each essay were coded according to a classificatory scheme from the research literature. This process yielded the finding that students who were successful in their revisions tended to make more formal changes to their essays and fewer changes overall, while those who were unsuccessful made more changes, and more of them were structural in nature. This result might suggest that students should be taught to focus more carefully on formal features of their writing when revising. Alternatively, it might imply that these features were receiving undue weight in how essays were being assessed, especially given that the unsuccessful writers were actually doing more revision.

In order to determine whether either or both or neither of these interpretations was valid, the Georgia team drilled down even deeper into the data, this time taking advantage of the affordances of the portfolio structure, looking closely at the content of several of the authors' paired drafts and their reflective explanation of the logic behind the revisions. Through this process, the researchers discovered that one reason for the discrepancy between extensiveness of revision and level of success was a focus on detail at the expense of global coherence. One writer, for example, believed that her original essay went into insufficient depth about the film she was analyzing and added a much more detailed treatment of a key scene. Her reflection on the revision makes clear her intentions and her understanding of the importance of strong textual evidence in a rhetorical analysis. However, in the process of adding evidence, she also eliminated some of the global signposts that signaled the coherence of the original argument. Her significant improvements in integrating evidence into her argument were outweighed by the structural problems they introduced when the essay was rated holistically. This suggests that the situation was more complex than what might be suggested by the numbers alone. While formal changes may or may not be overvalued, another dimension of the challenge of helping students revise well is to guide them in identifying how structural changes intended to improve one aspect of an argument can simultaneously create the need for additional revision to address another. On the basis of these results, Georgia faculty might add a more structured reflection process to the course that invites students to consider multiple dimensions of quality together as they revise.

The insights produced by the process of drilling down to the content of the portfolios and the reflective commentaries that explain them provide concrete directions for curricular and programmatic improvement that the numerical results alone could not. However, these results are more meaningful than informally collected examples or anecdotes because they were selected to be representative of patterns that emerged from the more general quantitative results. At the same time, analyzing at this individual level of specificity points to the complexity and ambiguity that is inherent in teaching and learning. The process of learning to write, like the process of learning any transferable and higher-order skill, is complex and messy; understanding the dynamics of any individual writer's process of learning to write makes this clear. At the same time, there are patterns and principles that can guide students in writing well. Part of the challenge of teaching writing is to help students see writing as not just a process of applying mechanistic rules while also helping them understand a more mature writing process as something other than a mysterious black box of creative expression with no discernable structure. One could say something similar about the challenge of teaching students to manage a small business or conduct an ethnographic study.

As Anthony Ciccone, Renee Meyers, and Stephanie Waldmann (2008) point out, helping students come to terms with complexity and ambiguity is a key component of higher education. It therefore makes sense to choose means by which we try to document, understand, and judge the effectiveness of teaching and learning in higher education that similarly acknowledge and make visible complexity and ambiguity. In linking authentic and integral representations of learning to the common structure of a shared understanding of the important dimensions of performance in a manner that allows meaning making across the two scales, eportfolios provide one such means. One of the greatest potential strengths of eportfolio assessment is the ability to create a bridge between the positivistic, strictly quantitative epistemology that underlies some conventional assessment regimes and the more complex and situated understanding of teaching and learning held by many educators and researchers.

Linking Up: The Whole, the Parts, and the Relationships Between

The more complex understanding of the relationship between revision and the quality of students' writing was possible because the Georgia faculty looked at multiple pieces of writing from each portfolio in relationship to its author's reflections on the relationships between his or her two pieces and between the two pieces and his or her experiences and intentions. The portfolio was more than an unstructured collection of pieces of evidence that could be extracted for assessment: the relationships of the pieces mattered. The multiple components were chosen for inclusion in the portfolio because they together communicated something important through how they were connected. A central challenge in using eportfolios for assessment is finding ways to examine eportfolios as compositions—as complex texts in themselves rather than simply aggregations of texts (Yancey, 2004a). Exemplified by the Georgia case, evaluating eportfolios as compositions is a more intensive and challenging process than simply judging their constituent parts individually. The process is made more challenging because of the need to interpret the meaning of the portfolio as a whole, the variations of quality and purpose across individual items of evidence included in the portfolio, and the effectiveness of the portfolio in explaining that variation.

Digital Media and Professional Learning Outcomes

The need for this complexity may be less immediately clear for professional portfolios tied to standards developed by professional organizations. If there is a clear consensus in the field about the set of things members of a profession should know, be able to do, or believe, then ensuring that students wanting to enter the profession are competent seems simply to be a matter of ensuring that they have these things. While the kind of analysis outlined above, which looks at relationships between elements of an eportfolio to work toward the improvement of educational programs, might be helpful, if the primary purpose of the assessment is to ensure competence, then such a complex process does not seem necessary.

This picture, however, is more complicated when the limitations of the standards as representations of professional competence, and the limitations of self-representations they engender, are taken into account. Practice in the education of teachers illustrates these limitations. Delandshere and Arens (2003) suggest that standards in teacher education, such as traditional National Council for Accreditation of Teacher Education or the Interstate New Teacher Assessment and Support Consortium standards, tend to present professional competence as a series of disconnected items related to knowledge and skills organized into a set of broad categories. Standards frequently take the form of a list composed of easily concretized concepts and abilities. The structure of professional portfolios, such as the example discussed in Chapter One, is often driven by such standards. Delandshere and Arens's (2003) research on portfolios in elementary education programs at three U.S. universities suggests that this connection leads to portfolios as "collections of artifacts, sequentially organized around key words from the standards, but [which] lack explanations or conceptual structure and represent teaching as an eclectic set of discrete and generic skills, beliefs, and activities" (p. 62). There are few connections between sections of the portfolio and little explanation for the conceptual logic behind how they are organized, how they represent the new teacher's understanding of his or her professional identity, and what theoretical perspectives on teaching and learning inform them. The portfolios are aggregations of documents more than they are compositions with a clear sense of overall purpose in which the relationships between the parts are intentional and explicit. This leads to "representations of teaching that are fragmented, and at times incoherent or inconsistent" (p. 63). Even when students are asked to include a statement of their teaching philosophy as a component of the portfolio, they tend to lean heavily on the standards, drawing most of their conceptual material from them:

> One could read these philosophy of education statements simply as restatements of the standards, using similar language and ideas. And although these are labeled as philosophy of education, [the researchers] were hard pressed to find the presentation of foundational ideas relating to, for example, the purpose of education, its importance in society, the meaning of knowing and learning, or the social and political implications of teaching. This is, however, not surprising given the absence of explicit philosophical considerations in the standards from which they work. (p. 63)

The language and organization of the statements of professional standards with which students are asked to work masks the deliberations about the purpose and dynamics of teaching and learning underlying them. Yet understanding and situating oneself within such debates is an integral component of professional competence and professional identity. As argued in Part One, an authentic and integral representation of oneself fully as a member of a profession means more than just demonstrating a set of skills, knowledge, and beliefs dictated by an external authority. It means articulating the underlying principles behind this assemblage of abilities and attitudes and connecting them to a professional's broader identity and social context.

Research conducted through the I/NCEPR demonstrates the importance of this broader understanding of what it means to be a competent member of a profession. The Coalition brings together teams of researchers from forty-eight colleges and universities from the United States, Canada, England, Scotland, and the Netherlands to investigate how eportfolios support learning and evaluate the effectiveness of using them for assessment. Each campus team, as part of a cohort of approximately ten institutions, conducts a three-year research project that addresses local priorities and shared questions (Cambridge, Cambridge, & Yancey, 2009).

Research at two campuses in the I/NCEPR, Virginia Tech and Clemson University, demonstrates how the affordances of the digital medium support creating and assessing broader representations of professional identity. Students at Virginia Tech created portfolios with multiple layers that both articulated their situation within their professions and provided evidence of abilities in relationship to professional standards. Students at Clemson composed portfolios whose structural complexity mirrored the increasing sophistication of their professional identities and growing level of professional competence.

In the master's in English education program at Virginia Tech, students create eportfolios to demonstrate their competence as new teachers of English (Young, 2009). These portfolios also help the program demonstrate that students meet INTASC standards, a requirement for accreditation of the program. During the first few years of the requirement, students were asked to create portfolios organized around the standards. Most eportfolios consisted of a fairly generic overview page that linked to pages for each of the top-level categories defined by the standards, a format similar to those examined by Delandshere and Arens (2003). Although they were adequate for the purposes of demonstrating that students were meeting the standards, neither students nor faculty found them particularly meaningful or complete. They failed to create context for a conversation about the key issues of the profession and did not contribute to students' sense of themselves as new members of it.

In the revised curriculum introduced as part of the research, students were asked to shift from a "standards-driven design" to a "design supported by standards" (Young, 2009, p. 183). The eportfolios produced through the new curriculum still included authentic evidence drawn from course work and fieldwork that could be used to evaluate their authors' possession of the knowledge, skills, and attitudes specified by the standards. However, the top layers of the portfolio were dedicated to communicating the students' own integrated understanding of their philosophy of and situation within English education. Rather than the standards dictating the organization, each student developed his or her own categories, and each established a theme through the reflective narrative that runs throughout the writing in his or her eportfolio and is communicated through its visual design. The ability to create multiple layers, linked together in multiple ways, allowed students to take ownership of the design of the eportfolio interface in order to situate themselves within the profession while also allowing readers to drill down to information needed to evaluate the students' work in relationship to professional standards. The results were dramatic. The ability to create a rich visual representation offered by the digital medium provided a means of reflection that aided in the process of integration. The students' designs contextualized the knowledge, skills, abilities, and attitudes from the standards within each student's own integrated, conceptual understanding of the profession. The research indicates that this "design supported by standards" approach enabled students to "define themselves more explicitly as . . . beginning English teacher[s]" and to "better situate themselves within the profession with regards to beliefs, philosophy of teaching and learning, knowledge of the field, and practice" (Young, 2009, p. 183).

For example, Katie Walter's portfolio opens with a splash screen featuring a picture of a flower at the end of a tree branch and a quote from Thomas Huxley: "Why not go out on a limb? There is where the fruit is." This introduction establishes the dual theme of risk taking and growth that she sees as central to the teaching profession and that runs throughout her portfolio. The other pages of her portfolio extend this theme, using earth tones and images of leaves, nuts, and soil in motion or being worked by human hands. The portfolio is organized into sections reflecting her understanding of the central components of the profession of teaching English: Literacy, Community, Technology, Knowledge, and Leadership. The importance of and relationships among the categories, as well as how INTASC standards related to them, are explained through the portfolio's reflective narrative and discussion of the artifacts Walter includes. In an interview, Walter said that the process of composing her portfolio "allowed me to bring together all of what seemed to be discrete pieces" of her professional learning and performance and to connect them to her evolving sense of what it means to be a responsible and effective teacher. Compared with portfolios created by students in the old curriculum, Walter's portfolio and those of her peers present a much more integrated, authentic, and engaging account of professional identity in the field. (See Figure 4.1.) The affordances of the digital medium for expressive visual design and hypertextual organization make this possible.

Research in other disciplines also suggests that the affordances of the digital medium contribute to the representation of professional competence and identity. In Clemson University's I/NCEPR project, psychology students composed eportfolios during a ten-week intensive summer internship program. The students created an initial version of their portfolio at the beginning of the program, drawing on

FIGURE 4.1. KATIE WALTER'S EPORTFOLIO

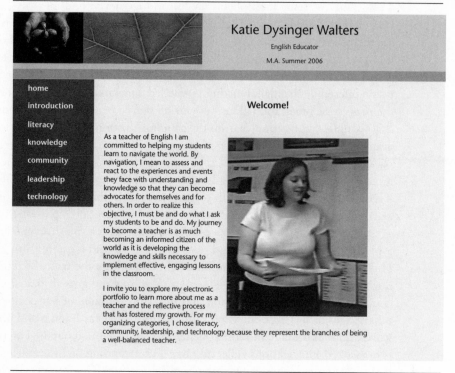

Reprinted with permission of Stylus Publishing, LLC.

their past course work and field experiences. They then revised and modified it each week, leading up to a final portfolio that reflected their increased understanding of and identification with the discipline and profession (Stephens, 2009).

Clemson's research shows that the organizational complexity of students' portfolios increased markedly over the course of the program as measured by a quantitative measure of the degree of hierarchy used to interlink documents in the portfolios. The increase in complexity correlated with increases in both students' level of mastery of the technical skills of psychology and their interest in the profession, as measured by their self-assessment and scoring of the portfolio on both measures by program faculty. The ability to create hyperlinks enabled students to represent complexity and depth of their professional knowledge and identity not only through textual reflection but also through the associations the links communicated. In accommodating not just technical skills but also the representation of professional identification, the use of eportfolios by the psychology program at Clemson signals an expanded sense of its important outcomes, of what counts as valuable learning in the profession that needs to be assessed.

VALUE and Writing

This pattern of broadening outcomes is also evident when the purpose of assessment is to measure a conventional, general learning outcome such as writing ability. The more complex description of the outcomes may do more than just measure the ability in a more nuanced way. It may, in fact, imply a different understanding of how to define the ability and what counts as genuine evidence of it. This makes comparisons of results with those of simpler assessments, even authentic assessments that draw on portfolios, problematic. The choice between simple authentic assessment and genuine eportfolio assessment is not simply between multiple means to the same end. Rather, just as examining authentic evidence allows institutions to measure a broadened set of aspects of an ability than does standardized testing, so eportfolio assessment further expands what counts as integral.

The Association of American Colleges and Universities (AAC&U) recently completed the Valid Assessment of Learning in Undergraduate Education (VALUE) project, which has a foot in both authentic assessment generally and eportfolio assessment specifically, helps show how this is the case. VALUE was an effort to move toward a national framework for assessing student learning that "privileges multiple expert judgments of the quality of student work over reliance on standardized tests administered to samples of students outside of their required courses" (Association of American Colleges and Universities, 2009b). As part of AAC&U's Liberal Education and America's Promise (LEAP) initiative, VALUE builds on earlier work defining a set of essential learning outcomes for liberal arts education that engaged a wide range of stakeholders from education, business, the nonprofit sector, and government, attempting to strike a balance between the values and traditions of the academy and the demands of contemporary society. (See www.aacu.org/leap/vision.cfm for the complete list of learning outcomes.) These outcomes are designed to be equally applicable across disciplines, professions, regions, and institutional types. They include not only the cognitive, generalizable skills most often measured in the assessment of general education outcomes, both within and beyond the major, but also aspects of learning and development often excepted from assessment because of their seemingly ineffable nature, such as "civic knowledge and engagement" and "ethical reasoning and action" (Association of American Colleges and Universities, 2007). A primary focus of VALUE was to produce a set of "metarubrics" roughly corresponding with the thirteen LEAP outcomes that faculty at higher education institutions across the United States can use for assessment of authentic evidence of student learning (Rhodes, 2009, 2010).

The rubrics themselves were being developed by teams of faculty from institutions around the country and by an advisory board of assessment experts, drawing on examples of rubrics collected from a large number of institutions that focus on similar outcomes. The VALUE project also worked with twelve "leadership campuses," which include a range of institutional types and are spread across all the major regions of the United States. Each of these campuses is experienced at using eportfolios to assess student learning, although the portfolio processes and formats in use at each institution, including the outcomes on which they have traditionally focused and programmatic contexts in which students compose portfolios, is equally varied. Eight of the twelve leadership campuses—Alverno College, Bowling Green State University, LaGuardia Community College, George Mason University, Kapi'olani Community College, Portland State University, San Francisco State University, and the University of Michigan—were already members of the I/NCEPR at the start of VALUE. The leadership campuses' role in the project was to use the VALUE metarubrics to assess student portfolios alongside their preexisting evaluation processes, providing feedback on the suitability of the rubrics for supporting such assessments and comparing the process of using the common rubrics with their own practices. Through several iterations of eportfolio evaluation, this feedback was used to revise the rubrics. Out of their work, VALUE also hoped to derive "a set of new comparable templates and frameworks" for using eportfolios to assess learning outcomes (Association of American Colleges and Universities, 2009a).

This second outcome is part of VALUE-Plus, which connects AAC&U's work with that of the American Association of State Colleges and Universities (AASCU) and the National Association of State Universities and Land-Grant Colleges (NASULGC) to build a new common means for assessing the performance of institutions that contains measures of student learning more effective than the standardized tests currently included as the sole measures in AASCU and NASULGC's Voluntary System of Accountability (VSA), which has been endorsed by over three hundred institutions in all fifty U.S. states (McPherson & Shulenburger, 2006). The VSA is a response to recent increased pressure from policymakers for comparable data about the performance of colleges and universities in the United States, particularly their impact on student learning. This effort was triggered in part in response to the Commission on the Future of Higher Education. Also known as the Spellings Commission, it called in 2006 for increased accountability in the form of a national database of data on institutional performance, including some measure of student learning that the public could use to judge the effectiveness of each American institution of higher education (U.S. Department of Education, 2006).

The challenge the VALUE project faced was a desire to develop rubrics that can be used for assessing a wide variety of student work, whether or not that work is part of an eportfolio, and in effectively assessing students' learning through eportfolios. The primary focus of the project was on promoting authentic assessment of the full range of LEAP outcomes. While eportfolios may be a powerful means for doing so, implicit in the design of VALUE is the assumption that other means can produce comparable results. The teams creating the rubrics attempted to write them in such a way that they can be used to assess isolated examples of students' work and to assess eportfolios.

Given that relatively few institutions are using eportfolios on a large scale to assess the outcomes on which VALUE focuses, and that implementing a process of eportfolio assessment requires a significant institutional investment, targeting the rubrics for use in a broad range of authentic assessments is likely to considerably broaden the number of colleges and universities that might use them in some way. AAC&U is inviting institutions to stay close to their existing practices and work with genres with which many of their constituents are already familiar, rather than challenging them to adapt processes to the characteristics of the eportfolio genre and ideals for educational practice it embodies. As is the case with eportfolios beyond the academy focused on employability and professional development, which will be discussed in Chapter Six, this strategy may be necessary for developing the familiarity of evaluators with authentic evidence and the relationships between institutions needed to begin to move toward embracing genuine eportfolios.

However, this approach neglects attending to the differences in student performance and identity that the eportfolio genre can make visible. The use of eportfolios signals a commitment to examining a broader range of indicators of student learning than does examination of unintegrated samples of student work. Examining the Written Communication rubric illustrates these distinctions. The introduction to the rubric states that it has been designed to "focus assessment on how specific written products or collections of work respond to specific contexts." Unlike some of the other draft rubrics, Written Communication makes explicit the assumption that equivalent judgments can be made from a portfolio, here reduced to a collection of work, or from examples of writing on their own. It also explicitly excludes the eportfolio itself from consideration as a written product and makes the distinctive components of a portfolio, such as its reflective elements, optional. The products of writing can be compiled into a portfolio or not. Such portfolios might or might not include reflective components, which assessors may "take into consideration." Reflection and its relationships to selected examples of writing and the portfolio as a composition are presented as glosses on, rather than integral to, the aspects of writing on which the authors have chosen to focus.

Like each of the VALUE rubrics, Written Communication consists of a set of criteria describing key components of learning for the outcome, which run down the left side of the table, and four levels intended to represent different degrees of competence, which run across the top. At the intersection of criterion and level, a performance descriptor defines what performance at the given level for the chosen criterion looks like. This is a common format for rubrics used in many kinds of authentic assessment (Broad, 2003; Huba & Freed, 2000; Maki, 2003).

The criteria for written communication are "the context of and purpose for writing," "content development," "genre and disciplinary conventions," "sources and evidence," and "control of syntax and mechanics." These categories are similar to those in many writing rubrics in use at colleges and universities across the United States. As with the performance descriptors, they are informed by position statements about writing assessment from the primary professional bodies for writing researchers and teachers, the National Council of Teachers of English, the Council of Writing Program Administrators, and the Conference on College Composition and Communication (Conference on College Composition and Communication, 2008; National Council of Teachers of English and Council of Writing Program Administrators, 2008). Most of the authors are well-established scholars in the study and pedagogy of writing, and they clearly were diligent in grounding their work in research. The criteria reasonably reflect a consensus view of the central elements of college level writing.

The performance descriptors, however, reveal some of the more arguable assumptions about what is important in writing that underlie the rubric. For example, the indicator for the capstone level of performance in "context of and purpose of writing" reads: "Demonstrates a thorough understanding of context, audience, and purpose that is responsive to the assigned task(s) and focuses all elements of the work." The design of the VALUE project assumes that this descriptor ought to be equally applicable to assessing an eportfolio and assessing a single essay. Yet attempting to apply this indicator to a whole portfolio raises a number of questions for the evaluator. Should one take into account the audience and purpose of the eportfolio itself, the audiences and purposes of each individual piece of writing included in the portfolio, or both? How should one take into account variations in levels of sophistication in handling of purpose across the multiple products of writing included in the portfolio? Should one compute a mental average of the level of each piece of writing considered individually, or look for patterns of changing performance over time? Does it matter whether the author of the portfolio identifies and explains the variations in the reflective components of the eportfolio? Is it important for a range of contexts for and purposes of writing to be represented by the products of writing included in the portfolio, or can written communication be accurately measured looking only at a single context or a very limited set of purposes?

These questions point to several of the dimensions of writing made visible in an eportfolio but deemphasized by the rubric. Many advocates of the use of portfolios to assess writing suggest that one of a portfolio's key contributions is the ability to capture development in writing ability over time (Hamp-Lyons & Condon, 2000; Yancey & Weiser, 1997). This characteristic of portfolios was key to the University of Georgia study, which examined multiple drafts of an essay composed at different points in a semester (Desmet et al., 2009). Understanding growth over time is important because it makes visible the dynamics of change in students' writing performance and suggests a trajectory that may predict the pace and direction of the continued development. The VALUE rubrics, in contrast, are designed to capture a student's level of competence at a particular point in time. Colleges and universities can use the rubrics to look at their impact on student learning by applying them at multiple points over the course of a student's education. However, the process of writing and coming to learn to write is not considered an integral component of his or her writing ability, as it is in some portfolio assessments.

While eportfolios are indeed commonly used for capturing a snapshot of a student's level of competence at a particular time, one of the arguments for their validity in doing so is that they can include a diversity of evidence—the products of a range of writing performances. Eportfolios can contain writing drawn from an assortment of contexts, addressing a range of purposes, making use of a variety of genres and media. The VALUE Written Communication rubric is designed to help evaluators determine the degree to which student writers are able to "respond to the needs" of audiences. Accurately assessing an understanding of audience arguably requires examination of texts targeted to different audiences in multiple contexts. The VALUE rubric, in contrast, suggests that such a determination can be made by examining a single performance in relationship to a single audience and purpose. In this case, the simpler version of authentic assessment in which the authors of the rubric imagine it being used would be insufficient to accomplish the rubric's stated purpose.

Other parts of the rubric suggest other important aspects of writing that eportfolios can make visible but the rubric overlooks. While attention to development over time and consideration of a diversity of evidence are common themes in the portfolio assessment literature, the inclusion of reflection on evidence is central to the very definition of an eportfolio. Almost without exception, scholars agree that the process of reflection that goes into composing an eportfolio is central to its impact on learning. In framing reflection as an optional gloss, the Written Communication rubric implies that students' understanding and assessment of the product of their own writing are not integral components of their writing ability. However, research on self-assessment and metacognition suggests that the ability to evaluate the quality of one's own writing, one's self-efficacy as a writer, and one's beliefs about and goals for writing are important to predicting how well one will be able to negotiate the demands of future writing challenges (Ross, 2006; Yancey, 1998). The ideal of authenticity, which Chapter One showed to underlie both highly standardized and highly personalized portfolio assessments, also points to the importance of the beliefs and interpretations of the portfolio author to understanding his or her abilities.

The VALUE Written Communication rubric performance descriptors would need significant revision to account for the substantively more complex way of defining what counts as writing ability implicit in the design of a genuine eportfolio. The indicator for the capstone level of performance for the criterion "context or and purpose for writing" would need to be revised to something along these lines:

> The portfolio has a sophisticated and nuanced definition of purpose that is used to focus all elements. The portfolio is responsive to the assigned task and demonstrates initiative in defining task and audience. The portfolio makes clear how samples of writing within the portfolio each demonstrate their own definition of purpose and are responsive to their defined task, and the portfolio explains differences in the level of sophistication of purpose and initiative across the collection of writings, demonstrating growth over time and/or the ability to respond to a variety of rhetorical situations.

Both the purpose and contexts of the portfolio as a whole, the purpose and contexts of each piece of writing within it, and the relationships between them need to be taken into consideration in order to fully assess this dimension of writing in a way that acknowledges the importance of expert writers' ability to respond to multiple contexts over time.

Another aspect of writing brought into focus by the eportfolio genre but neglected by the draft Written Communication rubric is medium. The criterion of "control of syntax and mechanics," for example, is explicitly limited to "graceful language" in the corresponding performance descriptors. (Earlier drafts of the rubric used the even more explicitly print-oriented *prose* in place of this phrase.) As the research on eportfolios composed to help develop and articulate professional development discussed earlier in this chapter shows, effective use of the digital, networked medium is important to composing an effective eportfolio. If a portfolio is to be assessed as a composition, not just as a container for compositions, then how effectively the portfolio author makes use of the affordances and works around the constraints of this medium must be taken into account. While effective use of medium is central to the genre of eportfolios, it is certainly not specific to it. Scholarship in rhetoric and composition and information science over the past three decades, particularly looking at the intersections of computers and writing, has shown that written communication extends beyond disembodied prose. Visual design, multimedia elements, hyperlinking, interactivity, and interface design are all integral to composing effective digital texts (Handa, 2004; Levy, 2001; Reid, 2008). Print texts also have visual elements and physical dimensions. The meaning and reception of print documents are shaped by choices about typography, layout, illustration, and format. In contrast to the emphasis on prose in the Written Communication mechanics criterion, Jenny Edbaur Rice (2008) has argued for an expanded conception of mechanics, which addresses the visual and technical skills used in composing documents across multiple media. Given that the evidence in a portfolio is likely to include a diversity of media and modalities, consideration of the whole, the parts, and how they are related is also needed when considering medium. A strong portfolio demonstrating writing ability would effectively use the digital medium to interpret examples of writing for multiple media.

In addition to combining and being distributed across multiple media, writing is performed within and across multiple disciplines. The varied contexts and purposes for writing that an author needs to negotiate across time and in multiple roles are rarely confined to a single discipline or community of practice. Strong writers are able to adapt their writing to the demands of the range of discourse communities they are likely to encounter. The ability to transfer writing competence across disciplinary boundaries is an important mark of an expert writer (Beaufort, 2007; Thaiss & Zawacki, 2006). Outside the classroom and in interdisciplinary courses and programs, even a single context of composing is likely to require considering the conventions of multiple disciplines. The Written Communication rubric, in contrast, treats discipline as explicitly singular. For example, the performance descriptor for capstone use of "genre and disciplinary conventions" specifies that students should use and understand "a wide range of conventions particular to *a* specific discipline" (italics added).

One of the strengths of the eportfolio genre is its ability to include and reframe writing originally written for disparate audiences and to chart the relationships between them, articulating the author's identity as a writer across the varied contexts. This process of synthesis is key to the ideal of integrity that Chapter Two argues should be central to eportfolio practice. The problems adults face in multiple contexts—professional, personal, and academic—are increasingly beyond the scope of a single discipline to address. A symphonic representation of self that demonstrates integrity of principles across contexts and between discourse communities is a powerful response to this complexity, and the composition of such representations is a crucial writing skill for lifelong learning and personal development. Programs and institutions that assess eportfolios that address this lived curriculum signal that this type of writing is essential, not just one option among many.

Taking into account the importance of a command of multiple media and disciplines, the accomplished level genre and disciplinary conventions performance descriptor for a genuine eportfolio assessment of writing might read something like this:

> The portfolio effectively employs the conventions of the genre and the affordances of the digital, networked medium. Individual artifacts blend genre conventions and the conventions of the appropriate disciplines or communities of practice in sophisticated ways to structure the writing and situate it within the appropriate discourse communities. The portfolio effectively explains differences in genre, discourse community, and the level of effectiveness in using the conventions of both across the multiple samples of writing, demonstrating growth over time and/or the ability to respond to a variety of rhetorical situations.

As with the professional outcomes discussed earlier, using eportfolios to assess skills such as writing, as part of a general education program or an aspect of expert practices in a variety of fields, does not simply mean assessing the same thing in a different way. Rather, it means embracing an expanded notion of what is important to assess. It suggests that we need to reframe the outcomes of higher education to take into account the dimensions of learning, identity, and performance that eportfolios distinctively, if not uniquely, can make visible. It means, as well, doing so in a way that allows quantitative assessment data to remain clearly linked to the rich representations of the social context and individual identity offered by the eportfolio genre.

These differences make the goal of producing data about student learning outcomes that can be compared across institutions more challenging. The multiple assessment methodologies from which colleges and universities have to choose are not simply neutral means toward an independent end. Rather, they embody specific beliefs and judgments about what dimensions of learning are valuable and measurable. For example, it would be possible to generate a number between one and ten that represented a student's level of competence in critical thinking with three different assessment methods: using the Collegiate Learning Assessment, an analysis of samples of work pulled from a course management system evaluated with the VALUE rubrics, or an assessment process in which students compose eportfolios in which they articulate authenticity and integrity through reflecting on evidence using the digital medium. Each of these numbers, however, would reflect a distinct conception of what counts as and in critical thinking. In order to compare these numbers across assessment methodologies, we would need to find ways to map similarities and differences between these conceptions of critical thinking and connect those descriptions back to the evidence that informs the judgment of those doing the assessing. Chapter Eight explores some of the ways that Semantic Web technologies might be employed to represent these differences and connections. Semantic Web technology allows information to be encoded in ways that computers can analyze without the authors needing to have previously agreed on common terminology or definitions. At the same time, it allows authors to precisely define the relationship between the concepts and categories they use and those defined by others. In some cases, even within a single institution and using the same methodology, the definition of some key learning outcomes may be necessarily contested. The next chapter suggests that such outcomes are a good match for eportfolios.

Questions for Practice

The account of assessment in this chapter suggests several questions for practitioners assessing eportfolios in higher education:

- What dimensions of the learning outcomes that your institution values are made visible by the assessment methodologies you use? What else that you believe is important to lifelong learning is left invisible, and in what ways might eportfolios help surface these broader aspects of learning, performance, and identity?
- How might drilling down from quantitative assessment data into authentic evidence and examining how it is linked up through reflective interpretation in students' eportfolios help you understand the causes of and meaning of patterns in the data, suggesting directions for improvement and innovation?
- How can the digital medium be used to help students represent their learning through the design of the eportfolio interface and the ways in which the components of the portfolio are linked together? What aspects of the outcomes you wish to assess might such representations reveal?
- What does comparability mean in your context, and why is it important? Are there forms of comparability other than simple numerical ranking that might serve your purposes? Is comparability more or less important than yielding context-dependent insights that can point toward directions for reform?

CHAPTER FIVE

ASSESSING INEFFABLE AND MATERIALLY CONNECTED LEARNING

Open Concepts and Open Texts

Chapter Four considered the use of eportfolios for assessing learning outcomes that have typically been the focus of assessment efforts, such as knowledge and skills specific to a profession or cognitive outcomes of general education programs, arguing that using eportfolios should mean thinking more broadly about what we value when we examine such outcomes. In addition, institutions increasingly are exploring the potential of eportfolios to aid in the assessment of outcomes of higher education previously considered ineffable. The Association of American Colleges and Universities' (AAC&U) Valid Assessment of Learning in Undergraduate Education (VALUE) project, introduced in the previous chapter, illustrates this shift. The Liberal Education and America's Promise (LEAP) outcomes, which VALUE seeks to measure, include conventional general education outcomes, such as written communication and quantitative literacy. LEAP moves into less familiar territory, however, with outcomes such as civic knowledge and engagement and ethical reasoning and action (Association of American Colleges and Universities, 2007). The importance of cultivating personal and social responsibility and encouraging integrative learning has been widely acknowledged for some time. It is an explicit focus of programs at many universities, yet the outcomes of these efforts are rarely assessed systematically, if at all. Because these outcomes are central to lifelong learning, their importance extends well beyond higher education, and how they are assessed within academia can speak to the larger challenge of recognizing and cultivating these capabilities throughout life.

Eportfolios show promise as a means to account for these broader outcomes. For example, at Portland State University, a VALUE leadership campus, the university studies program has used eportfolios for a number of years to document and evaluate students' civic engagement, and the University of Michigan, another VALUE institution, has begun to use them for this purpose in selected programs. Six campuses in the American Council on Education's Assessing International Learning Outcomes project have used eportfolios to examine their program's impact on intercultural competence (American Council on Education, 2006). Eportfolios played a central role in the work of several of the campuses involved in the Carnegie Foundation for the Advancement of Learning–AAC&U integrative learning project (DeZure, Babb, & Waldmann, 2005). This chapter examines the role eportfolios can and should play in creating the broader picture of student learning that these initiatives seek to support.

Eportfolios can be particularly powerful if the assessment processes in which they are used treat such broader outcomes, conventionally thought of as ineffable, instead as essentially contested, embracing the value of multiple, reasoned perspectives that Part One showed authentic and integral eportfolios can effectively embody. Capitalizing on these representations requires assessment to take into account the distinctive capacities of the eportfolio genre, as demonstrated in the previous chapter. The principles of deliberation introduced in Chapter Three provide the tools to put individuals' perspectives into programmatic and institutional dialogue. In practice, assessing ineffable outcomes as essentially contested concepts raises new challenges. The conventional understanding of what counts as evidence and how it can be used must be broadened to account for how students represent their learning and identities. When such representation and deliberation about it are enacted through digital, networked environments, the boundaries between individual and social representation and between text and context must also be reexamined.

Assessing the Ineffable

Much of the focus of institutional assessment has been on core skills cultivated by general education programs, such as written communication and critical thinking, and on specialized knowledge and skills taught by professional programs and specified in accreditation standards (Maki, 2003). However, many educators believe that colleges and universities have a responsibility to support their students' learning and development more broadly, considering not only cognitive capabilities but also affective and relational aspects of identity and performance. Arthur Chickering and Marcia Mentkowski (2005) suggest that these include empathy, ethics, integrity, service, and values. Such components of personal and intellectual development are often considered "ineffable" because they are "not easily defined and operationalized." However, they are also aspects of learning and development that are foundational for lifelong learning, for which higher education ought to prepare students. The idea of measuring such outcomes through a standardized test is difficult to imagine. While instruments such as the College Students' Beliefs and Values survey are useful in tracking student attitudes and beliefs as they relate to these outcomes, they lack the ability to account for individual experience, which is highly dependent on context, and offer little information to help institutions determine what impact they are making along these dimensions and why. The challenge of assessing the ineffable is to find the right level of human detail to understand the dynamics of learning and development as it is influenced by individual identity and social context.

The range of learning outcomes in higher education falls along a continuum. At one end is explicit, specific, technical knowledge, such as corporate tax statutes, statistical analysis techniques, and methods for administering medication. Nearer to the center is competence in generally applicable and primarily cognitive skills, such as the abilities to think critically and communicate orally. At the other end are outcomes that many, if not most, institutions see as valuable and an intentional focus of their work but that are more complex and context dependent. These outcomes are often considered ineffable and, consequently, outside the reach of academic assessment, not only because they are technically difficult to define and operationalize but also because the process of trying to define them runs up against not insignificant differences in political outlook, social context, and individual identity. The illusion of technocratic neutrality that has been the goal of many standardized assessment programs is particularly difficult to achieve with these outcomes.

Most would agree, for example, that producing students who are ready to be leaders in their communities and in the rest of the world is a desirable, if not essential, outcome of an undergraduate education. However, what different parties mean by *leadership* and what they believe counts as *genuine evidence of leadership capacity* varies widely. What ought to count as leadership likely depends on such factors as the interpersonal demands of the social context of the leadership activity and the understanding of what kinds of collective action in pursuit of which goals are desirable. Any assessment of leadership that attempts to impose rigidly defined standards of excellence is unlikely to be accepted across a single institution, let alone at the cross-institutional level that is the focus of recent calls for higher education accountability in the United States (U.S. Department of Education, 2006). At the same time, excluding leadership from the purview of assessment risks devaluing an important dimension of the work of higher education. The same argument can be made about such similarly important abilities as effective citizenship or social responsibility. Indeed, considered from the perspective of supporting lifelong learning, helping students develop their abilities in these areas may be higher education's most important contribution.

As suggested in Part One and Chapter Three, operationalized definitions of any competency, regardless of its place on the continuum, mask such debates about what an institution, discipline, or profession values. Chapter Four showed how using eportfolios to their fullest capacity suggests a broader conception of both the more traditional professional and general education competencies. However, in practice, assessment efforts often neglect to take such complexity into account because of the challenges of managing the process and engaging faculty and students. The VALUE project wisely chose initially to focus on simpler forms of authentic assessment because getting them to take hold on a large scale proves a formidable challenge.

One cause of this challenge is that other means of assessment that are sufficient to fulfill external demands for accountability are available for many of the more conventional learning outcomes. Because judgment about needed specialized knowledge is generally considered the sole domain of experts in a field, and because there is often a reasonable degree of consensus within a field about the key knowledge and skills members should possess, many in the academy see such opacity for this kind of outcome as acceptable. For cognitive, general education outcomes, however, there is often a more spirited debate about their boundaries and the factors that define excellence. For example, some might see information literacy as limited to skills of locating and evaluating print and electronic resources; others might argue that an understanding of how information works in organizations and how genres change in relationship to such organizational environments is necessary for students to be truly fluent in the use of information (Cambridge, 2006b). However, as with the specialized disciplinary and professional outcomes, there is a reasonable degree of agreement about what constitutes basic competence, and there are simple, standardized measures that do a reasonably good job of tracking such competence, such as the Educational Testing Service's iSkills ICT assessment. Although it is certainly not an authentic assessment, it does go beyond multiple choice to ask students to engage in extended, higher-order tasks that simulate authentic challenges of finding, evaluating, and communicating information (Somerville, Smith, & Macklin, 2008).

Advocates of the use of eportfolios in assessment may be wise to focus their work on ineffable outcomes, for which there are no easier, even if less complete, alternative means of assessment. If it proves possible to operationalize a process of assessing these outcomes using eportfolios, it would present an opening for their use at a broader range of colleges and universities. Should they prove successful and sustainable for this purpose, these institutions might then be more open to expanding their use to assess the more conventional outcomes as well. If institutions want to assess ineffable outcomes in even a nominal way, eportfolios may well be the only viable alternative.

One objective of the VALUE project is to provide such a means for operationalizing the assessment process. The faculty and assessment experts participating in the project have developed rubrics for the outcomes related to personal and social responsibility and integrative learning that are being piloted at VALUE leadership campuses and have gone through several rounds of revision. These "metarubrics" are derived from rubrics developed at individual campuses, often through extensive processes richly informed by theoretical accounts of teaching and learning, such as the development of an assessment of ethics using the Diagnostic Digital Portfolio at Alverno College (Chickering & Mentkowski, 2005). Although AAC&U has not released formal results comparing the effectiveness of use of the VALUE rubrics with that of the leadership campuses' existing portfolio assessment processes, narrative accounts of the experience of using the rubrics are promising (Burnett & Williams, 2009; Cambridge, Kirkpatrick, Peet, & Rickards, 2009).

VALUE intends for the rubrics to be used in simple forms of authentic assessment examining single samples of student work abstracted from portfolios, as well as in assessment that considers eportfolios as integral compositions. However, in contrast to the rubrics for conventional outcomes such as written communication examined in Chapter Four, the rubrics for the LEAP outcomes that might otherwise be considered ineffable seem to require the kinds of evidence of learning offered by a genuine eportfolio in order to allow legitimate judgments. The previous chapter argued that some of the rubrics for the conventional outcomes failed to take into account the need to consider evidence from diverse contexts, collected over time, and to interpret that evidence in light of students' own reflection on it. The other class of rubrics seems to demand both diverse evidence and reflection impossible to derive from isolated samples of student work. For example, in the Civic Engagement Rubric, the capstone-level performance descriptor for the "diversity of communities and cultures" criterion reads, "Demonstrates evidence of adjustment in own attitudes and beliefs because of working within and learning from diversity of communities and cultures. Promotes others' engagement with diversity." Reflection would seem essential as evidence of "adjustment in own attitude and beliefs." With regard to attitudes and belief, students are "privileged informants on their own learning" (Yancey, 1998). A legitimate representation of these aspects of students' identities surely requires the authenticity—in the full sense of the cultural ideal rather than in the narrow sense of authentic assessment—that the eportfolio genre offers. Determining how attitudes and beliefs have changed in response to "a diversity of communities and cultures" seems similarly to require evidence of learning drawn from multiple activities in multiple contexts over time and certainly would be aided by students' reflection on how this evidence represents their integrity across contexts. Other sections of the rubric are even more explicit about the centrality of elements of the eportfolio genre. Asking evaluators to judge whether a student articulates "reflective insights or analysis about the aims and accomplishments of one's actions" or "a clarified sense of civic identity and continued commitment to public action" obviously requires reflection, and being able to judge the extent to which students negotiate "complex or multiple civic engagement activities" seems to require diverse and multidimensional sources of evidence.

Ineffable Outcomes as Essentially Contested Concepts

Some distinctive characteristics of eportfolios, such as reflection on evidence drawn from multiple contexts over time to achieve authenticity and integrity, seem necessary for an assessment process to yield valid results concerning ineffable outcomes. The VALUE project may be a first step toward creating standards that may produce results comparable on a national scale. However, for these results to truly be comparable, institutions, programs, and individuals who make use of them must agree on definitions of good civic engagement, intercultural competence, or integrative learning. Behind the effort to create nationally validated metarubrics is the assumption that settling on a common conception of what is valued in each of these areas, at the level of detail necessary to use such an assessment instrument, is both possible and desirable.

This assumption, however, is questionable for many outcomes and is particularly suspect for ineffable ones. As the example of leadership illustrates, many core concepts that make up these outcomes are highly contested. While there is general agreement that these outcomes are valuable on the whole, which elements, how defined, and in what combination are subject to intense debate. Earlier drafts of the civic engagement rubric, for example, included multiple references to students influencing "the public good." What counts as "the public good" for a conservative Christian college in the South is likely to look very different from that at a public, urban comprehensive university in the Northwest, and even within these institutions, faculty espousing different disciplinary epistemologies and political commitments are likely to hold similarly diverse understandings of the concept, as are students. Indeed, as the discussion of deliberative democracy theory in Chapter Three makes clear, some are likely to question both the existence and desirability of a single "common good." Given these differences, at what level is agreement needed to produce usable assessment data? And to what extent might the achievement of agreement on the meeting of the outcome actually impede its development?

One way to address these questions is to consider whether many ineffable learning outcomes can be considered what Bryce Gallie (1956) terms "essentially contested concepts." While this phrase is sometimes used loosely in legal studies and other social science fields to refer to concepts whose definitions are particularly hotly debated (Waldron, 2002), Gallie's original definition suggests something stronger: that such concepts are contested is essential to their nature; the fact that they are contested contributes to, rather than impedes, their development. For essentially contested concepts, there is a general agreement about the value of a notion but disagreement about its proper instantiation. For example, most educators can agree on a fairly vague definition of "leadership ability" and would affirm that it is an important learning outcome, but they would differ about the specific components and practices that make it up. Such a concept differs from one where agreement about how properly and precisely to define it simply has not yet been achieved because "its vagueness reflects its actual inchoate condition of growth" (Gallie, 1956, p. 184). Essentially contested concepts have sustained value and foster innovation and excellence in part as a result of, rather than in spite of, the lack of a general principle for judgment that can be applied in all contexts.

Gallie argues that essentially contested concepts share seven characteristics, several of which are a bit difficult to understand in the abstract but will become clearer shortly when applied to specific concepts. First, the concept is appraisive; its use constitutes a value judgment. Second, it is internally complex, but the value judgment is made holistically. Third, it is variously describable: an explanation of the worth of the whole is made based on the contributions of the various parts, and those parts can be assigned varied weights. Fourth, the concept is significantly modifiable as circumstances change. Concepts that have these four characteristics can be considered "open."

For an open concept to be essentially contested, it also needs to meet three other tests. First, the concept must be used both aggressively and defensively; the parties making arguments for their own understanding of the concept address those who argue for alternative understandings, taking into account the criteria those others use. Second, the concept needs to be derived from an "original exemplar" whose authority is acknowledged by all users. Finally, and crucially, the process of continuous contestation may lead or is likely to lead to more optimum development of the concept building on the exemplar.

While it is not possible here to examine the full range of ineffable outcomes of higher education in need of assessment or even those specifically targeted in the VALUE project, working through one example in detail will illustrate why members of the larger class of ineffables might be profitably considered essentially contested concepts. Leadership, one such concept, has each of the characteristics Gallie specifies. Leadership is appraisive, being clearly valued by most people and institutions. Referring to someone as a good leader clearly makes a value judgment. It is also internally complex. When one refers to a "great leader" or an "effective leader," one is usually making a holistic judgment. However, being a leader means having or enacting a complex set of understandings, skills, actions, beliefs, and character traits. Different assessors of the quality of a leader may define what should be included within this set differently and may rank the importance of the different components in contrasting ways. Therefore, leadership is also variously describable. Because different kinds of leaders are needed in different social and historical circumstances and many of the leaders most people admire demonstrate the ability to adapt their strategies to changing circumstances, leadership is clearly significantly modifiable. It is therefore an open concept.

Beyond being open, leadership shares the other characteristics of an essentially contested concept. Theories of leadership abound in both scholarly and popular literature, and individuals in democratic societies develop their own understanding of what makes for effective leadership through their participation in or observation of the electoral process. In both scholarly and everyday arguments, individuals defend their own judgments about leadership and critique those of others with the knowledge that multiple perspectives exist, using the concept of leadership both defensively and aggressively. These debates generally build on a tradition of great leadership throughout history, the models of leaders who have moved their societies in a positive direction, and this tradition serves as a type of exemplar. While there are always disagreements about specifically whom and what this tradition includes, the appeals to a leadership tradition from those with multiple perspectives on leadership suggest that some belief in its existence is held in common. The practice of leadership may also have developed, and may continue to develop, more optimally because of its contested nature.

That this last characteristic holds for leadership is more difficult to prove—if proof is even possible. However, it does seem likely that development of leaders guided by diverse understandings of what counts as good leadership is likely to lead to the cultivation of a wider range of virtues, increasing the likelihood that there may be individuals in a given context with the distinctive leadership capacities to deal with the novel circumstances of any given set of circumstances. It may also be the case, as Gallie (1956) argues generally, that treating the concept of leadership as contested may lead to more thoughtful and thorough rationales for each individual's understanding and assessment of leadership:

> Recognition of a given concept as essentially contested implies recognition of rival uses of it (such as oneself repudiates) as not only logically possible and humanly "likely," but as of permanent potential critical value to one's own use or interpretation of the concept in question. . . . One very desirable consequence of the required recognition is any proper instance of essential contestedness might therefore be expected to be a marked raising of the level of quality of arguments in the disputes of the contestant parties. (p. 193)

The need to understand opposing conceptions of leadership in order to attempt to demonstrate the superiority of one's own position is likely to lead one to articulate an account of one's understanding of leadership that is clearer, more complex, and better supported by evidence. This is likely, however, only if the multiple perspectives are put into dialogue governed by the principles of democratic deliberation outlined in Chapter Three—principles implied by Gallie in his emphasis on reasoned argument and appeals to a common tradition.

This line of reasoning suggests that the criterion for judging arguments about essentially contested concepts should be the degree to which an individual's position is justifiable in light of the social context and that individual's identity and biography. Even in the absence of standards on which all parties can agree that could be used to decide what constitutes the "best use" of the concept, one can still judge the quality of each individual's use of it, determining whether such use is rationally justified in light of the circumstances. Indeed, some version of this ability to make contextualized judgments, recognizing the reasonableness of multiple perspectives without conceding that everyone's position is just as good as everyone else's, is characteristic of the highest levels of a range of scales of intellectual and moral development that are often used in higher education (Baxter Magdola, 2001; Belenky, Clinchy, Goldberger, & Tarule, 1988; King & Kitchener, 1994; Mentkowski & Associates, 1999; Perry, 1998). This kind of judgment, in other words, is not only possible but is what higher education aspires to teach.

In assessing leadership development, then, educators may be wise to focus on determining the degree to which students can make justifiable arguments for their own understanding of leadership and justifiable self-assessments of their performance in terms of this understanding. To be justifiable, such arguments must acknowledge the criteria informing other perspectives and situate the student's own position in relationship to them, appealing to a shared history of practice and using a sufficiently common language to allow mutual intelligibility.

Treating ineffable outcomes as essentially contested concepts resonates strongly with the cultural ideals for individual and institutional lifelong learning discussed in Part One. The demonstration of understanding and analysis of one's own performance called for by this way of thinking about the assessment process can be powerfully cultivated through the articulation of authenticity and integrity. An authentic and integral self-representation articulates its author's identity with depth and rigor, taking into account his or her values, commitments, and experience across contexts and over time, while also connecting this account to shared horizons of significance offered by the institutions in which he or she plays a part and by the larger culture and society. Students achieving authenticity and integrity provide powerful data for assessment.

The principles of deliberative democracy introduced in Chapter Three are particularly well suited to animating and guiding the process of connecting individual articulations of authenticity and integrity to institutional decision making. Deliberation is not a process of applying a predetermined, immutable standard but of ensuring that the perspectives of all those affected by a collective decision are taken into account in the process of coming to it. A deliberative process of improving leadership education at a college or university, for example, would need to take into account the multiple meanings of and objectives for leadership as represented throughout the campus community, and in the larger community it serves, and to try to shape the university's programs and infrastructure in a manner that serves them collectively. Some shared understanding of the broad contours of what constitutes leadership is necessary to make it possible to put the multiple perspectives in conversation with each other. At the same time, there needs to be a means for capturing the complexity and diversity of individual and group experiences that makes visible and intelligible their full range. Having this richer and more comprehensive picture provides participants in the collective decision-making process with a systematic, empirical basis for making judgments without presenting a single indicator as the sole, naturalized test of quality.

In fact, faculty on a number of the Leadership Campuses of the VALUE program are finding that the insights into student learning and the multiple perspectives on what about that learning faculty value generated through deliberation during the process of rating students' eportfolios using the metarubrics is at least as valuable as, and probably even more valuable than, the quantitative data the rating process yields (Cambridge, Kirkpatrick, et al., 2009). Much like the New Century College competencies discussed in Chapter Three, the rubrics are valuable not so much for offering a neutral standard that can be objectively applied as for providing a shared language that enables faculty to identify commonalities and explore conflicts between their diverse perspectives on student learning and between their perspectives and those articulated in the portfolios themselves.

Eportfolios and Evidence

Putting the ideals of authenticity and deliberation into action, eportfolios offer one means of generating a comprehensive account of students' experience of ineffable outcomes, having the promise to capture the complexity and context of students' learning in ways that more conventional kinds of assessment cannot. Even when they are used in the process of generating numerical ratings of abilities, eportfolios expand what counts as meaningful assessment data beyond strictly quantitative measures to include the artifacts of authentic learning activities and students' reflective interpretation and synthesis of that body of work. Because eportfolios are complex compositions that articulate the relationships between their parts and connect them to representations of the work of other individuals and institutions, they make visible the multiple contexts in which learning occurs and can accommodate more complex and individualized understandings of excellence. Taking into account differences in context and allowing eportfolios to bridge them requires a broadened understanding of what counts as evidence of learning, and the eportfolio genre supports the integration of such diverse types of evidence.

At its root, an eportfolio is fundamentally a selection of evidence and reflection on that evidence (Cambridge et al., 2009). The evidence is intentionally selected to work together, and the reflective components supply the logic behind the choices of what to include and connect what is included to the larger process and contexts of learning and to the student's background, experiences, and aspirations. Portfolios offer an ability to learn about student learning through the matches and mismatches among the different components and between the whole and its parts. Rather than judging the evidence within an eportfolio solely in relationship to a single, externally defined standard, focusing on matches and mismatches allows assessors to determine the justifiability of an individual student's understanding of the outcome being assessed and of his or her self-assessment of his or her performance in relationship to it. This approach is consistent with treating ineffable outcomes as essentially contested concepts.

As the previous chapter made clear, examining the relationships of portfolio elements offers a more complex understanding of students' competencies than looking at the elements in isolation. A clear alignment of purpose and meaning across the elements provides a stronger confirmation of intellectual and personal growth than an evaluation of the elements alone. Similarly, a lack of alignment can point to areas needing attention that might have been missed without taking the relationships into account. Matches and mismatches can be examined between different characteristics of the elements. Do they, for example, display a consistent degree of rigor in their moral reasoning, or does each suggest a strong commitment to a particular understanding of social justice? Perhaps more powerful, however, matches and mismatches can be identified and interpreted between the content of the evidence and the reflective elements that frame it. For example, do the intentions of the author as expressed in reflections match the results of a service-learning project as reflected in a report produced for a community partner, or does the conception of social justice in his or her reflections match those he or she is seen enacting in observations of his or her political activism included in the eportfolio? Matches and mismatches can also be examined between specific instances of evidence use and the global structure and objectives of the eportfolio. For example, is a persuasive skill that a student argues he or she has and uses in a video of a speech consistent with the overall philosophy of democratic participation articulated by the portfolio as a whole? Answering these questions can help assessors judge the justifiability of students' conceptions of ineffable outcomes and their self-assessments that apply those conceptions.

In order to engage in such an analysis, a broader understanding of evidence use in eportfolios is needed. Most scholarship on eportfolios tends to treat the use of evidence as a fairly simple matter. A portfolio author includes something he or she has produced through an academic activity in order to prove that he or she has a particular kind of knowledge or skill. Recent research at George Mason University, however, suggests that when the use of eportfolios moves beyond conventional academic outcomes to consider the whole of a student's learning, as is necessary for tracking ineffable outcomes, the dynamics of evidence use gets more complicated (Cambridge et al., 2009). The kinds of evidence included, the purposes for including them, and the activities that generate them all become more diverse.

A George Mason research project, conducted through the Inter/National Coalition for Electronic Portfolio Research (I/NCEPR), began as an investigation of how students in a semester-long cocurricular program linked together their curricular and cocurricular experiences to represent their leadership identities. Faculty from an integrative studies program, student affairs educators, and paid student mentors collaboratively led the project. The team guided the student participants through a process of reflecting on and gathering evidence of their learning, making connections between that evidence and ideas about leadership, and composing an eportfolio that synthesized that evidence and reflection for an audience of their choice.

Consistent with the treatment of leadership as an essentially contested concept, students were not asked to analyze their leadership identity and performance in relationship to a single standard defined by the institution. Rather, they were invited to articulate their own understandings of leadership, assess their own activities in terms of those understandings, and connect them to the context of the university using the shared categories of identity, relationships, and community. The team and participants met for three one-day workshops over the course of the semester and interacted online throughout the term through the Open Source Portfolio, a set of tools within the Sakai Collaborative Learning Environment. The team analyzed the content of a selection of the eportfolios the participants produced using the grounded theory methodology (Strauss & Corbin, 1990). Use of evidence emerged as a central theme.

Students were encouraged to include evidence drawn from both curricular and cocurricular contexts. The team expected that the use of academic evidence would follow the typical pattern: something the student had created in a class would be used to demonstrate that he or she had some skill that he or she saw as related to leadership. For example, they imagined that a student might suggest that being a strong leader means being able to understand other people's value systems and would include an essay from a comparative religion course that showed he or she had achieved such understanding. In fact, academic evidence proved to play a more varied and complex role. Although there were some instances of curricular evidence being used this way, it was much more common for such evidence to be used to show that a student embodied a character trait he or she associated with leadership. For example, one student included a final group project that was the result of a long, arduous, and conflict-filled research and writing process. It was not to demonstrate her writing skill or even her ability to marshal the resources of a group, however, but to show that she was steadfast in her commitment to succeed and be resilient in the face of obstacles. Rather than as a means to gain skills, academics was often represented as a test of self. For many of the portfolio authors, successfully negotiating this test showed that they had the strength of character necessary for leadership.

This pattern, one of several that the team identified through its analysis, suggested the need for a more sophisticated way to describe evidence use in eportfolios. In order to be able to judge the quality of students' self-representations, faculty and student affairs educators needed a shared language to talk about the variations in use of evidence. With such a language, it would become possible to determine the justifiability of students' understandings and self-assessments of leadership by looking for matches and mismatches in evidence use.

While a few previous studies had examined evidence in eportfolios explicitly, they did not address all of the dimensions of evidence use that the first-round research suggested were significant. Research at Alverno College on the development of student reflective ability examined the evidence to which students appeal in their reflections (Rickards et al., 2008; Rickards & Guilbault, 2009). Students who were more skilled at reflection appealed to a wider range of experiences than did those just beginning to learn to reflect well and relied more on their own assessments of that evidence. However, this work shares the limitation of the VALUE project discussed in the previous chapter because it analyzed student reflective writing in isolation from the context of the portfolio as part of which it was composed. It provides insight into evidence on reflection but neglects to examine the actual items of evidence included in the portfolio to represent the experiences on which students reflect. In order to examine matches and mismatches to assess the justifiability of the argument made by a student's portfolio, both the content of the evidence and its reflective framing need to be taken into account. Writing about science portfolios, Collins (1992) provides a classification scheme for items of evidence themselves, suggesting that a piece of evidence can be an artifact, reproduction, attestation, or production. This classification scheme captured variation in the context in which evidence was created, but it assumed uniformity in the purpose of including evidence, and the first round of research at George Mason showed that purposes varied as well. Delandshere and Arens (2003), in contrast, examine the relationship between evidence and purpose in teacher education eportfolios, suggesting that items in the portfolio should be considered as evidence only if they are appropriate to the purpose of the portfolio and the relationship between the item and the purpose is made explicit. While the Mason team agreed with this as an account of effective use of evidence, the added complexity its research uncovered suggested that a less restrictive definition of genuine evidence was needed. Before passing judgment of how evidence was used, it should first be possible to describe the range of uses systematically.

A Typology of Evidence Use in Eportfolios

The George Mason researchers took evidence to mean the items included in an eportfolio on which its author reflects. In order to meet the need for systematic description, the second phase of the research focused on identifying the key dimensions across which students' use of evidence in their eportfolios varied. The study was broadened to examine eportfolios produced in two additional contexts: a course on leadership targeted at current and aspiring student leaders through which students compose portfolios to represent their leadership identity and capability and an integrative studies capstone course in which students compose graduation portfolios representing their full undergraduate learning experience, in relationship to both traditional and ineffable general education outcomes.

(Examples of such graduation portfolio are examined in depth in Chapters One and Three.) Both sets of eportfolios were composed using PebblePad, an eportfolio system originally developed at the University of Wolverhampton (it is discussed further in Chapter Seven). The team analyzed the content of a sample of eportfolios from each context using grounded theory and reexamined the portfolios from the cocurricular program using the emergent categories from the full set (Cambridge et al., 2009). The results chart the use of evidence in eportfolios by students ranging from their first year at the university to the master's level within three cocurricular and curricular contexts using two different technology platforms.

The research resulted in a typology of evidence used in eportfolios (Table 5.1). In the student eportfolios examined in the research, evidence use varied along three dimensions, each with two facets. Use of evidence varied in terms of the characteristics of the item used as evidence, the purpose of incorporating the evidence, and the characteristics of the learning activity or activities associated with it. The characteristics of items of evidence varied in their agency and media.

TABLE 5.1. TYPOLOGY OF THE USE OF EVIDENCE IN EPORTFOLIOS

Dimensions	Frames

Characteristics of item used as evidence	Agency
	    Self-authored
	    Collaboratively authored (portfolio author and associates)
	    Other-authored
	Media
	    Media and modality of evidence (for example, text, audio, image, streaming video, multimedia)

Purpose of incorporating evidence	Function
	    Intended (or deduced) function of the evidence (for example, demonstrates or symbolizes)
	Object
	    Evidence reflects author's knowledge, skills, character traits, beliefs, goals, or identifications

Characteristics of associated learning activity	Sponsorship: The activity is:
	    Institutionally sponsored (curricular, cocurricular, community organizations, and so on)
	    Self-sponsored
	    Unsponsored
	Participation: Evidence indicates:
	    Individual participation
	    Group activity
	    Larger community or associational activity

Source: Adapted from Cambridge et al. (2009).

Agency is determined by who created an item of evidence. Items can be self-authored, collaboratively authored, or other-authored. The facet "media" specifies the media and modality of the evidence, such as text, audio, video, or image. The purpose of including evidence consists of a function and an object. The function of an item of evidence is the action it performs or is intended to perform, such as demonstrating, illustrating, or symbolizing. The object is the thing demonstrated, illustrated, or symbolized, such as a skill, character trait, or belief. It may be helpful to think of the function and object grammatically, as the verb and object of a sentence describing the purpose of an item of evidence, for example "This document proves [function] that the portfolio author is reliable [object]." Important characteristics of the learning activities with which an item of evidence is associated are their sponsorship and level of participation. Activities can be institutionally sponsored (either curricularly or cocurricularly by an educational organization or outside the educational system by some other organization), self-sponsored, or unsponsored. An unsponsored activity is one where learning, documentation of performance, or articulation of identity is an unintentional by-product of, rather than a purpose of, engaging in the activity. Participation can be individual, through a small group, or through participation in or association with a larger community.

After the typology was developed to describe the full range of significant variations in the use of evidence identified through the grounded theory analysis of the eportfolios, it then became possible to apply it to looking for matches and mismatches between different elements of evidence. Three patterns of alignment and misalignment emerge: the first related to media, the second to purpose, and the third to level of participation.

Most eportfolios in each of the three contexts studied included images as one form of evidence. In part as a result of the limited choices offered by the software students used for the visual design of the interface of their eportfolios, most of the reflection included was textual. The relationship between the content of the images and that of the reflections proved significant. While in some cases the images and the text worked together to achieve the author's purpose, more often their meanings diverged, a mismatch that shed light on the student's understanding of leadership and self-assessment.

In L'Vontte's eportfolio, for example, an image of a padlocked rusty locker was used as evidence in reflecting on how her relationship to education was transformed when she entered the integrative studies degree program. Prior to joining the program, her experiences with education had left her worn down and neglected, like the locker door, and knowledge to which she could connect was locked away. The new perspective offered by the program provided the lock's combination. Other-authored, the image is not intended to demonstrate that she has any particular knowledge or skill. Instead, the image symbolizes (function) the relationship on which she reflects (object). This metaphorical use of evidence is effective in supporting her argument about her personal development. The visual and textual elements work synergistically. This example differs significantly from the standard way of thinking about evidence use in eportfolios in its agency, medium, and function. It is other-authored, rather than the product of the author's own activity, is visual rather than textual, and symbolizes rather than proves.

The second pattern of match and mismatch was between the purpose of including a specific piece of evidence and the purpose of the portfolio as a whole. For example, Harry included an essay profiling a professional project manager whose work he observed to demonstrate his project management skills. Although the essay described the project manager's work using terminology and concepts from the field, such as "risk management" and "deliverable life cycle," Harry did not make an explicit connection in the essay or his reflection on it between these concepts as applied by the subject of his profile and his own experiences managing projects. The evidence does not help the reader understand the degree to which Harry is prepared to apply these concepts. There is a mismatch here between the object implied by the content of evidence and the object his reflection specifies in discussing the purpose for including the essay in this section of the portfolio. While Harry claims that the evidence demonstrates his project management skills, it more accurately signals his knowledge of project management. More significant, however, is the apparent mismatch between both of these local objects and the global object of his eportfolio. The stated purpose of the portfolio as a whole is to present Harry as a leader. In the course within which he composed the portfolio, management and leadership were considered as distinct constructs, as they often are in academic research (Northouse, 2007; Rost, 1993). However, Harry included evidence, successful or not, of his management skills within a portfolio focused on leadership, conflating the two capabilities. While it is possible that Harry could justify the inclusion of skills generally associated with management within his conception of leadership, the relationship between management and leadership is left implicit. This suggests that Harry had not yet made his argument for his understanding of leadership informed by a clear understanding of other reasonable perspectives. Such awareness would likely lead him to make a stronger argument, reflecting more critically on his leadership identity. It may also suggest that the program needs to do a better job of helping him understand the importance of thinking about his whole eportfolio as an integral composition rather than as a set of discrete treatments of skills and character traits without an overarching explanation of how they relate to each other.

The final pattern of mismatches is also between the local use of evidence and the portfolio as a whole, this time in relationship to level of participation. Another example from Harry's eportfolio illustrates this pattern. In one reflective section, Harry argued that he had displayed a considerable degree of patience, which he believes is an important quality for a leader. As evidence of his patience, Harry included several photographs he took of wildlife. The photographs are sharp and well composed, likely having required significant patience to capture. However, patience here is highly individual, a product of removing oneself from the social world. In contrast, the conception of leadership his eportfolio as a whole advances is highly collaborative and communal. Does having patience in isolation necessarily translate into patience while interacting with others? It is not clear that Harry sees the need to explain this mismatch between the level of participation represented by the local use of evidence and the level of participation that is the focus of his eportfolio as a whole.

One factor behind students' tendency to concentrate on individual-level evidence even while trying to represent what they themselves frame as an activity that is highly interpersonal and situated within community may be in part a legacy of the print portfolio genre. The print genre is strongly individualized. It generally consists of the work and reflections of a single individual author, although some of that work may be collaboratively authored. While often a response to an assignment that specifies certain types of content, the material included in the portfolio is ultimately the choice of its author. In part because of the logistical challenge of duplicating and distributing print, such portfolios are generally shared with only a select audience, often a single instructor or a small group of assessors.

Such a legacy of a highly individualistic focus may also help explain students' failure to take into account alternative perspectives on leadership that have currency in the academic communities within which they compose their eportfolios. Students may not have been, in Gallie's (1956) words, using the concept of leadership aggressively and defensively, because they thought of their eportfolio as compositions that should stand apart from, rather than participate in, the communities of practice through which they were developing their leadership. These students are unlikely to have yet come to see the contested nature of leadership as a "critical resource" for articulating their own understanding of it (Gallie, 1956).

This insularity suggests that curricular and cocurricular programs need to do a better job of helping students put their self-representations into dialogue with those of their peers and with ideas and practices of leadership to which they are exposed in the larger community. Through seeing their portfolios in relationship to other representations of the concept and practice of leadership, students would be more likely to create more justified and consistent arguments for their own understanding and performance. It would help students establish the authenticity of their self-representations through making connections to shared horizons of significance. Through reading and responding to others' portfolios, articulating their own understandings of leadership with an awareness of other perspectives and with an eye toward shaping the shared understanding, students can move toward participation in the process of democratic deliberation about the outcomes of education that ought to be central to the process of assessment, especially for ineffable outcomes that hinge on essentially contested concepts.

Material Participation in Social Networks

Print portfolios tend to be closed and relatively private, in part as side effects of the physical effort required to modify, reproduce, and transport them. The digital environment does not have these limitations, and the effective assessment of ineffable outcomes as essentially contested concepts depends on dialogue between eportfolio authors and their peers and instructors that networked environments can powerfully support. The records of this dialogue also can become part of the eportfolio composition itself. Yet many digital portfolios carry with them these conventions of their ancestor genre. Programs that are successful in getting students to make connections between their self-representations in eportfolios with those of other students and educators and to interact meaningfully with each other around their similarities and differences, such as the teacher education program at the University of Wolverhampton, are increasingly doing so using technology that incorporates the formats and features of blogs and social network sites. Chapter Seven examines both the potential of these genres and tools for eportfolio practice and the need to take into account the emerging genre conventions associated with their use outside the academy in order to remain true to the characteristics of the eportfolio genre that support lifelong learning. Accounting for the social nature of learning in these environments is also a challenge for programmatic and institutional assessment, which tends to focus almost exclusively on patterns in individual student performance.

Some additional emerging characteristics of social network site (SNS) profiles, which are reflective of trends in the digital networked medium more generally, have implications for eportfolio programs that wish to capitalize on their success in connecting self-representation to social interaction. On an SNS, an individual's self-representation is necessarily intertwined with the activity and expression of others and with the functionality of the network. Unlike a self-enclosed print portfolio, an SNS profile cannot be abstracted from the technical and social context in which it was created without losing much of its meaning. Perhaps even more dramatically than for other kinds of eportfolios, the assessment of eportfolios that build on the SNS model must take into account these contexts.

In an SNS, the network of "friends" that a person's profile displays is part of the message that person is communicating about himself or herself. These personal social networks are not simply reflections of a social reality beyond the system. Rather, they are "public displays of connection" that provide evidence of one's interests and how well one is esteemed and by whom (Donath & boyd, 2004). Including prominent members of one's professional field, for example, indicates that one has developed a professional network that might help one to be effective or influential. That these people are willing to be listed as friends is also an implicit validation of the content of one's profile. Evidence that a number of well-respected people in the field have affirmed their affiliation with the author of a profile makes that person's claim of identification with and competence in the field more persuasive. Similarly, including as friends people from one's family, neighborhood, church, or volleyball league within the same profile as one's professional colleagues makes a statement about how one manages the boundaries between these social contexts. In this sense, who one's SNS friends are is relevant to understanding how the profile articulates integrity. A claim to consistency across contexts may be stronger if it is made in a forum in which people from multiple contexts have chosen to publicly participate.

The representation of friends within an SNS profile differs from, say, a list of references on a résumé because parts of how these people are represented are not under the control of the profile's author. Friends are often represented by pictures they choose and have the ability to post comments, which are often placed on the screen in a way that gives them nearly equal standing with the author's own writing. The interface of the SNS system itself also figures prominently. Its components can be considered part of the message the profile conveys. Whether one makes a commenting feature available to the general public or just one's friends, for example, says something about what kinds of social contexts the profile is intended to mediate. This other-generated content can make up a significant portion of a profile. For example, in the screenshot of my Facebook profile, 19 percent of the screen is taken up by content posted by my friends and 29 percent is composed either of interface elements or ads chosen by the system. Although I am clearly identified as both the author and subject of the profile, close to 50 percent of the profile screen is devoted to material I did not compose. Self-representation within the genre of the SNS profile is therefore a collaborative enterprise. "Impression management is an inescapably collective process" (boyd, 2007, p. 142).

In an episode from her ethnographic research on Friendster, the first SNS to gain widespread popularity, danah boyd (2007) illustrates how confusion can be caused by intersection of self- and other-authored material within a profile.

Friendster in its early days became an online home for a variety of young adult subcultures. One group active on the site was young women who were models for Suicide Girls, an amateur soft-core pornography site that was popular with middle-aged men. Not a member of this group, boyd was initially confused when she began to receive e-mail messages asking for the address of her Suicide Girls page. Her potential fans pegged her as a Suicide Girl because of two pictures that were part of her profile. One of her own pictures showed her wearing a bikini top. One of her friend's profile pictures, which was displayed on her page, was of a middle-aged man wearing a tie entitled, "old, white balding guy." (The friend intended the photo to be interpreted ironically. The friend was, in fact, much younger—and likely more hirsute—than the person in the picture.) To some readers of her profile, posting revealing photographs of oneself plus having middle-aged white guy friends equals Suicide Girl. Some aspects of her self-representation were under her own control; others were not. While other instances of interpretation that involve both self- and other-created content are not likely to be as colorful, the underlying dynamic in this example is a common one.

Alongside Facebook, MySpace is one of the two most popular SNSs. As on Facebook, profiles consist of both content composed by the author and that composed by friends; pictures and comments from friends become part of one's profile. In addition, much of even the profile owner's own self-representation is accomplished through including media, design, and interactive elements others created. MySpace offers much more control of the visual design and functionality of a page to its users than does Facebook. Through including HTML and CSS code, users can change the colors and fonts of their page, rearrange its layout, and add embedded music and video players and interactive elements like hit counters and quizzes. Rather than being written by the profile author, these elements are often included through cutting and pasting code written by others. Dan Perkle (2006) calls the skills needed to develop such pages through reusing others' code "copy-and-paste literacy," which he argues blurs the boundary between production and consumption of content. Participating in the emerging digital culture means not just creating self-representations but doing so through creative engagement with resources offered by the network.

It is significant that MySpace users create their profiles through incorporating code rather than adding media directly. In many cases, the code plays media stored elsewhere on the Internet or creates interactivity that depends on services hosted on other servers. Like friends' profile pictures, these resources can be changed after the profile has been composed without the consent of the profile's owner. In addition, it is technically difficult or impossible to disconnect the profile from these distributed resources. For both its meaning and functionality, the profile depends on its computational links, which cannot be easily replicated. Such an SNS profile is therefore "materially connected" to the network (Perkle, 2006).

The activity of composing and using an SNS profile is thus different on several levels from that of authoring a print portfolio, or even a more conventional electronic one. The traditional understanding of authorship and ownership, which has been central to eportfolio assessment, assumes that authors have full control of the content of a text and that that text can communicate its meaning even if it is abstracted from the context in which is created. Neither of these assumptions holds for SNS profiles. As eportfolios are increasingly composed in technical environments that employ many of the same features as SNS systems, the assumptions are not likely to hold for eportfolios much longer either.

Perkle (2006) suggests "participation" as an alternative to "authorship" to describe the kinds of activity on MySpace he has analyzed. *Participation* could be a useful term for eportfolio assessment as well. Just as there are limitations to what can be understood about learning and identity from looking at artifacts abstracted from their context with an eportfolio, so too may there be limits to what is made visible by eportfolios abstracted from their function within the network of tools, people, and institutions in which they play a part. While the strongest portfolios represent and explain that context in order to demonstrate authenticity and integrity, these ideals can also be enacted through participation in the network, including through participation in deliberative assessment processes. Social software-like functionality makes the mechanisms and products of this deliberation, some under the portfolio owner's control and some outside it, part of the eportfolio itself.

When used to assess ineffable outcomes, eportfolios articulate the connections between their owners' beliefs and performances and the open, essentially contested concepts that frame institutional dialogue about learning. Effectively understanding and responding to such eportfolios requires a broader perspective on what constitutes evidence and how it should be interpreted. When these eportfolios materially participate in online social networks, open concepts are expressed through open texts. Such an eportfolio will not only acknowledge and respond to alternative conceptions; others' expressions of contesting conceptions become part of the eportfolio's message. The distinctions between text and context and between content and functionality are becoming less clear, both offering an opportunity for a richer understanding of teaching and learning and posing significant challenges of technique and technology.

Questions for Practice

The analysis in this chapter of how eportfolios can be used to assess ineffable outcomes suggests a number of questions educators should ask:

- Do the learning outcomes you are assessing constitute or contain essentially contested concepts? If so, how might you shift focus from evaluating eportfolios according to a precisely defined, single standard to judging the justifiability of each individual conception of the outcome in relationship to a more open conceptual framework?
- What constitutes evidence in your context? How might you track matches and mismatches in students' use of evidence to support their claims about their understanding and performance?
- How can you help students craft public displays of connection as intentional self-representations through their eportfolios? How do you assess when they are successful?
- If you embrace participation as a meaningful means of self-representation and reflection, how does that change how you think about evidence and ownership in eportfolios?

PART THREE

EPORTFOLIOS FOR LIFELONG LEARNING

CHAPTER SIX

LIFELONG LEARNING WITH EPORTFOLIOS BEYOND HIGHER EDUCATION

Negotiating Audience and Integrity

In higher education, eportfolios are being used to support learners in articulating identities that enact authenticity and integrity, two deeply held cultural ideals. The rich representations of learning and practice that result can inform institutional decision making through deliberation, a key democratic process. Linked to the symphonic style of integrative learning, which reveals how the whole is more than the sum of the parts, the eportfolio genre is well suited to represent such identity and inform such deliberation. Students who have composed authentic and integral eportfolios and engaged in deliberative conversations supported by them leave colleges and universities better prepared for learning throughout life. And institutions that take these portfolios seriously as resources for organizational learning are better equipped to change in ways that support their students. The three ideals of authenticity, integrity, and deliberation provide a theory to inform the use of eportfolios not just for assessment in higher education but also for lifelong learning throughout society.

This chapter examines the use of eportfolios for lifelong learning beyond higher education. While much has been written about the need to support lifelong learning and the potential of eportfolios to help address that need, research on how eportfolios are being used beyond the academy is in its early stages. Numerous initiatives have been launched worldwide, but documentation is uneven, so it is often difficult to distinguish actual accomplishment from mere aspiration. Rather than trying to survey the full range of emerging practice, this chapter focuses primarily on a selection of well-documented examples that together illustrate key issues in the use of eportfolios to support lifelong learning beyond higher education. Specifically, it considers these questions:

- Is there evidence that individuals are using eportfolios for lifelong learning? If so, what aspects of eportfolios do those individuals find valuable? Research on the eFolio Minnesota project in the United States provides some preliminary answers, suggesting that eportfolios are being used for lifelong learning and that audience and integrity are key factors in predicting the impact of such use.
- How are institutions, such as professional bodies and employers, supporting the use of eportfolios for lifelong learning? What kinds of infrastructure and partnerships are needed for their support? Research on the coordination of eportfolio practices across multiple levels of education and between education and employment in the Nottingham region of England points to the challenge of both accommodating the existing needs of institutional audiences and encouraging them to transform their practices to capitalize on the potential of the eportfolio genre. The Nedcar project and its extension by the Center for Work and Income in the Netherlands provides the most mature and well-documented example of large-scale use by employers to date, showing both the efficacy of eportfolios in supporting employability as commonly defined in national educational policies and suggesting ways that the broader understanding of professional identity implicit in the eportfolio genre calls such policies into question.
- How well do these institutional practices, and the eportfolios they elicit, embody authenticity, deliberation, and integrity? How could the practices be improved through engaging the ideals? Each of the examples considered in this chapter points to the promise of existing practice for advancing the ideals and suggests that much work is left to do to fully embrace them.

Potential of Eportfolios

In recent years, leaders in U.S. higher education have pointed to the need to support learning over time and across contexts, moving beyond the boundaries not just of classes or disciplines, but also across institutions and between episodes of engagement with colleges and universities. Higher education institutions increasingly see as part of their teaching and learning mission helping learners plan, manage, and make sense of their learning over the course of their lives. Today's students take courses from multiple colleges and universities, at once and over time; learn through their professional practice and community engagement; and live in a knowledge society where they will need all of these resources to be successful. Peter Smith (2004), former president of California State University Monterey, writes that these new realities call for an "educational passport" that documents and aids in the planning of an individual's learning over time as he or she engages with multiple institutions. William Plater (2006), professor and past dean of the faculties at Indiana University Purdue University Indianapolis, sees eportfolios as the means for providing such a "self-managed, meaningful, coherent, integrated lifelong record of learning that demonstrates competence, transcends educational levels, and is portable across institutions of learning—formal and informal" (p. 62). According to these leaders, higher education should promote lifelong learning not only through cultivating skills and dispositions that aid students' self-directed learning after graduation but also through facilitating the creation and use of eportfolios that capture learning, which will have a life before, after, and in between the times when learners are enrolled in colleges and universities.

These calls parallel an increasing emphasis on the role of self-representation of learning throughout life in cultivating a learning society in the educational policies of other nations. For example, in the United Kingdom, the Dearing Report recommends that learners have the opportunity to develop an ongoing record of their learning in order to plan their personal and professional development (National Committee of Inquiry into Higher Education, 1997). The European Union (EU) makes lifelong learning a priority throughout its educational programs, particularly emphasizing expanding participation in formal learning and increasing the mobility of the workforce (Commission of the European Communities, 2000). Representations of skills and capabilities that transcend national contexts are key (Schärer, Little, & Goullier, 2004). Increasingly, funding agencies such as the Joint Information Systems Committee in the United Kingdom and the EU's Leonardo da Vinci program are looking to eportfolios as a means to support planning and recording learning and performance.

The vision of using eportfolios to bridge institutional contexts and episodes of learning throughout life is well represented in the scholarly literature. A keynote address at the first international conference on eportfolios in 2003 presented the story of a learner using an eportfolio to understand her learning and manage her relationships to multiple institutions (Cambridge & Cambridge, 2003). The learner uses her eportfolio, begun in school, to apply to a university and subsequently to link together courses she takes from a local community college and several online universities, negotiate the terms of a job, make decisions about her continuing professional development, obtain career advice, and make connections with others with similar political interests in a new city. Stefani, Mason, and Pegler (2007) present a series of similarly wide-ranging scenarios that imagine the future use of eportfolios in such situations as applying for a job at the conclusion of a degree program, documenting the skills of newly arrived immigrants, and sharing expertise across generations.

Such narratives illustrate the potential of an eportfolio to serve as a "digital identity" (Ravet, 2005) or "e-dentity" (Ittelson, 2001) independent of any particular institution, with which an individual can share information about himself or herself in order to negotiate relationships and receive services. For eportfolios to be used effectively for these purposes, infrastructure is needed. First and foremost, learners need a flexible lifelong space in which to manage and publish their self-representations (Cohn & Hibbits, 2004). However, to be fully useful, those representations must be linked up with institutional systems in ways that render them intelligible. This linkage capability is likely to require standards for both the vocabularies used to label parts of a portfolio and their technical structure (Cambridge, 2006a; Treuer & Jenson, 2003). With such infrastructure in place, eportfolios could more easily be used to help learners engage in activities such as locating online learning resources within "lifelong learning networks" (Koper & Tattersall, 2004) and presenting evidence of prior learning for credentialing by educational institutions and professional bodies (Hoffmann, 2004; Vervenne, 2007).

In both broader educational policy discussions and scholarship specifically focused on eportfolios, the potential of eportfolios to support lifelong learning is made apparent. What is also notable in both contexts, however, is the lack of clarity about what distinguishes an eportfolio from other kinds of compilations of information about learning. In some cases, "eportfolio" seems simply to mean any collection of data about a person. As argued in the Introduction and Chapter Two, a genuine eportfolio is more than this limited notion (this line of reasoning is continued in the next chapter). In order to provide an authentic and integral representation of its author, an eportfolio presents a theory, story, or map that articulates the relationships between the different materials included and synthesizes their meaning. An eportfolio is a symphonic representation of self. This distinctive character is important to the eportfolio's role in many of the activities envisioned for it in learning throughout life, such as charting an educational path or developing a career identity, for reasons explored throughout Part One of this book. A key question to ask when examining the use of eportfolios in these activities in contexts beyond higher education is the degree to which programs embrace the distinctive characteristics of the eportfolio as a genre. Such engagement is challenging because it is likely to require significant change in institutional processes and data structures. While it may be much easier to constrain eportfolios to fit processes and genres already in use, these are just as likely to require aggregation of atomized information as to encourage the symphonic representations that characterize genuine eportfolios. Failing to embrace this character risks disconnection from the ideals that underlie the best of eportfolio practice.

Independent Lifelong Learning Through eFolio Minnesota

Before considering what is needed to support eportfolios for lifelong learning, it is important to examine this chapter's first question: whether individuals are actually using eportfolios over time and across contexts, as envisioned in policy discussion and scholarship. If they are, then how? How much of an impact do individuals believe their experience using eportfolios has had on their learning, and what factors influence the extent of this impact? In 2004 and 2005, I conducted research on the eFolio Minnesota project that investigated these questions (Cambridge, 2008a).

eFolio Minnesota is the largest-scale eportfolio initiative in the United States that supports not just students in higher education institutions but also learners beyond them. Any resident of Minnesota, or student of a college or university based in Minnesota, may compose an eportfolio through eFolio Minnesota. As of spring 2010, over 150,000 people had signed up for accounts, with steady growth since the project was launched in fall 2002. Run by the Minnesota State Colleges and Universities (MnSCU), a system of two- and four-year institutions throughout the state, eFolio is in partnership with Avenet, a private company that developed the software it employs, and the State of Minnesota Department of Labor, which provides technical support. While many schools, colleges, universities, and workforce development centers incorporate the use of eFolio Minnesota into their curricula or offer training and assistance in its use, MnSCU largely leaves it up to individual eportfolio authors to decide how to design and use their eportfolios.

eFolio Minnesota provides an easy-to-use Web application for creating and publishing eportfolios. When signing up, portfolio authors identify the primary role in which they will use their portfolio: as a student, educator, or worker. The system then presents them with a template containing a set of categories designed to be relevant to the needs of individuals in the chosen role. Authors can drop existing categories or add new ones, into which they can enter textual and multimedia content, and they have basic control over the look and feel of their portfolios. While by default portfolios are publicly accessible on the Web, sections may be password protected.

Because of the large number of users from across the state and the flexibility of the software, eFolio Minnesota proved an ideal site for studying if and how individuals use eportfolios beyond a specific institutional context. To investigate the use of eFolio, MnSCU funded a study with two phases. (A more detailed account of this research can be found in Cambridge, 2008a.) First, a large sample of users was surveyed about the purposes to which they were applying eFolio and how satisfying and effective they found the software to be for their goals. Then a smaller group of users was interviewed; these users reported a high level of impact of the eportfolio experience on their learning and were representative of other patterns in the survey data. The focus of the research was appreciative: rather than seeking to determine reasons for potential users not selecting to have portfolios, it sought to determine who was finding eFolio Minnesota valuable and why.

The results of the survey indicate a diversity of portfolio authors and purposes. While MnSCU had anticipated that users of eFolio would be disproportionately of traditional college age, the age distribution of survey respondents roughly paralleled the distribution of Minnesota's population as a whole. In fact, age did not correlate significantly with any variable, including impact on learning and ease of use of the software. Users were also similar to the state's population in their racial and ethnic identification. In contrast, eFolio users reported significantly higher levels of formal education than the greater population. The significant number of Minnesota residents without any college education was underrepresented. Because many portfolio authors are initially introduced to eFolio Minnesota through colleges and universities, this disparity is a less surprising result than the lack of disparity in relationship to age and ethnicity. Although the system proved more attractive to some groups than others, the degree to which it appealed to a wide range of people was striking.

eFolio Minnesota was also being used for a wide range of purposes, with educational planning playing a central role. eFolio Minnesota users were asked about six purposes for which eportfolios could be used, drawn from the American Association for Higher Education's Electronic Portfolio Clearinghouse: educational planning; documenting knowledge, skills, and abilities; tracking development; finding a job; evaluation within a course; and performance monitoring in the workplace (American Association for Higher Education, 2003). For each purpose, respondents indicated how often they used eFolio, how long they had used it, how effective they found it, and how satisfied they were with it. A significant portion of the users reported using eFolio for each of the purposes, ranging from 36 percent for performance monitoring to 75 percent for documenting knowledge, skills, and abilities. There were also strongly significant correlations among the different functions. People used eFolio for multiple purposes that connected to each other. Of the six uses, educational planning was strongly correlated with each of the others, suggesting that it played a central role. This result was particularly striking because the templates in the eFolio software contain no prompts that are explicitly forward looking. Planning proved important in spite of this lack of prompts.

For each of the six categories, the survey also asked which role—student, educator, or worker—the portfolio author most often assumed when using eFolio for that purpose. Over 27 percent of the time, users reported using eFolio in a role different from the one they chose when registering. (See Table 6.1.) This fact suggests that they were using eFolio beyond the context in which it was introduced to them. Interview data from the second phase of the research confirmed this. For example, a special education teacher who began using eFolio in a course while a student continued to use it to document her teaching as a professional educator in anticipation of a future job search, and a graphic designer who first used eFolio to document his skills during a job search continues to revise it as he returns to a community college to deepen his technical expertise. Users also reported using eFolio for different purposes in multiple roles at a given time. Tracy Wright's use of her portfolio to articulate the relationship of her work as a practicing nurse, a nursing educator, and member of a family, as described in Chapter Two, illustrates this pattern.

TABLE 6.1. EFOLIO USE, SATISFACTION, AND EFFECTIVENESS

Function	Used	Satisfied	Found Helpful	Used One or More Times per Semester	Used One Semester or More
Educational planning	56%	65	40	37	44
Documenting knowledge, skills, and abilities	75	45	42	38	42
Tracking development	42	53	48	47	46
Finding a job	47	33	37[a]	27[b]	40
Evaluation within a course	40	47	45	54	53
Performance monitoring	36	49	47	36	34

[a] Found to be somewhat helpful.

[b] Used less than once per year.

The frequency of these role shifts suggests that eFolio Minnesota is indeed supporting lifelong and lifewide learning. Users are continuing to use their portfolios to document, plan, and communicate their learning over time, beyond their engagement with a single institution, and across the multiple roles and affiliations in which they are invested at any given time. These users are diverse in age and cultural backgrounds, as are the purposes to which they are putting their portfolios. Evidence exists, then, that some of the potential of eportfolios for lifelong learning beyond the academy is being realized in the lives of individual eportfolio authors.

The extent of the perceived effects of this activity varies. While most users reported finding the experience of composing and sharing their portfolios helpful for the purposes to which they put them and were satisfied with them, a significant minority, 18 percent, reported that their experience with eFolio had a substantial level of impact not just on particular activities but also on their learning and their relationships with others at their institutions as a whole. The second phase of the research focused on this group. Interviews with these highly affected portfolio authors revealed a common process of composition, moving through an experimentation phase into a "living document" stage. The research also pointed to two central factors that influence the degree of impact: audience and integrity.

Experimentation and the Living Document

Most eFolio authors who reported a high level of impact on learning began the composition of their portfolios with a period of experimentation. Rather than having a detailed plan for their portfolios, they began by "playing around" with the software and the content they had available, "seeing how different items can work." They experimented with what material to include, which media to use, and how to connect the elements. Through experimentation, many moved beyond narrow conceptions of the purposes of their portfolios to embrace wider possibilities.

This experimentation process was supported in two ways. First, the software provided structure, which served a heuristic function, and flexibility, which made changes relatively painless. The categories, prompts, and visual templates included in the software provided a starting place—something authors could use to think about how to organize their work and what to include, rather than starting from a completely blank screen. At the same time, the software made it easy to try new things and make changes to the structure. Changes were not difficult to make, and most features were easy to master through trying them out. Second, authors benefited from developing their portfolios alongside their peers. Many of the high-impact users reported the value of composing their portfolios in concert with others, giving them the opportunity to "bounce ideas off of someone else" and discover strategies their peers were using that they could incorporate into their own portfolios. Learning about the kinds of artifacts others were choosing to include, the ways in which they integrated them into their portfolios, and the audiences with whom they hoped to connect often significantly broadened users' sense of the possibilities of their own eportfolios.

Once a set of purposes for the eportfolio came into focus and the portfolio's content felt sufficiently robust and well integrated to the author, the portfolio entered the living document stage. Portfolios in this stage are up-to-date in terms of the key information and materials they contain and accurately reflect the author's perspective and aspirations. Keeping an eportfolio up-to-date requires periodic updates, but these are more likely to be made in response to significant accomplishments rather than on a weekly or daily basis, as one might update a blog or social networking site profile. Authors believed these additive updates were largely sufficient if the overall story the portfolio told remained faithful to their experience. However, major life transitions, such as changing careers or returning to school, would require more significant reenvisioning of the portfolio as a whole.

Audience and Integrity

The importance of sharing eportfolios as they are being developed with others who are going through the same process points to the role of audience, one of the two factors identified in the research as most central to the perceived level of impact on learning and institutional relationships. Two kinds of audience were shown to be important. First, the degree to which authors saw their eportfolios as powerful was strongly related to how confident they were that audiences about whom they cared were reading and valuing them. Sometimes authors saw that their portfolios were being read through comments posted on their sites or how often their pages had been accessed. More often, authors got a sense that their portfolios were valued by these audiences when the eportfolio mediated some other interaction. In some cases, the eportfolio served as a conversation piece during a job interview or an advising session that supplied examples of the author's experiences and work, placed in a larger context. In others, the eportfolio proved effective in communicating a new sense of self to distant family and friends, brought on by events as diverse as entering a new program of study or becoming a parent for the first time.

Second, successful portfolio authors thought about their work in relationship to an imagined public audience for their portfolios. They saw themselves as "being out there" through their portfolios being published on the Web, and they sought to ensure that they were well represented to their potential readers. One author explained that she composed her eportfolio with a public audience in mind this way: "You choose the pieces that you feel most accurately and positively reflect on your human being, and so I selected things that I felt demonstrated my values and shed a positive light on me in a public way." On the one hand, she is invested in the portfolio as an "accurate" representation of her authenticity, her distinctive "human being" that conventional representations of professional competence, such as résumés, might miss. On the other hand, she feels a need to ensure that her self-representation is positive. People who may make judgments about her—clients, neighbors, potential employers—might read her portfolio, so it needs to emphasize how her accomplishments align with her values and how those values are congruent with those held by others in the professional and civic communities of which she is a part. Balancing accurately articulating her authenticity with accentuating the positive aspects of her identity that are intelligible to others in public forums is a key challenge.

This balancing act points to the second factor that was strongly connected with the high impact of lifelong learning, integrity, a concept considered in detail in Chapter Two. Authors found the experience of composing and sharing an eportfolio particularly meaningful and transformative when they were able to show how their values and commitments are consistent across the different roles they played—personal, professional, and civic—and to narrate how this coherence was achieved over time. When such coherence is not available in their lived experience, some feeling of integrity can be gained through examining this lack. Eportfolios are personal documents for articulating how one is unique through sharing one's "vision of life" and what one's "dreams are [and] goals are." At the same time, they have a "professional edge," representing a more public persona that matches the audiences valuable in the communities in which authors take part. Eportfolios that achieve integrity show how these different elements of identity connect and how they conflict.

However, even for authors who could not tell a meaningful story about how their personal, professional, and civic lives interconnect, the experience of reflecting on each aspect of their identity in the process of composing their eportfolios often proved valuable in itself. One author, for example, realizes that his portfolio includes a significant number of personal, professional, and academic items but admits that how they relate to each other is not always clear. This lack of integration mirrors what he sees as a lack of connection between the different spheres of his life. He reflects that "it would be ideal if they were related . . . unfortunately they're not. Right now my work is my work. And my personal life is my personal life. And school is just sort of everywhere all the time." While he begins by noting an absence of relationship, through reflecting on his eportfolio he is in fact beginning to see the potential of the new academic identity he is cultivating as he returns to higher education to tie together aspects of his personal and professional lives. In future iterations, his eportfolio might serve as a place to articulate that integration.

Both making connections with multiple audiences, concrete and public, and articulating integrity—the two key achievements predicting self-reported impact on lifelong learning—are often accomplished through layering. Authors craft their eportfolios in such a way that they accommodate varied kinds of evidence that meet the needs of different readers and capture diverse experiences. Through careful use of categories and subcategories, eportfolios can be organized so that readers "would be able to find their way around for their specific needs." Layering is also facilitated by the ability to include diverse kinds of content within the portfolio, including text, Microsoft Office documents, images, and videos. The ability to control their portfolios offers further opportunities for expression. Portfolio authors say the ability to customize the visual layout and color scheme of the portfolios and include multimedia content are key to representing the personal, embodied aspects of their identity, which can then be layered on top of more professionally oriented content. One author stressed that she included audio and video artifacts and thought carefully about her choice of colors so that "you can hear my voice." Sharing her personality in this way was key to communicating the authenticity and integrity of her identity.

The research demonstrated that eFolio Minnesota is supporting lifelong and lifewide learning that is meaningful to individuals beyond the requirements of a single institution. The accessibility and usability of the software enabled a wide range of learners to easily begin composing their portfolios through experimentation, and the software's flexibility enabled layering that contributed to connecting with multiple audiences through self-representations that achieved integrity. These eportfolio authors were introduced to both the software and the possibilities of eportfolios through a wide range of local institutions, such as schools, universities, and workforce development centers, providing entry points for residents at a variety of life stages and with diverse backgrounds. These settings often helped connect the authors with peers with whom they could engage in the process of composing their portfolios. A significant number of these authors felt that the development and use of their eportfolio had such an impact on their learning and relationships that they chose to continue using it independently beyond the context through which they had been introduced to eFolio Minnesota.

However, the way eFolio Minnesota was designed did constrain the ways in which portfolio authors could connect with audiences. The manner in which each portfolio was arranged, the kinds of evidence each contained, and the terminology used to interpret it were largely up to the individual. While many schools, colleges, and universities did integrate the use of eFolio Minnesota into their curricula, there was no formal coordination among institutions in how the integration was achieved. The expectations and values underlying use in one context could be quite different from that in another, just as they could differ among individuals composing their eportfolios independently. While this diversity of formats and practices was a central source of strength, it also made the integration of eportfolios into institutional processes more difficult, particularly at points of transition. For example, some authors moving from higher education to the workforce or seeking to change careers wished that they could make it possible for employers to conduct automated searches of their portfolios based on quantitative ratings of skills agreed on as important for their professions. Such a capability would make it practical for employers to scan through significant numbers of portfolios without having to read in depth those of authors who lacked crucial qualifications. These authors believed that such a filtering mechanism was necessary to convince employers to invest their time in considering whole portfolios in their authentic and integral forms.

Providing this capability would require new kinds of coordination across institutions. The eFolio software would need to add the ability to rate skills in standardized ways that employers' technology could access and understand, and means for their systems to interact with eFolio would need to be defined. Schools, colleges, universities, and employers would also need to agree on which skills are relevant to a given profession, how to name and define them, and how and who should rate them. Other applications, such as using eportfolios originally developed in secondary schools to guide placement into university course work, would also be more easily achievable in the presence of similar technical and conceptual coordination.

While the Minnesota State College and University system has begun to build more structured ways of representing learning outcomes in eFolio Minnesota in response to the need to produce data for accreditation and accountability, this work is in its early stages. In addition, it is focused more on facilitating organizational learning than it is on supporting individual learners across organizational boundaries and across their lifetimes (Olsen, Schroeder, & Wasko, 2009). Work in the Nottingham region of England, however, provides a further developed model for the kind of institutional coordination for which eFolio authors identified a need.

Linking Up Learning in Nottingham

With leadership from the University of Nottingham and the City of Nottingham Local Education Authority, an extensive network of institutions in the Nottingham region is working together to broaden participation in further and higher education through the use of eportfolios. Like the university leaders from the United States, educators in Nottingham see a need for a "longer-term commitment" to learners' success that extends before and after their enrollment in a particular educational program (Hartnell-Young et al., 2006). Their work focuses on enabling the use of eportfolios to personalize key transition points, such as moving from schools to enrollment in further or higher education, moving from education into the workforce, or changing employers.

Such work requires developing partnerships among schools, colleges, universities, providers of career information and guidance, training organizations, and employers. Regional work began through the Regional Interoperability Project on Progression for Lifelong Learning (RIPPLL) with the involvement of the University of Nottingham, Nottingham Trent University, the City of Nottingham Local Authority (which runs many of the local schools), UfI/Learndirect East Midlands (which provides educational services to those outside higher and further education), and all of the further education colleges in the Nottingham area. (In the United Kingdom, further education often serves purposes similar to community colleges in the United States, although it is considered distinct from higher education.) Although establishing connections with employers has proved difficult, a number of employers have expressed an interest, including the Toyota-Lexus Academy, Rolls Royce, Siemens, and Tribal Technology (Harley & Smallwood, 2005, 2006; Smallwood & Kingston, 2006). These relationships may prove easier to develop through a newly established Nottinghamshire and Derbyshire Lifelong Learning Network, which involves an even broader group of institutions across the region. The more specific focus on engineering of the related JOSEPH project, which is designed to help individuals navigate pathways toward work in engineering beginning in specialized schools and colleges and continuing into the workforce, may also be effective in engaging business across the region (Smallwood & Kingston, 2007).

Central to this regional work is the City of Nottingham Passportfolio, which builds on the success of the City of Nottingham Passport. The focus of the Passportfolio is to empower learners ages fourteen to nineteen by facilitating their transition from schools to further or higher education. The Passport, an online system for recording achievements, was launched in 2003 and used by over thirty-five hundred students in its first two years. Adding richer eportfolio and personal development planning capabilities, the Passportfolio was launched in September 2006 through over seventy schools, seven colleges, and a number of other educational institutions through the Nottingham Training Network and Nottinghamshire Education Business Alliance (Harley & Smallwood, 2005).

Passportfolio aids students in recording their achievements, reviewing their learning, and presenting information about both to a variety of audiences.

An "achievement zone" helps students capture evidence of specific skills and experiences in relationship to defined sets of objectives and skills relevant to their goals. A "reviewing zone" provides personal development planning support, offering quizzes, learning styles inventories, games, and other heuristics for "articulating skills, aptitudes, values, aspirations, and plans" (Harley & Smallwood, 2005). A "presentation zone" helps students arrange and share the materials they collect or create in other parts of the application. Templates are offered that correspond with formats elicited by other institutions, such as curriculum vitae for employers, applications forms and personal statements for further education colleges, and new entrant profiles for universities.

Evaluation conducted after the launch of Passportfolio suggests that students find the system quite useful for examining and planning their learning. Students suggested that the recording and reviewing capabilities of the software helped them articulate their identities in deeper and more sophisticated ways than they would have without the structure and assistance. Students said that the system "gives me words about myself," that they "have written down things about myself that I usually wouldn't have thought of," and that, through working with their eportfolio, they were "able to find out more about myself and realize the kind of person I am" (Harley & Smallwood, 2005). Like the categories and prompts in eFolio Minnesota, the structure of the software, combined with the advice and support it provides, plays a heuristic role, helping students generate ideas they can use to produce fuller accounts of learning and experience. Also as with eFolio, the social context matters. Students reported interactions with peers around their eportfolios as a valued element of their experiences.

However, when moving from recording and reviewing to presenting, the power of the process of composing and sharing eportfolios is limited by the formats that students' self-representations must take as they are introduced into admissions and hiring processes at other institutions. Nottingham leaders are still struggling with the mismatch between these processes and the characteristics of eportfolios. While they have been successful in helping students use data collected in the process of composing eportfolios to populate nonportfolio formats already in use by colleges, universities, and employers, helping audiences at those institutions to reenvision how those processes might embrace the broadened possibilities that the portfolio genre offers has proven more difficult. While the personal statement component of application forms could present a richer and more personalized account of a learner's experiences and capabilities, it often functions in its current form as an inflexible one-off that cannot be customized sufficiently to support the needs of multiple audiences, facilitate reiteration over time, or incorporate the diversity of evidence that eportfolios invite. As RIPPLL project staff write,

Showing [further education] colleges and training providers that an electronic application process is more than an electronic application form is crucial. . . . Future developments must consider the role of teachers as mediators more carefully, as the development of rich content and reflective processes among learners will require their support. Similarly at the points of judgment, assessors, admissions officers and employers need to be skilled in evaluating a wider range of evidence if the goals of widening participation are to be achieved. (Hartnell-Young et al., 2006, p. 865)

For eportfolio processes to recognize the unique capabilities of learners, learners need to be supported by the institutions at both ends of a transition: schools need to help students document and interpret their work and experiences, and those on the receiving end need to understand and value the distinctive and more complicated kinds of self-representations that result. Substantial changes may be needed in the processes of admission and hiring so that "the transition [between institutions] acquires meaning and purpose within the individual's personal and career development" (Harley & Smallwood, 2006).

The need to make connections to important institutional processes related to transitions without asking the institutions involved to change radically how the processes work and how learners and workers may represent themselves within them is a practical reality in the short term. Given the ambitious regional scope of the Nottingham initiatives, finding ways to build relationships that can include a large number of institutions is a necessary first step. Time and resources are limited, but the kind of changes needed to build continuity in reflective processes and help audiences understand more diverse kinds of evidence require intensive investments that many institutions may not yet be ready to make. As in the VALUE project, discussed in Part Two, the Nottingham leaders have chosen to compromise in order to broaden participation. Through beginning with the processes and formats as they are, they have positioned themselves to advocate for change by building on established working relationships.

Creating this change is likely to take a number of years, and its achievement would have a significant and much-needed impact. However, facilitating the use of a wider range of evidence and more reflective material is different from creating the conditions under which it becomes possible to use eportfolios across transitions as symphonic texts with authenticity and integrity. The extent to which the Nottingham practitioners are ready to embrace the more expansive conception of eportfolios presented in Part one is unclear. Their focus seems to be more on supporting processes often associated with eportfolio development, such as reflection on work experiences or the identification of competencies, and on exchange of information that is often incorporated into eportfolios, such as research papers or assessment results, than it is on supporting the use of eportfolios as integral wholes. Even scenarios that describe desired practice five to ten years in the future developed by participants in the regional work to guide the associated technical projects rarely feature institutional readers considering eportfolios as integral compositions. Rather, the focus generally is on the exchange of selections of atomized information divorced from its context within an eportfolio (Joint Information Systems Committee, 2007).

The work at Nottingham points to an important dilemma facing those who would promote the use of eportfolios across institutional boundaries. On the one hand, advocating a strong conception of eportfolios as a genre with associated practices that depend on the use of that genre may make it difficult to engage institutions that are not yet willing to undertake the sometimes foundational changes that embracing this vision might entail. It is likely to be much easier to shape the definition of *eportfolio* to match existing practices closely enough to incremental improvements that align with the kinds of learning portfolios have traditionally been used to support. However, by so doing, the truly transformative potential of eportfolios is diluted and the need for institutional transformation easier to ignore.

The report of eportfolio use authored for Becta, a U.K. government agency that supports the use of technology in schools, by a research team at the University of Nottingham that overlaps with those working on the projects discussed here illustrates this tension (Hartnell-Young et al., 2007). When the research was commissioned, Becta gave the researchers eight schools to use as case studies. Surprisingly, almost none of them were asking students to compose and teachers to respond to eportfolios as the researchers would previously have defined them. Even the practices they were undertaking and the materials produced that did have some similarity to those traditionally associated with portfolio composition were not referred to as "eportfolios" by teachers and students (Hartnell-Young, 2008). The researchers responded to this dilemma by redefining *eportfolios* to mean a wide range of practices of documenting, planning, and reflecting on learning that are in the spirit of traditional eportfolio practice and were observed in the chosen schools. This approach makes eportfolios less threatening to schools and allows the authors to highlight a wide range of practices for using technology to support student learning that are surely worthy of greater support and more widespread adoption. However, such a commandeering of the idea of an eportfolio makes it easier for institutional leaders and policymakers to ignore the deeper ideals of authenticity, integrity, and deliberation that the symphonic eportfolio genre uniquely supports. Loosening up too much what an eportfolio entails threatens the link between eportfolios and transformative change.

The goal of accommodating existing processes and formats has also driven the technical aspects of the Nottingham work. Early in their work, the University of Nottingham developed an eportfolio reference model that defined a set of scenarios to inform development of Web services to support entry processes into higher education and employment, charting key paths individuals might follow between institutions and the kinds of exchanges of information they would require. The genres for representing individual learning and accomplishment in use in many of these institutions, such as CVs and application forms, and software used to manage them, such as student information and human resource systems, do not accommodate portfolios. In order for eportfolios to be used in conjunction with these genres and systems without requiring them and the processes they mediate to change, information about individuals has been divorced from its situation within an eportfolio composition and atomized in highly granular forms that can be reassembled into nonportfolio formats. Perhaps as a response to the difficulties in drawing employers into the project, the Nottingham technical work is now taking a demand-led approach to increasing the employability of individuals within the region by conforming to the formats and processes already in use in order to see more immediate gains in the ability of individuals to gain jobs they desire (Jones, 2007).

This need for the exchange of small pieces of personal information led to a rejection of the technical specifications and standards designed for eportfolios that the Nottingham developers initially evaluated, the U.K. Learning Information Profile (UKLeaP) and the IMS ePortfolio Specification (Cambridge, Smythe, & Heath, 2005). The poor fit between these formats and the perceived needs of the Nottingham work are unsurprising, as both formats—particularly the IMS specification—were designed to represent portfolios as wholes, not discrete bits of personal information (Cambridge, 2006a). For the technical leaders of the Nottingham project, an "eportfolio" is not a portfolio, in the sense of an instance of a genre of self-representation with associated learning and assessment processes that depend on the character of that genre. Rather, it is a set of services that can be provided through technology, acting on personal information about learning and performance, linked up to existing institutional processes. While these services may indeed have resonance with some kinds of learning that portfolios support, the portfolio itself is missing.

What matters instead is the facility of the technology to capture data about individuals from diverse sources in a variety of formats, use them to match individuals to institutional processes, and transform them into other formats those processes demand. Doing this successfully requires not a common syntax for representing portfolios but a semantic way of understanding all of the kinds of personal information that might be involved and the ability to express them in a variety of syntaxes. An "eportfolio" is simply whatever "dynamic view on distributed data" is needed at the time, aggregated and formatted by software rather than composed by an individual (Vervenne, 2008). Nottingham has begun to collaborate with colleagues in the Netherlands and elsewhere in Europe who are having success with this approach. The challenge of balancing the existing needs of institutional audiences with the transformative potential of the eportfolio genre is equally central to the pedagogical, policy, and technological aspects of the regional eportfolio work in Nottingham.

Employability and Lifelong Learning as Competency Matching

While the Nottingham projects have had difficulty connecting with employers, some of the greatest successes in the Netherlands have come from within industry and government services designed to help Dutch workers find employment. The most mature of these initiatives is the Nedcar project, which uses eportfolios to help autoworkers develop their skills and find new jobs when faced with unemployment. Building on the success of Nedcar, the Dutch government is now offering employability eportfolios to the entire national workforce.

Matching Competencies

Nedcar is an auto manufacturer in Limburg province that makes cars for companies such as Volvo, Mitsubishi, and DaimlerCrysler. Traditionally employees had been hired with the expectation of lifelong employment. However, in recent years, Nedcar has seen dramatic fluctuations in the number of models it has been able to contract to build. The company believes that this change means that auto manufacturing in Europe is moving from a jobs-based to a project-based industry in which companies will need to expand and reduce capacity on a regular basis (Vervenne & Mensen, 2006). In 2006, the company needed to lay off over one thousand workers, almost one-third of its total workforce, in order to remain profitable. On average, these workers were forty-two years old, had over twenty years of experience at Nedcar, and had had only a few years of junior-level vocational education prior to employment (Claus, 2008). Nedcar saw eportfolios as a means to help the employees who were losing their jobs find new employment. While employers might not be able to ensure lifelong job security, through public-private partnerships businesses might be able to facilitate "flexicurity" by making the process of moving from one job to another more routine.

The Belgian company Synergetics developed an employability eportfolio system for Nedcar. The system was designed to help workers, in collaboration with human resource coaches and consultants from Dutch national employment services, identify and document the competencies they possessed, both industry specific and more general. This documentation process took into account internal training as well as expertise developed through on-the-job experience. The system stored this information in the form of a competency profile—a list of competencies linked to evidence of their possession. All employees were offered the ability to create such a profile, which was intended to help them find employment or support their continuing professional development. The system matched laid-off workers to job openings available elsewhere through partnerships with the Center for Work and Income (CWI), the Dutch public employment agency, and Kenteq, which accredits prior learning. For workers who remain at Nedcar, the system helps identify training and education possibilities that will help them improve their performance and advance into positions offering increasing challenge and · responsibility.

In addressing the short-term need for securing new employment, the project has been a success. Despite the fact that Nedcar is the only large-scale auto manufacturing company in Holland, over 80 percent of the dismissed workers had been placed into new positions within one year. The public agencies that worked with Nedcar on the project have been sufficiently impressed with the impact of the program that they are working to provide employability portfolios to all Dutch residents. In September 2008, the Center for Work in Income launched its employability eportfolio system (Claus, 2008; de Groot, 2007). Its primary purpose is to help the unemployed obtain jobs through matching their competencies to possibilities for employment and to additional education and training as needed to fill gaps in their skills. At the time of the launch of Werk.nl, CWI's eportfolio system, the center had approximately 200,000 clients whom it expects the eportfolio system will help find employment. In addition, CWI hopes to link with higher education to promote lifelong learning. Dutch higher education has endorsed a national standard for the structure of eportfolios, ePortfolio NL, which is based on the IMS ePortfolio Specification. CWI expects that all Dutch graduates from higher education will soon leave with an eportfolio that can feed into their system.

Werk.nl has at its center a "competency atlas." As with Nedcar, individuals develop a competency profile through adding information about their degrees and certifications, prior learning accredited as equivalent to formal education through testing by Kenteq, competencies documented through testing by the Basic Competencies Authority (BCA), and competencies they assert they possess through self-reflection. This information is indexed to a "universal" competency classification system developed by the American company SHL, as well as to a number of sets of industry-specific competencies. Based on individuals' competency profiles, the system matches individuals to profiles of the competencies needed for different job titles and links to a variety of job boards to show what positions are available for each type of job. The system also includes a "workbook" through which individuals can communicate during their job searches with career counselors, who help point individuals to job opportunities and resources for enhancing or better documenting their skills.

As in Nottingham, the leaders of the CWI project would like to help transform how employers make decisions about hiring and supporting continuing professional development. However, they need to balance this desire with the short-term imperative to find jobs for people. While they would like to provide more ability for individuals to personalize the structure of their portfolios and include richer representations of themselves than simply a collection of competencies, such as adding the ability to share values and goals, the technical challenge of integrating information systems across multiple organizations and the political challenge of affecting how employers make decisions have put these aspirations on the back burner (Claus, 2008).

In part because of these constraints, a competency in both the Nedcar and CWI systems is defined as a clearly described skill, knowledge, or ability that an individual has or does not have. An individual is represented in these systems primarily as a collection of such competencies, and the only competencies that matter are those requested by employers, without regard to the values, experiences, or aspirations of individuals. Although I believe that leaders of these initiatives do not intend such an outcome, in both cases lifelong learning risks are limited to the responsibility of individuals to increase the number of competencies they have as dictated by these institutions. As discussed in Chapter Two, this way of thinking about lifelong learning, which is common in policy discussions, risks reducing the role of the individual in professional and civic life to "a continuous economic capitalization of self" (Rose, 1999, p. 161). This danger is not limited to competency matching systems hosted and controlled by a particular institution. The TENCompetence project, an EU-funded project, provides free desktop software that enables individuals to use a profile of their competencies to locate learning content and services through "lifelong learning networks" that connect to many distributed institutions. It too depends on a similar understanding of competencies and thereby risks encouraging a similarly reductive understanding of the purposes of learning and personal development (Koper & Specht, 2007).

This simplification of what counts as a meaningful representation of professional identity and capability is likely to make using eportfolios to support the transition from higher education to the workforce more difficult. Dutch scholars investigating eportfolios highlight the broader potential of eportfolios that they wish to engage. For example, Meeus, Van Petegem, and Van Looy (2006) believe that portfolios as a genre may not be as effective as testing and other more traditional means for assessing specific professional competencies. However, portfolios can be powerful means for documenting what they call "learning competencies": the ability to learn independently, transfer knowledge and expertise to new situations, and ground action in a mature professional or disciplinary identity. These kinds of competencies are not neatly predefined or something a person either does or does not have. They are interrelated in a complex way, and the links to social context and individual identity must be made clear for documentation of them to be meaningful. Here, a portfolio is more than a collection of binary competencies. It is an integrated representation of self that provides this richer representation of learning power. The ePortfolio NL standard used in higher education provides the capability to support such portfolios. However, this capability will not be as useful for lifelong learning as it might be unless the systems used by employment services agencies, such as CWI, and employers themselves, such as Nedcar, can also support such richer representations.

Developing Careers

Finding ways to represent these other dimensions of identity may also prove important for the second primary purpose of the Werk.nl and the Nedcar employability eportfolio: to support the career development of individuals while employed and through multiple jobs over the course of life. Projects like Werk.nl and Nedcar could better support career development through embracing a broader understanding of good work in a field, finding better ways to provide social support, and providing individuals with the opportunity to help define institutional needs.

As argued in Chapter Two, understanding professional development requires moving beyond a sole focus on skills to understand "good work" in a field, which also includes institutional and individual values and the intersection of professional activity with other spheres of life. This broader sense of professional identity is a key component of employability (Fugate, Kinicki, & Ashforth, 2004). Stevens's (2008) research on the use of eportfolios to increase the employability of adults older than forty-five interested in moving into new jobs supports the claim that articulating a broader sense of self is important to promoting career development. Steven found that the SWOOP Forward project in Exeter, England, aided these learners in a number of ways: they developed a fuller understanding of their personal skills and attributes, gained in self-confidence, increased their motivation, were less worried that their age would have a negative impact on their prospects, and gained a clearer sense of what employers valued. Central to these successes was the capability of the portfolio genre to capture not just skills or qualification but to support discovering and sharing "what kind of person you are" and "not just your working life, but you as a person."

Representing some of a person's sense of identity in a way that software can understand serves a valuable purpose. As with eFolio Minnesota and the Passportfolio, the structure offered by competency frameworks and the prompts, quizzes, and activities that help individuals document their work and experiences in relationship to them can serve a powerful heuristic role. It can help portfolio authors see patterns in their own experience and recognize the value of evidence of their learning that they might otherwise miss. The ability to match competency profiles to job profiles and to corresponding learning opportunities can also work as a filtering mechanism that benefits both portfolio authors and audiences, allowing each to more effectively focus attention on understanding content and building relationships that have a good chance of meeting needs. The capability of technology to analyze patterns that suggest promising avenues for human action has much to offer eportfolio practice. Competency profiling can provide an opening to a conversation or negotiation.

For these patterns to be meaningful, they need to be situated within fuller accounts of identity and capability that inform the resulting conversations and negotiations. When structure and semantics constrain portfolio authors' ability to create these more integrated accounts, they shift from assets to liabilities. As I will suggest in Chapter Eight, we need better means for layering the complex, personalized structure of portfolios designed for human audiences and the standardized structures designed for analysis by technology; in this way, structure and semantics can serve not only as heuristic and filter but also as a means for communicating through the eportfolio genre in its fullest sense.

Each of these projects points to the importance of the social support, informed by the content and form of portfolios and facilitated by the communication features of the technologies through which it is shared, to promoting learning and development. eFolio Minnesota portfolio authors were successful in producing self-representations they believed had a significant impact on their learning through a period of experimentation shared with others who were also composing portfolios. Students using the Nottingham Passportfolio were more engaged by working alongside their peers. Laid-off Nedcar employees successfully used their eportfolios to find new employment with the help of career coaches whose coaching is facilitated by the Workbook component of the Werk.nl software. Other research on the use of eportfolios to support learning and professional development beyond higher education confirms the role that eportfolios can play in mediating learning in community. The effectiveness of the programs investigated by Stevens (2008) in England and Firssova (2007) in the Netherlands depended on the effectiveness of portfolios to strengthen the relationship between career coaches and individual job seekers and early career professionals.

When supported by institutions, whether schools, universities, businesses, or governmental agencies, most of these social processes are aimed at shaping individuals to help them meet the already defined needs of these or other institutions. As argued in Chapter Three in the context of assessment in higher education, eportfolios can also play a central role in deliberative processes that empower individuals to play a part in defining those institutional needs themselves, drawing on their own commitments and lived experience. For genuine deliberation to be possible, however, an alternative understanding of competencies is needed. No longer is it sufficient to see competencies as predefined capabilities that individuals either do or do not have. Rather, as in deliberative assessment in higher education, competencies need to serve as interfaces between unique, individual self-articulation and shared institutional decision making beyond the academy. They make possible institutional decision making that embraces the principles of deliberative democracy.

Eportfolios and Deliberation Beyond the Academy

The ideal of deliberation has yet to be embraced in most contexts beyond higher education in which eportfolios are being used to promote lifelong learning. An exception is in the development of institutional portfolios similar to those already in place in higher education, a practice beginning in some noneducational organizations. For example, working with the e-learning consulting company Percolab, members of a community-run arts center in Montreal, Canada, developed an institutional portfolio as a way to examine the organization's twenty-five-year history and chart its future course (Slade & Otis, 2007). Through collaboratively examining documents and reflecting on experiences, members determined a set of core competencies for the organization and analyzed how well it was meeting them. They discovered a disconnect between the competencies the artists valued in their own practice and those around which some institutional activities were organized. A better alignment of the way the organization represented itself to the community and to its members with the competencies they valued renewed the members' investment in the organization. Competencies helped connect the diverse interests and experiences of the organization's members, offering a shared language for deliberation.

Such an institutional portfolio approach might be fruitful for a broad range of organizations committed to democratic governance, such as other nongovernmental organizations, and even governments themselves. Ravet (2006) has examined the potential of civic eportfolios to engage citizens in defining the goals and evaluating the performance of "learning cities" and "learning regions."

This idea is being put into practice through projects such as the Augusta Community Portfolio, which attempts to represent the achievements and aspirations of an entire small, rural, impoverished town in the Arkansas delta region in order to mediate deliberation about its future (Cambridge, in press-a).

However, the benefit of a deliberative approach to the use of eportfolios in lifelong learning could extend beyond institutional and civic portfolios. Just as they do in educational settings, deliberative processes of making organizational decisions informed by authentic and integral individual eportfolio self-representations have the potential to lead to decisions that are both more effective and more just in the vocational world. Fully understanding what makes work good requires a fuller picture of individual commitments and practices than can be captured by a narrow focus on knowledge and skills. Eportfolios that have integrity, capture how their authors' values and competencies connect, and are consistent across multiple social roles can provide such a richer representation, which can then shape the organizational vision through deliberation.

One obvious context for such a deliberative definition of vocational excellence is unions and professional organizations, which have begun to offer eportfolio services to their members. The Royal College of Nursing in the United Kingdom, one of the first such organizations in the world to use eportfolios, currently employs them on the largest scale in the sector, offering eportfolio services to over 390,000 members (Cable, 2003, 2007). Both a trade union and a professional body, the college is responsible for supporting the career development of nurses and for certifying the continuing professional development work that all members of the profession must complete to maintain their certification. As more nurses from across the EU come to work in the United Kingdom, it seeks both to help nurses navigate an increasingly competitive environment and to expand participation in the field of nursing. RCN Learning Zone, the college's eportfolio software, is designed to support nurses' continuing professional development in relationship to specific nursing competencies and support the development of self-directed learning as a transferable skill in itself. The system is organized around a reflective learning cycle, in which nurses are guided through the process of planning learning, engaging in learning activities, reflecting on and recording the results, and taking action on the basis of what they have learned in their professional practice. The system enables them to gather multiple kinds of multimedia evidence of their learning and link it to professional standards. The system offers numerous online learning materials and activities, also linked to the standards, that nurses can use in the course of their continuing professional development based on the plans they create. These online learning resources are proving particularly valuable to nurses who are not currently practicing but wish to keep current in order to be able to reenter the field in the future. Less directly, the system also helps to support nurses' activism. Through message boards, members connect with others who have common concerns and commitments and organize to take collective action.

However, the rich evidence of the values and experiences of individual nurses being articulated through the portfolios they produce in the RCN Learning Zone is not yet connected to the processes by which the college charts the future of the profession. Just as the authentic representations of individual student learning and identity in portfolios can inform curricular and programmatic decision making in higher education through deliberative assessment, so could analogous nursing portfolios inform deliberation about professional values and standards. (For an example, see the discussion of nurse and nursing educator Tracy Wright's eportfolio in Chapter Two.) Particularly given the drive to expand participation in the profession, taking into account the diversity of the lived experiences of individual nurses in how the priorities of the profession are determined and the programs of the college are shaped seems essential. The eportfolios already being composed by nurses across the United Kingdom could be powerful in deliberations about future directions.

Because they are formed to serve the needs of both their members and the professions of which they are a part, institutions like the Royal College of Nursing should certainly aspire to live up to the principles of deliberative democracy. The case for decision making that adheres to the principles of deliberative democracy in business is less straightforward. Some theorists believe that principles of justice require democratic oversight. For example, Gutmann and Thompson (2004) argue that because corporations are awarded special privileges by government and have a substantial impact on public life, decision making in corporations should be deliberative. Ensuring that this is so requires regulation, which some theorists would like to see expanded to give workers broader democratic control over how decisions are made in the workplace (Russell, 1998). The case for cultivating a deliberative system around the workplace may be made by examining its potential contributions to the bottom line. Particularly in countries where unions are strong, empirical evidence shows that workplace democracy can contribute to competitiveness (Melman, 2001). The positive effects of discussion-centered practices such as intergroup dialogue are also beginning to be documented (Groth, 2001; Hardiman & Jackson, 2001; Ramos & Mitchell, 2001). The role that eportfolios might play in making business both more democratic and more profitable is a topic ripe for research.

Moving Toward Transformation

Although research is only in its early stages, the projects discussed in this chapter suggest that eportfolios beyond the academy have the potential to significantly enhance learning, increase opportunities for employment, support career development, and inform organizational decision making. Portfolios are perceived as effective when they help their authors share with audiences whom they value representations of their lives that integrate personal and professional experiences and values, demonstrating integrity. Authors are most likely to be successful in developing such portfolios when they work closely with peers and coaches and are provided with structure that stimulates their self-examination, serving as a heuristic. Structure can also help connect to institutional audiences by an interface of authors' self-representations with existing institutional processes and formats. But if in so doing it constrains representation of learning and identity, oversimplifying either, both authors and audiences risk missing out on the distinctive capability to capture authenticity and integrity and to guide deliberation that the portfolio genre offers. Fully capitalizing on the potential of eportfolios to support these cultural ideals is likely to require innovation in both technology and process.

The final two chapters of this book set an agenda for this innovation. Chapter Seven considers the potential and limitations of blogs and social network sites for providing audiences and social support for eportfolios. Chapter Eight examines the potential of emerging technologies for supporting lifelong learning in a way that addresses the needs of a wide range of institutional audiences while remaining faithful to the eportfolio genre, supporting individuals' articulating authenticity and integrity through their participation in deliberation. The Conclusion acknowledges that a significant transformation of institutional processes is needed to value and be guided by the broader picture of learning and identity that portfolios can capture and briefly points to other movements for change in higher education that might contribute to that transformation.

Questions for Practice

The use of eportfolios beyond higher education suggests a number of questions that both educators and leaders of projects like the ones described here should consider in order to support the use of eportfolios to help individuals manage transitions between levels of education and between education and work:

- In what ways can planning future learning and professional development become central to the reflection you invite authors to undertake through composing their eportfolios? How might this planning process be driven by individual values and commitments, as well as by external requirements?
- What audiences are available to eportfolio authors that they value? How will they know that they are reaching their audiences? How might you create contexts in which audiences are motivated to give careful attention

to genuine eportfolios? What kinds of social support are built into your eportfolio model?

- Rather than as the sole representation of individuals to institutions, how can competency profiles in eportfolios serve as interfaces between individuals' symphonic articulations of authentic and integral identity and institutional selection processes?

- How might you build partnerships with other organizations that are likely to be audiences for the eportfolios of individuals you support through which you can negotiate a balance between the partners' existing formats and processes and the essential features of the eportfolio genre? In what ways can you demonstrate the value of the richer representation of academic and professional identity and capacity that eportfolios offer to these partners?

CHAPTER SEVEN

EPORTFOLIOS, BLOGS, AND SOCIAL NETWORK SITES

Networked and Symphonic Selves

Over roughly the past decade, blogs and social network sites (SNSs) have emerged as significant means through which people represent themselves and make connections to others online. Because representing oneself for an audience over the Internet is also a primary reason people create eportfolios, both within and beyond the academy, research on how people use blogs and SNS may help inform the use of eportfolios in support of lifelong learning. Because more people use these new technologies and their associated genres than use eportfolios, understanding why people are motivated to use them may identify ways to motivate people to compose and share eportfolios. In addition, the technology behind blogs and SNSs overlaps in functionality with software that supports eportfolio practice. All are powered by the database. Even more telling, higher education institutions are beginning to experiment with these blogging and SNS tools to support eportfolio practice. Pennsylvania State University and the University of Southern California have launched initiatives that invite students to compose eportfolios using blogging software, and many more colleges and universities are adopting eportfolio systems that incorporate blogging and social networking capabilities. Although there has been little formal research on these initiatives to date, this blurring of boundaries between eportfolios and social media suggests that examining social practices around these tools can inform their intersection with eportfolios. While yielding opportunities for convergence and appropriation, the analysis in this chapter also identifies ways in which the portfolio and social software genres contrast and suggests ways to combine the advantages of each without submerging one within the other.

Blogs and SNSs are popular on an unprecedented scale. While hundreds of thousands of people are composing and publishing eportfolios in the United States, tens of millions are writing and interacting using these social software systems. According to a survey by the Pew Center for Internet Research, 39 percent of American Internet users read blogs, and 8 percent of them write them (Lenhart & Fox, 2006). Of these writers, 54 percent have not published their work in any other form. Also according to data from Pew, 35 percent of adult Internet users and 65 percent of teens have created an SNS profile (Lenhart, 2009; Lenhart & Madden, 2007). Ellison, Steinfield, and Lampe (2007) found that over 94 percent of college students at a large midwestern public university had a Facebook profile. Facebook claims to have 175 million active users worldwide, who spend 3 billion minutes using the SNS each day and exchange more than 28 million pieces of content each month (Facebook, 2009). Through blogs and SNSs, millions of people are engaging in literate practices in authentic settings beyond the classroom that may align with some of the objectives of higher education and lifelong learning.

The vast majority of this expansive activity is being undertaken by individuals without direction or support from any institution and without monetary remuneration. This fact suggests that understanding why people are willing to invest their time and energy into reading and writing blog posts or constructing and commenting on SNS profiles might provide insight into their intrinsic motivation that might inform eportfolio practice. Chapters Three and Six examined what motivates people to create and use eportfolios without specific incentives or directives from institutions. Determining how the motivations for using blogs and SNSs compare and contrast with those for eportfolios can help us understand their respective strengths and limitations and how they might be used in concert.

Findings about what eportfolios offer individuals in learning and representing themselves are quite similar to findings about blogs and SNSs and their dynamics. The growing interest in both blogs and SNSs and in eportfolios seems to arise from changing boundaries between the public and private and between the personal and the professional. The composition and publication of both blogs and SNSs and of eportfolios can be seen as a response to the requirement for constant self-reinvention that seems to be pervasive in Western societies. People use both social software and eportfolios to take up the challenge of stabilizing the self while also cultivating social connections in the face of the inadequacy of the narrative models of a life available to them in contemporary culture.

The kinds of responses facilitated by the social software and eportfolio genres, however, take different forms. These two different styles of self-representation are the networked and symphonic (Cambridge, 2008b, 2009). Research on the use of eportfolios to support lifelong learning, within and beyond the academy, suggests that they are most effective and compelling when used symphonically. Research findings about formal features of blogs and SNSs and how they are typically used correspond with the networked style. Both styles seem to offer individuals important strategies, suggesting that educators should explore how they can be used together, regardless of whether educators frame their work primarily as supporting blog writing, social networking, or portfolio building. A model for such integration is the University of Wolverhampton, where students in a graduate teaching certificate program keep networked blogs as part of a year-long process of developing symphonic eportfolios as they learn the theory and practice of teaching.

Blogs and Social Network Sites at the Intersection of the Personal and the Social

An intriguing aspect of blogging and SNS use is that they are at once highly personal and intentionally social activities. In their focus on the personal and individual, they are much like eportfolio use. Their social dimension, however, seems to be more fully developed than that of eportfolio practice, raising important questions for educators committed to supporting lifelong and lifewide learning.

While media coverage of blogs often focuses on blogs with multiple authors that address political topics, research shows that the vast majority of blogging is personal and individual in purpose and scope. Bonnie Nardi, Diane Schiano, Michelle Gumbrecht, and Luke Swartz's (2004) research on why people blog identifies documenting one's life as a central motivation for blogging. Their subjects often composed blog entries to create records of their everyday lives, in effect, to "log [their] being." Susan Herring, Lois Scheidt, Sabrina Bonus, and Elijad Wright's (2004) analysis of 203 randomly selected blogs found that over 90 percent had a single named author. The "personal journal" was the most common type of blog, with 70.4 percent of the sampled blogs falling into this category. In the Pew Survey, 76 percent of respondents reported that they used their blogs to "document personal experiences and share them with others," and for 37 percent, the primary topic of their blogs was their "life and experiences" (Lenhart & Fox, 2006).

The audiences that authors intend for their blogs are also often personal. Nardi, Schiano, Gumbrecht, and Swartz (2004) found that bloggers frequently write to keep family and friends up to date on their lives. In the Pew survey, 54 percent said that they blog mostly for themselves rather than for the benefit of an audience (Lenhart & Fox, 2006). Nardi et al. (2004) point to catharsis as another central motivation. Posting frequently to a blog provides an "outlet and a stimulus" to work through problems. Even when writing about topics other than their own lives, it is a convention of the blog genre that the perspective of the blogger should unapologetically color his or her posts. As Carolyn Miller and Dawn Shepherd (2004) put it, blogs offer a "perspectival reality, anchored in the personality of the blogger."

The use of SNSs is more obviously personal. While some successful SNSs focus primarily on professional information and connections, such as LinkedIn, the most popular SNSs—Facebook and MySpace in the United States—invite users to share information that is explicitly personal, such as relationship status or favorite music. SNS sites are organized around profiles that focus on an individual author's background, experiences, interests, and preferences. The online community that is established on these sites is egocentric, built primarily through networks of "friends" that center on an individual rather than groups organized around shared interests (boyd & Ellison, 2007). While the ways in which we represent ourselves offline and the social connections we display depend on the social context, in almost all SNSs, such contexts are flattened and the boundaries between them removed (boyd, 2004). An individual has a single profile that displays all of his or her "friends," regardless of the type of relationship or its social context.

Similarly, it should be clear by this point that the individual is at the center of eportfolio practice. With the exception of the organizational portfolios discussed in Chapter Two, portfolios are almost uniformly individual. The portfolio is about its author's identity, and his or her goals, skills, and achievements. While institutions and software may shape how the individual creates his or her self-representation, making connections to standards or conceptual frameworks, as examined in Chapter Five, the individual is still the focus. As detailed in Chapter One, underlying both individual efforts to define themselves through composing portfolios and institutions' efforts to make decisions on the basis of such representations is the ideal of authenticity. Each individual has his or her own distinctiveness, and the path to genuine knowledge must take into account this unique nature and pass through the self.

While the focus on the portfolio is personal and individual, the research discussed in Chapter Five showed that making a connection with an audience was also a central goal for eportfolio authors. Similarly, at the same time that their purpose and focus is personal, many blog authors value audiences beyond themselves and cultivate them using features of blog software. According to Pew, 87 percent of blog authors allow readers to leave comments (Lenhart & Fox, 2006). Herring et al.'s (2004) research shows that 51.2 percent of blogs link to other blogs, through blogrolls (lists of other blogs) or other means, and almost a third of all posts contain links to others. Blog authors can also respond to the writing of other bloggers by sending trackbacks, which signal that one post is a response to another. Through these means, bloggers manage their relationships with readers and other bloggers, affirming or contesting views, signaling personal affiliation, and providing social and institutional context. By tracing links, comments, and trackbacks across blogs, scholars can identify virtual communities of bloggers organized around common interests or identifications (Efimova, Hendrick, & Anjewierden, 2005). Some bloggers also choose to affiliate with more formally defined communities, such as the community of sewing enthusiasts that Carolyn Wei (2004) analyzed. Nardi et al. (2004) suggest that writing in connection with these audiences can aid with invention. The blogging community serves as a "muse" to stimulate and challenge the blogger's thinking.

That SNSs are socially connected as well as individually centered is evident from the name itself. Research on how these sites are used supports the intention of their designers for them to be social spaces. The scope of the personal social networks that individuals build is substantial. The average college student has 150 to 200 friends on Facebook (Ellison et al., 2007). The maintenance of the relationships articulated by these lists of friends is generally interactive. Eighty-five percent of teens have written on someone's "wall" in an SNS, and 82 percent have sent messages within the system (Lenhart & Madden, 2007). While linking has always been part of the Web, the new capabilities of blog and SNS software offer a broader range of social possibilities, many of them accessible with little extra effort on the part of the writer. As Stephen Downes (2007, p. 22) puts it, blogs, SNSs, and other Web 2.0 technologies can be combined into personal learning environments that "convert the act of creating content into a social and connected act."

The degree to which this is the case for eportfolios varies. Research on such projects as eFolio Minnesota and LaGuardia Community College's eportfolio suggests that establishing a genuine connection with audiences such as teachers, employers, and family is one of the most important factors in predicting how much an author values his or her eportfolio and its impact on her or his learning and personal development (Cambridge, 2008a; Eynon, 2009). However, many of the most otherwise compelling portfolios lack the integrated mechanisms for signaling connection and inviting interaction that are available in blogs and SNSs. None of the individual eportfolios examined in depth in the previous chapters have means for interacting with their audience as an integral component.

Samantha Slade's portfolio illustrates this gap particularly strikingly. As explained in Chapter Two, Slade's portfolio represents her symphonic understanding of her identity, showing how a specific understanding of learning informs both her personal and professional lives. As a whole, her portfolio communicates a theory for supporting learning through cultivating environments rich in information, tools, and people on which individuals can draw in their pursuit of learning and personal development. The portfolio is composed using a wiki, a type of software often associated with highly collaborative and open environments (Cummings & Barton, 2008). However, while the portfolio is indeed rich in information, features of the tool that invite interaction are disabled, and other people are largely absent. Only Slade can edit the portfolio, and there are no means to directly offer feedback. While the portfolio does include some testimonials from others, these have been collected and excerpted outside the portfolio. Slade acknowledges on the "resources" page of her portfolio that she has thus far struggled to integrate her social networks into the portfolio: "I'm still trying to figure out the best way to represent to myself my web of people, organisations, projects etc." While the portfolio powerfully argues for learning environments rich in opportunities for social engagement, it does not yet embody such a space. Examining how the social is enacted through blogs and SNSs may help portfolio authors like Slade create a stronger relationship with their audiences, offering those others a presence within their self-representations.

Mediated Self-Representation and Managed Interaction

Through blogs, SNSs, and eportfolios, people are sharing aspects of their personalities and lives more frequently and more publicly than they might have chosen to prior to the advent of the new technology. This raises some obvious questions: Why do people want to write about the personal in public? Why do other people want to read this writing?

Research shows that this activity is intended to help clarify, validate, and solidify identity and build and maintain relationships through self-representation in comparison with the representations of others. The digital, networked environment provides means for managing interaction that offer a desirable level of control and lower transaction costs, but they also change social dynamics, and thereby require new strategies.

Miller and Shepherd (2004) examine the historical moment of the late 1990s, when blogging began, to look for answers. The trends they uncover extend into the early 2000s, when SNSs originated and the use of eportfolios expanded beyond the academy. This period was characterized by changing relationships between the public and private and between the unmediated and mediated. As people began to feel they had less and less control over their personal information as technology tracked and commoditized more and more of their movements and transactions, they sought both more agency in how they were represented through media and more access to personal information about others. Miller and Shepherd suggest that this period was characterized by "mediated voyeurism"—the desire to view other people's seemingly authentic, unguarded, and unscripted lives through technology, eliminating the risks of actual interaction.

Mediated voyeurism is made possible by a simultaneous rise of exhibitionism. Making aspects of their personal lives more intentionally visible offered individuals new means for "self-clarification, social validation, relationship development, and social control" (Miller & Shepherd, 2004). Representing the personal through media was a key component of exhibitionism, because "validation increasingly comes through mediation, that is, from the access and attention that media provide." In addition to the advent of blogging, mediated voyeurism and exhibitionism are also suggested by such developments as the rise of reality TV, the popularity of "reality literature," and the rapid adoption of cell phones and digital cameras. In an analysis of why people use SNS, danah boyd (2007) argues that "the desire to participate [has] both a voyeuristic and performative quality" (p. 155). New technology and genres make it possible to offer greater access to personal information while also offering additional options for managing the dynamics of that access. While it is unfortunate that the terms Miller and Shepherd and boyd use—*voyeurism* and *exhibitionism*—have strongly negative connections in general use, the cultural changes they describe need not be seen in solely negative terms. Rather, they signal an ingenious use of communication and technology to confront the challenges of contemporary identity and relationships.

Part of the appeal of blogs may be the new options they offer for managing interaction. Herring et al. classify the blog as a hybrid genre that combines features of both traditional, static Web pages and other modes of computer-mediated communication (CMC), such as e-mail or instant messaging. As with a static HTML home page, one of the blog's ancestor genres, the relationship between author and reader is asymmetrical. While blogs offer CMC-like enhanced ability to interact with readers through comments and trackbacks, the author's writing is clearly central, and the author has control over what is displayed. At the same time, blog audiences do not feel compelled to read new material immediately or to always respond, as they might with e-mail or instant messaging. Blogs are less intrusive. As Nardi et al. (2004) put it, contact between authors and readers is "modulated . . . interaction-at-one-remove" (p. 46). A blog has some of the feeling of stability of a home page while also promising an interactive, yet distanced and managed, relationship with readers.

SNSs also offer transformed means for managing interaction. In particular, they reduce the transaction costs of establishing and maintaining relationships (Donath & boyd, 2004; Ellison et al., 2007). SNS fields that refer to offline affiliations, such as hometown or high school, combined with high levels of participation in such sites, make it easy to locate acquaintances (Lampe, Ellison, & Steinfield, 2007). In a manner that parallels aggregator software for reading blogs, SNSs make it possible to quickly survey changes in many friends' profiles and view their status updates, which are similar to one- or two-sentence blog posts. By writing their own updates, making small changes in profiles, or uploading media, SNS users can also easily remind their friends of what is going on in their lives. Friends' lists also make it easier to ensure that people are who they say they are. That a set of known others has indicated some degree of affiliation with an SNS user is an implicit validation of the accuracy of the information in the user's profile (Donath & boyd, 2004). While research suggests that most relationships managed by SNS begin through offline contact and migrate online, rather than the other way around, as was the original intention of SNS software designers, SNSs make it practical for people to maintain and strengthen relationships that might otherwise have remained ephemeral (Ellison et al., 2007).

SNS may be most powerful in cultivating a network of people with whom the user has weak ties—those beyond his or her circle of close friends and colleagues (Donath & boyd, 2004). Weak ties are key resources to accessing information and assistance, such as research advice or employment opportunities (Granovetter, 1973). Ellison et al.'s research (2007) on university students' use of Facebook confirms that SNSs may help profile authors build or maintain social capital, particularly what Robert Putnam (2000) termed "bridging social capital," that is, relationships based on weak ties. The intensity of students' use of Facebook was positively correlated with all types of social capital and had the strongest connection to the bonding type—relationships with others with whom one has much in common (Ellison et al., 2007).

Interestingly, intensity of SNS use had a stronger relationship with bonding social capital for students with low self-esteem and low satisfaction with their university environment than for students high on these measures, that is, students who are likely to have developed a high degree of social capital with or without the SNS. This observation suggests that SNSs may be particularly powerful for groups that are otherwise disadvantaged in a particular social environment. The fact that, among adult Internet users in the United States, use of SNSs by African Americans (43 percent) and Hispanics (48 percent) outpaces use by Caucasians (31 percent) and use by those with incomes under thirty thousand dollars a year (48 percent) is higher than for all other income groups suggests that this pattern may be generalizable beyond college students (Lenhart, 2009).

The lowered transaction costs that facilitate such cultivation of bridging social capital come at the cost of a flattening of relationship types and social contexts. One set of "friends" is visible to everyone so designated, as is a single profile. This poses a new challenge to privacy. In offline social settings, one presents oneself differently in different social situations, withholding or deemphasizing some aspects of one's identity, highlighting others, sharing who one knows or is affiliated with as appropriate for one's social goals and local context. As boyd (2007) puts it, "Many social processes depend on forms of selective disclosure, strategic ambiguity, and/or mediation within networks" (p. 144), and these activities are more difficult in the unfaceted social space of SNSs. Profile authors have responded to this challenge through both "professionalization" of their profiles and using features of technology in ways different from those intended by their creators, such as through the creation of Fakesters on the early Friendster system—profiles for groups or fictional characters to which users can link to indicate social affiliation distinct from binary "friendship" (boyd, 2004; boyd & Ellison, 2007). SNS software designers have begun to respond to these challenges by incorporating features such as more finely grained privacy controls and the ability to form groups.

Individuals seem to be using blogs and SNS to negotiate a psychically desirable balance between privacy and publicity "in a culture that finds its reality in the media" (Miller & Shepherd, 2004). In the increasingly mediated and networked information society that has developed in recent decades, the choice between private and public becomes an ongoing and complex boundary management process (Palen & Dourish, 2003). Miller and Shepherd (2004) argue that bloggers write in an attempt to establish ownership of their identities, inscribing them as genuine, integrated, and persistent:

> The blog might be understood as a particular reaction to the constant flux of subjectivity, as a generic effort of reflexivity within the subject that creates an eddy of relative stability. Infinite play, constant innovation, is not psychically sustainable on an indefinite basis. In a culture in which the real is both public and mediated, the blog makes "real" the reflexive effort to establish the self against the forces of fragmentation, through expression and connection, through discourse.

The blog is a means for fixing and connecting up identity that provides a felt sense of reality in the face of a world that can often seem chaotic and incomprehensible. The use of SNSs, too, suggests an effort to articulate a persistent self through expression and connection, to make one's identity and social integration into the larger world visible and tangible.

Narrative and the New Capitalism

Part One and Chapter Three of this book made a similar argument for eportfolios, showing how they can be used to articulate their authors' authentic and integral identities in relationship to individual and institutional audiences. While the means for establishing social connections within and around eportfolios may not yet be fully developed, a rich set of strategies for creating complex and compelling self-representations has emerged. One key strategy is the use of narrative. In Chapter One, Sean Moore crafted a narrative of affiliation with and rejection of multiple intellectual and spiritual traditions to chart his own understanding of community, which he eventually defines in a way that draws on aspects of each engagement. In Chapter Three, multiple stories about communication that were incorporated into two students' portfolios and linked through a common conceptual framework suggested directions of curricular development, and the potential of an eportfolio as a testimony that could make the experience of marginalized groups intelligible within institutional decision-making processes was discussed. Chapter Two, through Samantha Slade's portfolio, introduced the goal of integrity. Examining how narrative can contribute to establishing and understanding consistency and coherence across a life can help elucidate the potential connections between blogging and SNS use and eportfolio practice and point to important distinctions between the form and dynamics of social software and the eportfolio genre.

Responding to societal pressures for continuous transformation of the self, bloggers can bring a "narrative coherence" to the personal information in their blogs to achieve this goal (Jarrett, 2004). The desire for and challenge of constructing a coherent narrative of one's life seems to be central to "psychically sustainable" living. Richard Sennett's sociological research illustrates how this deep-seated need is pervasive in contemporary society. Sennett (1998, 2006) studies what he calls "the culture of the new capitalism," focusing on the ways in which individuals respond to the changed economic environment that has caused the reconfiguration of their relationships to employers and other institutions. His interviews with a wide range of current and aspiring workers within this culture in the United States suggest that they are struggling to find ways of connecting their experiences in the workplace with the ideas about "character" that they wish to be guiding principles for their lives as a whole. The workers vary in their industries and circumstances: they include bakers, recently laid-off senior computer programmers, an early-career management consultant, and a long-time bar owner who is moving into advertising. What links them together is that the life courses on which they seek to model their own are characterized by long-term commitments and enduring relationships. Such commitments and relationships prove increasingly difficult to maintain in a professional workplace characterized by short-term, transactional contracts; frequent reconfigurations of temporary teams linked to discrete projects; and other ongoing changes in response to market indicators. In their personal lives, they seek to make commitments to family that supersede the immediacy of their day-to-day needs and desires and maintain ties to their communities that demonstrate loyalty and identification. These values and the types of commitments they engender no longer ensure, and may in fact interfere with, their professional success. It therefore becomes difficult for them to craft a coherent understanding of their identities across private and public roles.

The most straightforwardly professionally successful of Sennett's (1998) subjects provides an example. Rico is an in-demand management consultant who travels around the world, working with a wide range of powerful companies and being paid extremely well. He has a great deal of autonomy in his practice and is able to choose clients who present intriguing challenges and lucrative compensation. He is flexible and adaptable, quickly establishing collaborations within a new setting and applying his past experiences to new contexts. Yet Rico feels a deep sense of dissatisfaction with his life because of a disconnection between his career and personal life. His father, Enrico, a lifelong factory worker whom Sennett interviewed in the seventies, modeled for him permanent commitment and long-term loyalty as keys to happiness and success. He would like to do the same for his own children, but he cannot through his professional life. He lacks a means to make sense of and take authorship of his life as a whole. He is unable to create a narrative that helps him understand his life as having integrity:

> Narratives are more than simple chronicles of events; they give shape to the forward movement of time, suggesting reasons why things happen, showing their consequences. Enrico had a narrative for his life, linear and cumulative, a narrative which made sense in a highly bureaucratic world. Rico lives in a world marked instead by short-term flexibility and flux; this world does not offer much, either economically or socially, in the way of narrative. (Sennett, 1998, p. 30)

The disjunction between Rico's personal and professional roles cannot be made to fit the narrative models for a successful life available to him, which are linked to a social world very different from the one in which he is living.

Without the ability to understand his life as a story, Rico feels cast adrift, as do many of Sennett's other informants. Narrative is key to fitting people's identities into their social worlds. Experience is made socially compressible and sanctioned by narrative. As Eakin (1999) puts it, "We live in a culture in which narrative functions as the signature of the real, or the normal" (p. 54). Societies offer narrative models for life stories with which individuals compose their own. These models come from literature, history, folklore, and popular culture—from the life stories of role models and family members and from the genres through which institutions call on individuals to represent themselves. Successful alignment with institutional models is necessary for material success and social integration (Smith & Watson, 1996). As institutional templates for identity are transformed in the new capitalism in ways that diverge significantly from the narrative models offered by the traditions and relationships with which people identify, their ability to achieve both material success and psychological well-being is threatened. In the changed environment, clear narrative models are increasingly difficult to locate (Alheit, 1992; Sennett, 1998). Those received models that are available often smooth over important tensions and naturalize institutional demands, providing poor tools with which to take a critical stance and advocate for change (Goodson, 2005).

Narrative is one powerful means for not just enumerating what one has experienced, achieved, and valued but also for synthesizing these things in a way that shows how they add up to something more than the sum of the parts. Narrative helps us discover and communicate an overlying logic. Articulating underlying principles that one uses to make decisions about one's life, establishing a critical distance from one's feelings, beliefs, commitments, and relationships, is key to the symphonic self, as defined in Chapter Two. Through the extended analysis of Samantha Slade's portfolio and the research at LaGuardia and Kapi'olani Community Colleges presented in that chapter and the examination of eFolio Minnesota in Chapter Six, it is clear that such symphonic self-representations are strongly associated with a range of positive outcomes that eportfolios, both individual and institutional, have the potential to support. Narrative figures centrally in many of these portfolio models. Examination of how people use eportfolios suggests that, as with blogs and SNSs, the ability of the eportfolio genre to integrate multiple dimensions of individual experience and identity and to connect it compellingly to public audiences is key to its impact.

Databases and the Networked Style

Another similarity between many recent eportfolios, including most eportfolios created beyond the academy considered in Chapter Five, and blogs and SNSs is their underlying technical structure: the database. However, the social practices associated with the eportfolio genre, with its focus on integrity and symphonic self-representation, differ in significant ways from those emerging around social software. Examining the structure and dynamics of the database can help clarify the distinctions. In databases, the interface can provide some of the continuity that blog, SNS, and eportfolio authors seek. Empirical research shows that the blog and SNS genres make it easy to accumulate and dynamically filter loosely structured collections of small, discrete items, allowing their authors to efficiently make new connections and repurpose materials. However, the relationships between the resulting sets of items are not explicitly articulated as they are in eportfolios, leading to less narrative coherence. Eportfolio narratives are the product of composition, not search.

Blogs, SNSs, and eportfolios are appealing to authors in their ability to link up multiple aspects of life, pointing to what each author sees as most important, and using that self-representation to mediate interactions with others. They also share the database as a similar underlying technical structure. In analyzing the role of the database structure on blogging, Jarrett (2004) draws on the work of media theorists Lev Manovich and Mark Poster to suggest that blogs are evidence of the challenge of "database subjectivity" that we all face. Both theorists argue for the database as the "dominant conceptual paradigm" of our moment—the technological counterpart to the changing relationships between mediated and "real," between private and public, and between personal and professional that Miller and Sennett examine. Manovich (2001) suggests that a database consists of two components: a data collection and an interface. The data collection is unstructured—an aggregation of discrete data open to constant expansion, revision, and rearrangement. The interface applies an algorithm in order to bring structure to the collection, guiding the experience of a reader who encounters the database. The interface provides the coherence that is not inherent in the collection alone. That coherence, however, does not necessarily take a narrative form. In fact, Manovich writes, the database and narratives are "natural enemies" (p. 228).

The nature of the coherence—how narrative, how persistent, how integrative—offered by the interface varies. Poster's work (1990, 1995) suggests that database identities tend toward the dynamic and multiple. The database structure "produces identities which can be dispersed across numerous sites, but pulled together temporarily through the particular filter or search function in operation at the time" (Jarrett, 2004). Filtering and searching, rather than composing, are the key means of arrangement. Through the options the interface provides to the reader, a new version can be immediately produced as suits the reader's purposes. Building on these insights, Jarrett proposes that in the age of the database, the "self becomes a data set of collected experience and the partial, dynamic representation of it."

Jarrett argues that the representation of self in blogging works this way, and research on how blogs are typically used supports the interpretation. Bloggers tend to write posts that are short, an average of 210.4 words, and to write them frequently (Herring et al., 2004). In the Herring et al. (2004) study, the average time between the most recent and second most recent post was five days, and the mode was one day. Bloggers do not necessarily devote a great deal of time to their compositions. In the Pew Survey, 59 percent of bloggers said they spent only one to two hours per week working on their blogs (Lenhart & Fox, 2006). It seems unlikely that brief blog entries, written frequently and quickly, are likely to be carefully integrated into the blog as a coherent whole. The blog is more of a collection of data without an intentional structure than a composition with an overall message. As Jarrett (2004) puts it, "A blog is, firstly, a data set, a list of things—experiences, events, people, objects, information—that the blogger has collected." Blog software usually offers an interface that allows readers to sort this list in several ways. The default organization is reverse chronological: last in, first out. Viewers may also filter blog posts by tags or categories or search their full text. The representation of the author offered by the blog is a dynamically created list of discrete, brief texts organized according to the reader's interests at a given time.

The design of SNSs is similarly search oriented. An SNS profile is essentially a list made up of other lists. A profile includes a list of friends and information about the author. The order of the fields that present that information is effectively arbitrary, and most fields call for either a very brief answer, such as the name of one's employer, or a list of brief items, such as the names of books one has read lately. Search features are prominent in SNS interfaces. A search box is generally available on every page, and in some cases, profile responses, such as favorite bands or movies, show up as linked keywords that trigger a search for other users who have also included those terms in their profiles.

Research on SNS use shows patterns similar to those for blogs. Writing on SNS is generally short in length, often in frequency, and brief in duration. The mean length of the "About Me" profile field on Facebook, which invites the most extended and open-ended response, is only 157 characters, with a median of 36—very short indeed—and fields inviting profile authors to list interests or favorites averaged only 6.5 items with a median of 5 (Lampe et al., 2007). Adult users of SNS sites tend to access them quite often. Sixty percent of SNS users access the system at least several times a week, and 37 percent access them every day (Lenhart, 2009). The average college student logs into Facebook at least once a day (Ellison et al., 2007). Yet the amount of time spent on the systems is relatively modest: students spend between ten and thirty minutes per day on an SNS (Ellison et al., 2007), roughly equivalent to the overall average of seventeen minutes per day per user reported by Facebook (Facebook, 2009).

Lampe et al.'s (2007) research on the relationship between the contents of profiles and the number of Facebook friends users sheds light on these dynamics.

They found that the number of profile fields that users have completed is highly associated with the number of friends they have, while the amount of information included is weakly associated with the number of friends. Surprisingly, however, their stepwise regression analysis found that the amount of information in the open-ended fields did not add to the models' ability to explain variance in the number of friends. In other words, "it doesn't appear to matter how much information is included in profile fields, just that some information is included" (Lampe et al., 2007, p. 8). The fields that had the strongest relationship to number of friends were those that could be used to identify common points of reference with other users, such as home town or concentration (major), that is, fields on which other users are most likely to search. The ability to be found seems to be more important than what one has to say about oneself once located in generating connections using SNS, and the pattern of frequent and brief communication using the system seems to support the maintenance of these relationships in a way that is sustainable in the face of the demands of day-to-day life.

Like SNSs, blogs lower the transaction costs for making connections. The ability to tag and categorize posts, as well as the ability to make links from older posts to newer ones, empowers the blog author to make connections across the collection with a relatively small investment of time and energy. One of the central attractions of the blog genre to educators, in fact, is that it seems to be well suited to helping students make connections across courses, across disciplines, and between the classroom and personal experience beyond it (Chen et al., 2005). SNSs add the ability to make connections to diverse others across traditional social boundaries, make accessible to others information so that they can easily identify potential points of connection, and maintain weak ties that might yield new perspectives and bring new resources to light. Bringing into play conventions that encourage the personal and social, yet are composed in academic and disciplinary settings, educational blogs and SNSs have the potential to help students move beyond traditional boundaries in the service of integrative learning.

Technology Support for Networked and Symphonic Selves

This focus on continual generation of new connections with relative speed and ease helps individuals develop the networked self, the self of making intentional connections (Cambridge, 2008b, 2009). As suggested by Table 7.1, there are numerous differences between the networked and symphonic styles of learning and self-representation. They differ in the understanding of what is valuable in learning and identity that informs them, the activities undertaken in support of

TABLE 7.1. DISTINCTIONS BETWEEN THE NETWORKED SELF AND THE SYMPHONIC SELF

	Networked Self	Symphonic Self
Values	Play, emergence, entrepreneurialism, flexibility, agility Analysis Liberalism Student engagement Folio thinking	Integrity, commitment, intellectual engagement, balance Creativity Humanism Personal engagement Matrix thinking
Activities	Ease, speed, low-cost integration Embedded in day-to-day work Connection Aggregation, association Collection Reflection-in-action, constructive reflection Revision Continual learning	Time, effort, high-cost integration (author, context, and audience) Stepping out of daily work Articulation, reframing Synthesis, symphony Selections, projection Matrix thinking, reflection-in-presentation Iteration Moments of mastery, accomplishment, celebration
Genre characteristics	Space Openings Relationships as end, heuristic, invention Relationships between things Atomized, aggregated Collection, list, link, datum, snapshot	Text, composition Boundaries Relationships as organization Relationships between relationships Holistic, integral, systemic Theory, story, interpretation, map
Technologies	Web 2.0 tools, social software, Identity 2.0 providers, PLEs and other aggregators, MyLifeBits Atom, RSS, FOAF, Flikr API, OpenID	Eportfolio systems Concept mapping systems IMS ePortfolio, Topic Maps, Resource Description Format
Impacts	Low yield—incremental and by accretion Greater connectedness and intentionality Learning in the network	High yield—occasional and intensive Synthesis, coherence, integrity Learning in the individual

Source: Adapted from Cambridge (2009).

that understanding, the genres of representation that the outputs of those activities often assume, and the technologies that most often support use of those genres (Cambridge, 2009). Web database technology can support both styles. The genre conventions and technical capabilities of blogs and SNSs support the making and managing of connections essential to the networked self but do not support the synthesis of those connections necessary to articulate the symphonic. In contrast, some features of eportfolio systems have proved successful in guiding composition and synthesis.

The networked style of self-representation has several characteristics that correspond closely to the structure and typical uses of blogs and SNSs. As already noted, the conventions of blog writing blur boundaries, helping their authors to make connections, and blog software allows rapid generation of connections through tagging and linking. SNSs offer the ability to find and stay in contact with a larger group of others than it might be possible to otherwise manage, rapidly circulating ideas and resources. The brevity and frequency of blog posting and SNS communication also suit the rhythms of daily life. Blog posts, status updates, and wall posts can be composed quickly, in spare moments between more formal activities. Rather than needing to be intentionally integrated into a single composition, blog posts can remain relatively discrete, as can the fields and friends list of a SNS profile. Blogs and SNS profiles are fundamentally lists that readily accommodate new items and can be easily reorganized and repurposed to meet the needs of a changing environment. Blogs and SNSs become valuable to their authors and audiences through aggregation, of which the networked self is a product.

Some eportfolio software developers, particularly those involved in projects outside the academy such as those discussed in the previous chapter, conceptualize eportfolios as analogous to blogs and SNSs in their networked structure. According to Ingo Dahn, a German scholar who has a leadership role in the TAS[3] personal information infrastructure project, an eportfolio should be seen as a "dynamically generated view of distributed data," a definition strongly parallel to Jarrett's idea of database subjectivity (Vervenne, 2007). An eportfolio, like a blog, can be a "partial, dynamic representation" of "a data set of collected experience" (Jarrett, 2004). Several educational software development projects that publicize their tools as useful for eportfolio practice have similarly embraced the networked form of SNSs and blogs. Elgg, which originates in Scotland; Mahara, which comes from New Zealand; and Epsilen, from the United States, all include functionality common to both blogs and SNSs, such as the ability to post and comment on blog entries, complete a list-style profile, upload and categorize media files, and make "friends." Content in these systems is easily searchable and allows linking to and importing content from elsewhere on the Web. They lower the cost of locating, aggregating, and publishing information about their users from and to multiple sources.

Like most other existing blog and SNS software, however, most social-software-inspired eportfolio systems offer few tools that help eportfolio authors integrate and synthesize the evidence and reflection they have collected into a coherent composition. As Parts One and Two sought to demonstrate, eportfolios that articulate authenticity, demonstrate symphonic integrity, and can contribute to deliberative democratic decision making look very different from arbitrarily ordered lists. They are extended, complex compositions that link together diverse kinds of evidence into integral wholes. Which items the author chooses to select, how they are arranged, and how the interface of the portfolio and its reflective narrative frames the items are all essential to its meaning. While the blog- and SNS-like features of eportfolio technology and the use of blog and SNS software to support the social aspects of eportfolios have great promise, in the absence of corresponding capabilities that foreground the composed, integrative, and symphonic nature of eportfolios designed to support lifelong and lifewide learning, employing these tools risks neglecting what is distinctive and powerful about the eportfolio genre. Some systems, however, are balancing networked and symphonic capabilities more successfully, as evidenced by the example from the University of Wolverhampton discussed later in this chapter.

Eportfolios as compositions also differ from blogs in that they tend to be updated less frequently. The eFolio study suggested that portfolio authors did not feel the need to make frequent additions to their eportfolios as they might for a blog; being "relatively up to date" was sufficient for most (Cambridge, 2008a). Instead of a daily log of their lives, authors saw their portfolios as capturing more persistent aspects of their identity to which they were signaling a more enduring commitment through their public representation, addressing the needs for consistency across roles and over time that Miller and Sennett identified. Rather than many incremental additions, authors made more substantial revisions of their portfolios in response to significant transitions, such as returning to school, changing majors, having a child, or changing jobs. Rather than just adding new content, eFolio authors reexamined their whole portfolios on these occasions, sometimes making significant changes to their content, organization, and design. Research on the use of eportfolios in higher education conducted by members of the Inter/National Coalition for Electronic Portfolio Research reveals a similar pattern of less frequent, more in-depth rewriting at points of transition, such as the end of a course, the beginning of a new program, or the completion of a degree.

While the development of database-driven technology to support eportfolios can be problematic because of differences in form and frequency between blog and SNS writing practices and those associated with the eportfolio genre, the introduction of eportfolio systems has eased the learning curve for new eport-folio authors, particularly those developing their portfolios without institutional mandate or support. These systems enable authors to compose portfolios with-out needing to learn complex and specialized Web development software. For example, many users of eFolio Minnesota ranked ease of use as one of the most important factors in their decision to create their portfolios and continue to use them (Cambridge, 2008a).

Beyond ease of use, the database technologies that support the composition and publication of eportfolios offer new possibilities for social connection and interaction. While the print portfolio is primarily a private genre, perhaps shared with teachers, evaluators, or potential employers but rarely published, electronic portfolios in the form of static Web pages are often fully public, available to anyone with a Web browser who knows the address. Eportfolios using database technologies at once offer increased opportunities for interacting with an audience and more granular control over the level of publicity. Like blogging software and SNSs, many of the tools used to create and publish eportfolios provide readers the ability to post comments and the author the ability to decide who gets to read them. In some cases, portfolio authors may also submit their portfolios for feedback from evaluators and mentors, such as supervisors, faculty members, and alumni. Rather than choosing to make his or her portfolio fully private or fully public, an author may choose which specific people or groups can see the portfolio and for how long. Database eportfolio software provides new means of connection while offering greater control. A number of scholars have noted that some colleges and universities offering such technology choose to take this control away from students (Kimball, 2005; Yancey, 2004a). However, the choice to deny students control of their online self-representation is a regrettable policy decision rather than a limitation of the technology. Projects successful in help-ing authors cultivate and communicate their symphonic selves, such as eFolio Minnesota and LaGuardia ePortfolio, are scrupulous about placing the power to decide who can interact with an author through his or her eportfolio squarely in that author's hands.

Software specifically designed to support eportfolios shares with blogs and other database technologies these expanded mechanisms for interaction that offer new types of control over authors' relationships with their readers. Research on the use of eportfolio-specific tools in higher education suggests they are distinguished by the ways in which the structure of the tool can support the development of symphonic self-representations that connect the author to a community of others around a shared integrative conceptual framework. Through her collaboration with Susan Kahn, Sharon Hamilton (2006) coined the term *matrix thinking* to refer to the process of reflecting on one's work previously created in another context in relationship to the intersection of multiple dimensions of such a shared conceptual framework. Some eportfolio tools provide scaffolding that helps students compose such reflections and share them in a way that connects with that of others. For example, at Kapi'olani Community College, students reflect on their experiences and work in relationship to a set of six native Hawaiian values and four stages of the journey of an outrigger canoe, another metaphor from the indigenous culture (Kirkpatrick, Renner, Kanae, & Goy, 2009). The values help students think about the multiple aspects of their learning, within and beyond the classroom, cognitive and affective. The journey metaphor helps them track their development over time. By configuring the Matrix tool within the Open Source Portfolio around this shared framework, faculty can help students break the complicated task of creating self-representations in their portfolios that connect their cultural heritage and home identity to their experiences as new members of an academic community into manageable steps, receiving feedback along the way from their instructors and other students at similar stages in the process. Research also documents success using eportfolio tools to support matrix thinking about leadership at George Mason University, liberal education at Indiana University Purdue University at Indianapolis, and writing at the University of Washington (Cambridge, Fernandez, Kahn, Kirkpatrick, & Smith, 2008; Fournier, Lane, & Corbett, 2007).

In both the LaGuardia and eFolio projects, templates for organizing eportfolios have served a similar role. Rather than beginning with a blank screen, portfolio authors are offered a default set of pages and categories to help them think through what to include and reflect on. They serve as heuristics for authors and allow comparison across portfolios. However, as authors become more confident, they have the ability to depart from the default structure, developing their own organization and including whatever material they deem germane. By offering structure that can aid with invention and facilitate connection but allows flexibility and creativity as well, eportfolio tools can effectively scaffold the development of symphonic selves.

Layering the Networked and Symphonic Styles in Wolverhampton

While the symphonic style of self-representation associated with eportfolios is a powerful response to the social exigencies discussed earlier in this chapter, it also has weaknesses and poses challenges that become clear through examining an example of how the networked and symphonic styles have been used together.

At the University of Wolverhampton in England, Emma Purnell engaged in both eportfolio composition and blog writing while earning a postgraduate certificate in postcompulsory education (something like an accelerated master's program in community college teaching). Purnell's eportfolio uses narrative to symphonically frame her learning. Her portfolio, the second of two composed while completing the certificate, is organized around a central page that tells the "digital story" of her "learning journey" over the course of the year, beginning with taking classes on the theory and practice of teaching and learning and progressing into teaching in the classrooms of a local further education college. (See Figure 7.1.) The narrative page links to a "learning autobiography" that was part of her first portfolio, in which she details the life experiences that have informed her decision to teach and her beliefs about teaching learning; to action plans, test results, essay excerpts, and videos of her teaching collecting over the course of year, each framed by her reflections and many including comments from her instructor and peers; and to a blog in which she and her peers wrote about

FIGURE 7.1. EMMA PURNELL'S EPORTFOLIO

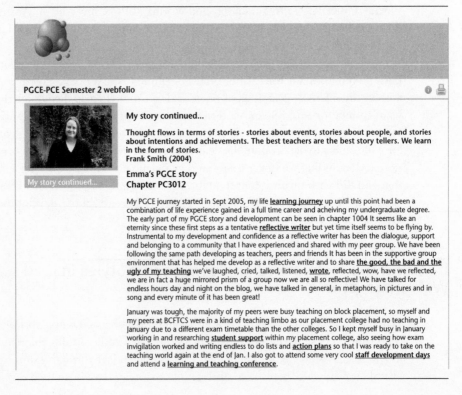

PGCE-PCE Semester 2 webfolio

My story continued...

Thought flows in terms of stories - stories about events, stories about people, and stories about intentions and achievements. The best teachers are the best story tellers. We learn in the form of stories.
Frank Smith (2004)

Emma's PGCE story
Chapter PC3012

My PGCE journey started in Sept 2005, my life **learning journey** up until this point had been a combination of life experience gained in a full time career and acheiving my undergraduate degree. The early part of my PGCE story and development can be seen in chapter 1004 It seems like an eternity since these first steps as a tentative **reflective writer** but yet time itself seems to be flying by. Instrumental to my development and confidence as a reflective writer has been the dialogue, support and belonging to a community that I have experienced and shared with my peer group. We have been following the same path developing as teachers, peers and friends It has been in the supportive group environment that has helped me develop as a reflective writer and to share **the good, the bad and the ugly of my teaching** we've laughed, cried, talked, listened, **wrote**, reflected, wow, have we reflected, we are in fact a huge mirrored prism of a group now we are all so reflective! We have talked for endless hours day and night on the blog, we have talked in general, in metaphors, in pictures and in song and every minute of it has been great!

January was tough, the majority of my peers were busy teaching on block placement, so myself and my peers at BCFTCS were in a kind of teaching limbo as our placement college had no teaching in January due to a different exam timetable than the other colleges. So I kept myself busy in January working in and researching **student support** within my placement college, also seeing how exam invigilation worked and writing endless to do lists and **action plans** so that I was ready to take on the teaching world again at the end of Jan. I also got to attend some very cool **staff development days** and attend a **learning and teaching conference.**

their experiences teaching in real classrooms for the first time, receiving support from one another and from their advisor. Her portfolio narrative demonstrates how the varied artifacts of her learning and performance fit together to demonstrate her understanding of what it means to be an excellent teacher. It chronicles the process by which she came to this understanding and communicates her commitment to the future practice of her profession according to values and principles she applies throughout her life. It interprets and synthesizes the digital documentation of her experience over time and projects forward into the future, connecting her professional identity to her personal history and her vision for her life as a whole.

Narrative is a particularly appropriate framing mechanism in Purnell's portfolio because her emerging understanding of professional practice embraces the metaphor of storytelling. Her portfolio opens with a quote from educational theorist Frank Smith (1990, p. 62): "Thought flows in terms of stories—stories about events, stories about people, and stories about intentions and achievements. The best teachers are the best storytellers. We learn in the form of stories." Becoming a reflective practitioner of education means telling stories about experiences in the classroom and examining them to develop and test ideas about how best to support students' learning. Perhaps more important, telling compelling stories to students and helping them interpret their own is a key idea that has resonated with her professional experiences so far.

During her and her peers' block placements (the rough equivalent to student teaching in U.S. teacher education), as they were trying to make sense of the challenges they were negotiating teaching students for the first time, their blogs were a key context for telling stories. Through telling "war stories" on their blogs and responding to those of other members of the cohort, Purnell and her colleagues shared their "thoughts, feelings, fears, [and] anxieties," working together through responding to the others' posts to make sense of them and figure out how to react. The group struggled in the blogs to apply what they had learned in their course work to the concrete challenges they were facing in the schools. They turned to this writing and responding when they could find time in the midst of their ongoing professional activity—perhaps late in the evening after assignments were graded and lessons were planned or in a few stolen minutes during lunch. The purpose was fairly immediate: to make sense of what happened today or this week to make it possible to face tomorrow or next week. Posts were generally brief and only occasionally related back to previous posts. The entries contained insights, but ones not yet tested across a range of experiences and contexts. The cohort's sense of what it means to be a successful teacher grew by accretion over the course of the year, typifying cumulative reflection. This collaborative process of making sense within the flow of professional practice is what Julie Hughes (2009), their professor, calls "everyday theorizing."

Purnell's blogging exemplifies the networked self. It differs in a number of ways from the process of developing a symphonic representation of self, as seen in both Samantha Slade's portfolio in Chapter Two and the narrative portfolio that she composed at the conclusion of her classroom placement. Both of these portfolios required stepping out of daily activities, making time for extended reflection and analysis in periods of transition. The Wolverhampton blog writing, in contrast, was embedded in the immediacy of everyday practice. It happened whenever a bit of downtime could be found between the day-to-day activities of teaching, learning, and family life that are the authors' primary focus during the period in which the blog is being written. The blog writing is more focused on the quick win—on insights and affirmations that can be captured and communicated in the time and with the energy that is available above and beyond what is required to discharge primary responsibilities. The value of the blog writing builds up over time. In the aggregate, it provides a rich record of the process of learning to teach. However, it does not provide in and of itself a sense of the whole—a coherent account of the relationship the author chooses to have to multiple ideas, experiences, beliefs, and relationships represented in the collection of blog posts.

While symphonic eportfolios require significant investments of time and effort to compose, the payoff is substantial: a sense of authorship of a life as a whole that can help the author negotiate a new chapter. Such symphonic articulation of self is very much needed for professional success and personal well-being in the increasingly boundaryless world in which we live for reasons that Miller's rhetorical analysis of blogs and Sennett's sociological examination of the transformed workplace make clear. However, the symphonic self also has limitations, and practices for articulating the networked self, such as Purnell's blog writing, can help remedy them. The networked and the symphonic styles need each other to support lifelong learning. The literary scholar Katherine Hayles (2007) suggests that database and narrative, the networked and symphonic, are less natural enemies, as Manovich proposes, than "natural symbionts. . . . organisms of different species that have a mutually beneficial relation" (p. 1603).

Purnell's experience reveals at least four advantages of the networked self, which is embedded in day-to-day life, develops social capital, builds cumulative value, surfaces dynamics of power, and helps move beyond received narrative models. First, whereas constructing the symphonic self requires an extended amount of time and energy, the networked style of self-representation can help individuals respond to the immediate challenges of their professional and personal lives with flexibility and agility. Through blog writing, Purnell and her colleagues were able to access immediate support, quickly apply theory to practice, and draw on their emerging experience to address novel challenges in the thick of the day.

The empirical analyses of blog writing habits surveyed earlier in this chapter, which point to short, frequent posts written quickly, suggest that this dynamic may be characteristic of the genre. Such rapid connection making is crucial in the rapidly changing environments in which adults live and work today.

Second, networked self-representation builds social capital. Through sharing their experiences and insights, the Wolverhampton blog writers built a community of practice around their teaching that they are likely to sustain beyond the academic program that convened it and benefits not just the writers themselves but also the students they teach, the schools in which they work, and, through linking their network with larger networks of educators, perhaps even the profession of teaching itself. The pattern of modulated interaction typical of blogs, splitting the difference between the immediacy and reciprocity of synchronous forms of computer-mediated communication and the complexity and control offered by conventional Web page authoring, provides a compelling model for developing online relationships that support practice. Research discussed earlier in this chapter shows that SNSs also have a role to play in building social capital, extending beyond groups that interact regularly, such as the Wolverhampton teachers, to broader networks of friends and acquaintances (Ellison et al., 2007). This research pointed to the special role these technologies may have to play for individuals who would otherwise be less likely to be able to develop social capital. This is probably also the case for the Wolverhampton students, many of whom are returning adults managing multiple commitments that would not otherwise allow much time for cultivating and maintaining a strong support network.

Third, through aggregation, networked self-representation builds a collection of evidence and reflections that is a powerful resource for examining an individual's identity. Over time, the networked constitutes what Yancey (1998) terms "cumulative reflection," a process of "developing a cumulative, multi-selved, multi-vocal identity" over time. In this multiplicity, the collection of networked self-representations captures the inherent messiness of learning and performance. Because human memory continuously reconstructs itself to accommodate new information, rewriting the old in light of the new, it can often be difficult to remember how little one may have known in the past, how earlier beliefs differ from those currently held, or how frustrated one was or how powerless one felt (Rosenfield, 1988). Reviewing the products of a regular networked reflective practice helps authors create more accurate accounts of their development over time.

By incorporating these in-the-moment networked reflections into an eportfolio, such an account resists the tendency to conceal the dynamics of institutional power in shaping individual action. In symphonic representations that seek to articulate self-authorship, critical reflection on institutional power may be cast off in favor of a narrative of agency that smoothes over conflicts, contradictions, dead-ends, and roadblocks (Hughes, 2009). Over the course of the term, Purnell reflects on experiences that are difficult to square with her rather progressive understanding of how she ought to teach and the role of education in her life. Through the comments of her peers and her instructor, she begins to question assumptions that might have been left unexamined.

For example, during her placement, Purnell shares her anxiety with her peers in her blog posts about being evaluated during observations of her teaching by her instructor. She finds that having an authority figure assessing her performance makes it difficult for her to teach as well as she normally does, an obstacle she resents. Her peers' comments help her realize that a source of both the anxiety and the resentment is her sense of absolute commitment to support her students' learning: "We do, as Liander [another new teacher] said feel responsible for them in so many ways and never want to let them down, you can't switch those sort of feelings off." Realizing that perfect teaching is not a reasonable standard to which to hold herself and that anxiety caused by the desire to do well is a necessary part of teaching helps her gain confidence and perform more strongly while being evaluated. The process of blogging about her experience in the classroom in conversation with others both helps her overcome her immediate obstacle and provides a spark of insight into her profession. In her eportfolio at the end of the term, Purnell returns to the challenge of being evaluated:

> One of the most challenging times in this semesters teaching was the ridiculous amount of observation nerves I had, I was feeling more confident in my teaching but as soon as I was observed I turned into a "high pitched, couldn't talk faster if I tried, nervous, emotional jelly." I am going into a profession filled with ongoing observation, if I didn't combat nerves now I could just see future [Office for Standards in Education] visits in my career actually causing me to pass out. Luckily as the observations went on I, with the encouragement and support of my peers managed to control my nerves (on the outside at least) it is one of my biggest achievements as I felt the teacher I was being every other every day was starting to show through on the scary observation days too.

Her eportfolio, on the whole, is a narrative of mastery, showing that she has achieved a high level of competence in teaching. However, having her blog entries, from which she quotes in this passage and links to throughout, to reflect on reminds her of the struggle of managing her emotions and expectations and the reality of hierarchical power relationships in her profession, aspects of her learning she might otherwise not have highlighted. While her symphonic narrative enables her to integrate these conflicts into her understanding of her identity and context, the networked database of blog posts makes them more readily accessible and more difficult to discount, leading to a more genuinely transformative narrative of professional development.

By layering the networked underneath the symphonic, as Purnell does through links between her central narrative and her many blog writings, both realities can be considered. The portfolio articulates Purnell's developing theory of storytelling as a key to knowledge and learning and the challenges of acting in accordance with the principles this view suggests in the face of the politics and policies of the school in which she taught. The messiness of the cumulative picture of her experiences that she develops in the blog helps her create a more robust and sophisticated narrative account that stresses the importance of adapting to contingency and context. This conceptual integration was supported by technical integration of the blogging and portfolio composition functions of PebblePad, the eportfolio system through which she blogged and authored her portfolio.

The eportfolio she composes presents a compelling vision of teacher as storyteller, establishing overarching principles for managing the competing demands she will encounter as she moves forward in her life and determining the role that her profession will play within it. At a moment of transition into a new profession in a changing workplace, her portfolio narrative articulates her symphonic self. This symphonic vision is more than mere aspiration, however, because it evolves out of and is built on her networked self as constructed through her blog writing. This writing was sustainable because it offers immediate value in dealing with day-to-day problems and was possible to undertake in the few spare moments within a busy schedule. This day-to-day value comes in large part through the community that she and other members of her cohort built through reading and commenting on each others' blogs. Through sharing their experiences, challenging each other, and offering advice, they developed a shared understanding of the practice of teaching and concern for one another's success. Over time, Purnell's collected blog writings give her a rich record of her experiences and reflections, connected to those of others undergoing similar challenges, to analyze and interpret. This collection is messy and mixed, capturing as often moments of chaos and confusion as those that went according to plan, making it impossible to impose a simple narrative of upward progress or complete mastery onto her experiences.

Through stepping out of the day-to-day world, investing the more intense time and effort required to reflect holistically on what she had experienced and created, she was able to move beyond reacting to daily challenges of decision making to establish and clarify the principles and sense of direction that she wishes to govern it. Her symphonic self-representation points the way forward, helping her identify which connections are most significant and productive.

The power and utility of her symphonic portfolio are enhanced through her connection with an audience.

Blogging and eportfolio composition in concert at Wolverhampton provides an early model for how to use social software and the eportfolio genre together to develop the networked and symphonic selves. Networked blog writing and SNS use fits into daily life, helping to capture and process ideas and experiences across apparent boundaries and in the face of immediate challenges through connecting with other authors and readers, offering validation, stimulating invention, lowering the cost of making and maintaining relationships, and providing an immediate sense of efficacy and control. Symphonic eportfolio composition, done iteratively through more intensive reflection at points of transition, helps authors find coherence and establish commitments that are informed by and have the potential to influence day-to-day decision making. By helping learners use both sets of resources, thereby cultivating both kinds of selves, we are likely to better prepare them for the challenges they will face throughout their adult lives.

Questions for Practice

Supporting the two styles of self-representation requires combining the new capabilities of social software with the traditional strengths of the eportfolio genre. Practitioners should consider both how to incorporate the social features that are proving powerful and how to keep them connected to eportfolios as compositions by asking questions such as these:

- What role does a desire for validation through being represented in digital media play in eportfolio authors' motivation? How might you help them receive that validation in a way that furthers their articulation of authenticity, integrity, and deliberation?
- In what ways can features of social software help eportfolio authors reflect on their experiences in dialogue with members of their communities of practice over time? How does it support cumulative reflection? How can it help them balance a desire to interact with others with a need for control over their self-representations?
- How might authors use social software features to create interfaces to their eportfolios that enable the eportfolios to be searched and scanned, reducing the transaction costs of making connections?
- How can you encourage connections between authors' symphonic eportfolios and their networked reflection using social software features in a way that helps them take a critical stance toward their learning and performance,

challenging standard narratives of success and questioning the dynamics of institutional power?

- How can you reframe the use of blogs and SNSs in the composition and use of eportfolios in light of the emerging conventions for their use found by researchers? How can you encourage them to use these tools for the symphonic style of self-representation, as well as for the networked?
- How can you help eportfolio authors think about social connections and the other-authored content that those connections introduce as part of the content of their eportfolio compositions? How can authors most effectively integrate their social networks into their eportfolios in order to contribute to the articulation of their identity and capabilities?

CHAPTER EIGHT

THE PORTFOLIO PROCESS AND THE PROCESSED PORTFOLIO

Future Directions for Eportfolio Technology

This final chapter considers the role that technology can play in supporting the composition and use of eportfolios. Such consideration is left for last because technology ought to support the practices of the eportfolio genre that have been the focus up to now rather than dictate the form of eportfolios or the processes they mediate. Nevertheless, the capabilities of emerging technologies that might be employed in eportfolio practice point to possible future directions for the genre and the learning and assessment it facilitates. Not only can technology contribute significantly to each stage of the composition and use of eportfolios, but it can also play a central role in the eportfolio as a composition, become part of its content, and shape the way readers use it to create meaning.

The chapter focuses primarily on future possibilities for technology rather than the capabilities of current mainstream eportfolio tools for two reasons. First, technologies used to support eportfolios are rapidly changing; a book that surveyed solely what is currently available would be out of date by the time it was printed. More significant, I agree with many other scholars who suggest that the current generation of eportfolio systems leaves enough to be desired that the idea of dedicated, stand-alone eportfolio systems comes into question. Rather than searching for a monolithic platform that supports all aspects of eportfolios, I argue that learners should use a collection of general-purpose and fit-to-task tools in concert to meet their distinctive needs.

Limitations of Current Systems and Proposed Alternatives

Over the past ten years, many eportfolio systems have been developed. Most are Web applications, written in Java or a Web scripting language, that users access through a browser and which store data in a database. The EPAC (2009) website's list of at least forty such applications does not even include many systems developed by individual higher education institutions or by software vendors outside of the United States. Many of the systems that it lists have faced considerable criticism for their perceived focus on the needs of institutions rather than individuals. Most constrain the ability of portfolio authors to control the visual design and organization of their portfolios, imposing an organization dictated by institutional, disciplinary, or professional standards. Some give institutions control of the content and form of the portfolio in ways that conflict with the traditional principles of eportfolio practice. Most fail to offer the flexibility and social reach of blogs, social network sites, and other Web 2.0 tools. These criticisms have merit. Many share an emphasis on making the eportfolio process person-centric rather than application-centric, focusing on the activity of composing and using eportfolios, supported by multiple technologies, rather than on what is possible within a single system.

However, the recommendations of many critics also have limitations. Some advocate for a return to static HTML eportfolios (Kimball, 2005; Rice, 2001). Others suggest that general-purpose Web 2.0 tools are sufficient (Barrett, 2008; Wilson, 2005). Still others suggest that the process of reflection associated with eportfolios should take precedence over any formal product that process produces, whether assessment data or an eportfolio itself, and that technology should focus primarily on supporting the process (Hartnell-Young et al., 2007). The first perspective neglects the capabilities of technology to support social interactions around eportfolios—capabilities to provide expanded means for deliberation and self-articulation. The second fails to take into account the differences between the conventions of social software genres and that of the eportfolio. The third discounts the impact the portfolio as a genre itself can have on learning and identity.

None of the perspectives fully takes into account that eportfolios may have computer, as well as human, audiences. Software, as well as people, can access and analyze the contents of eportfolios. In contrast to HTML portfolios, elements of eportfolios in Web 2.0 environments may be made available to other applications through syndication standards such as RSS and Atom and through application programming interfaces. However, such standards and interfaces generally work with atomized data divorced from the context of the eportfolios of which they play a part. They offer little capability to represent the structure of eportfolios as integral wholes in a way that computers can understand (Cambridge, 2006a). Similarly, process advocates do not see the value in such integrated self-representations.

These proposed alternatives also do not address one of the central problems of using eportfolios on a large scale: the scarcity of human attention. Addressing this issue requires moving beyond seeing technology as just a means for communication to seeing it as a tool for computational analysis. In an ideal world, in assessing the impact of an educational program or reviewing applicants for a job, each portfolio would be closely read by multiple evaluators, taking into account the complexity of its content and context in a manner similar to that used in the first three chapters of this book. In practice, this is not possible to do systematically for very large numbers of eportfolios, at least without a fundamental restructuring of the institutions in which they are used; the discussion of eportfolios beyond the academy and in assessment within it made this clear. What is needed is a way to use technology to more strategically direct attention in order to see patterns across many portfolios without isolating their contents from the context of the portfolios of which they are a part. Such use requires harnessing the computational power of information technology to quantitatively analyze the contents of eportfolios as part of the process of reading eportfolios rather than just as a way of making sense of the data that result from the reading.

Technology can and should support learning, the articulation of identity, and the assessment of performance. It can help connect portfolio authors with portfolio readers, individual and institutional. This book has argued that the eportfolio genre, through the cultural ideals of authenticity, integrity, and deliberation and the symphonic style of self-representation, has a distinctive role to play in these processes. In place of the dichotomy between process and product, it may be more productive to think about an eportfolio itself as a special kind of tool that mediates these processes. The educational theorist Lev Vygotsky argued that human activity is mediated by both technical tools, such as software, and psychological tools, such as the conventions of a genre (Wertsch, 1985). Because it can serve as a means for engaging with a range of technical tools for communication and analysis, as well as provide a set of conventions useful for documenting and making sense of experience and identity, eportfolios share characteristics of both types. The ways by which the processes of learning, identity articulation, and assessment can be carried out by both authors and readers are enabled and constrained by the functionality of the chosen technology and the conventions of the eportfolio genre.

An eportfolio is a text that mediates these activities and is meaningful only when considered within them. An emphasis on an eportfolio as an integral composition does not discount the importance of process. Rather, it points to the distinctive role that the mediation of the eportfolio genre, as enacted through technology, plays in making those processes effective. Considering eportfolios as both technical and psychological tools in the light of emerging technologies suggests new ways to think of conceptualizing what the eportfolio text is and what it does. Technology can both support the processes of composing and using eportfolios and become an essential component of the eportfolio composition itself.

A Model for Supporting Eportfolio Practice with Technology

Technology has a role for supporting each of the activities of eportfolio practice. Five types of activity are important to the process of composing and using an eportfolio. Because an eportfolio is composed of both evidence and reflective interpretation of that evidence, the first necessary step in composing an eportfolio is to capture and collect evidence. Second, this evidence, which may be distributed across a range of sites and formats, needs to be aggregated and managed. Once the evidence is captured and brought together so that it can be systematically examined, the third activity of sustained reflection on the evidence can begin. The evidence and the results of reflection on it can then serve as the basis for a fourth activity, the composition of an eportfolio that selects from and synthesizes these components to articulate authenticity and integrity symphonically. Part of the process of composition entails linking up these components with a network of other resources and other people, socially validating the eportfolio's message and making it available for deliberation. When connected to a network, the portfolio becomes available for a fifth process, that of analysis, by both human readers and computers. These five processes are not necessarily linear. For example, computational analysis of the evidence and reflections in an eportfolio may serve as a heuristic for reflection and synthesis, and the process of synthesis, itself a reflective act, may point to the need to capture additional evidence.

Capture

Capture is a distinct process from the selection of information that warrants reflections and might serve as evidence within an eportfolio. The purpose of the capture stage in the process is to fix and make available for examination as much potentially useful information as possible. During later stages in the process—management, reflection, composition, and analysis—portfolio authors determine what subset of this larger archive is relevant to the portfolio's purposes. It is rarely possible to know before the fact of the activities and artifacts to be captured what those purposes may end up being, let alone what specific pieces of evidence are going to be most useful to achieving them. In introducing students to portfolios, teachers often advise them to keep everything. Capture technology makes this possible on a larger scale.

As is the case with many other aspects of the eportfolio process, the challenge of capturing evidence of identity, learning, and performance is not specific to eportfolios, and many general-purpose tools prove useful. Most eportfolio systems allow the use of virtually any type of digital file, although few include functionality for creating new media other than text. In current practice, when multimedia evidence is included, capture already involves multiple distributed tools. Because the volume of material these distributed tools generate can be substantial, capture technology also needs to generate metadata that can help the eportfolio use the resulting records.

While many documents included in eportfolios are already digital, such as Word documents and PowerPoint presentations, and inexpensive scanners can digitize print documents, capture technologies are needed to document significant ephemeral activities, such as presentations, group interactions, performances, travel experiences, and fieldwork. Useful audio and video recording devices and software are increasingly easy to use and inexpensive. Web 2.0 applications allow recording, editing, and publishing of images, audio, and video using built-in or inexpensive hardware, such as webcams and USB headsets. The results can be shared through a vast array of sites, the most popular of which are YouTube, Flikr, MySpace, and Facebook.

The capacity to capture both multimedia and textual data is increasingly incorporated into mobile devices, such as mobile phones and personal digital assistants (PDAs). Many devices allow for upload to blogs and social network sites (SNSs), and some allow developers to write specialized applications for capturing and sharing more specialized data. For example, eportfolio projects in medical education in several countries use mobile technologies to record specialized textual information, such as clinical reports, as well as audio and video that document clinical practice. Technology connecting PDAs and smartphones to eportfolio software developed at the University of Newcastle and the University of Leeds has been used by medicine and dentistry faculty and students at several universities across England. Similar technology is being developed and tested through the University Hospital Fundación Santa Fe de Bogotá in Colombia and the University of Melbourne in Australia, where the technology is used in primary and secondary education (Cotterill, Jones, Walters, Horner, Moss, & McDonald, 2006;

Cotterill et al., 2007; Hartnell-Young & Vetere, 2007). At the University of British Columbia in Canada, PDAs are used to document nursing students' clinical experience in their eportfolios (Garrett & Jackson, 2008). Researchers at the University of Reading in the United Kingdom are developing technology that allows synchronization of offline and online data to enable its use where Internet access is not available (Johnson, 2006). Some capabilities for mobile upload are also being incorporated into commercially available eportfolio systems, such as PebblePad and Desire2Learn.

In addition to specialized textual data, some activities to be documented in an eportfolio may benefit from being represented through other media. For example, the Digital Interactive Video Exploration and Reflection (DIVER) project developed at the Stanford Center for Innovations in Learning seeks to record activity where multiple perspectives are important, such as teaching and learning (Pea, 2006; Pea et al., 2004). Using audio and video to document a classroom where students are engaged in group work is challenging. Conventional devices can capture only one perspective at a time, but it is often difficult or impossible to determine beforehand which perspective will capture the most significant activity at a given time. DIVER uses a panoramic camera and an array of microphones to record 360-degree video and audio that captures sounds throughout a space. After the fact, users of DIVER can create paths through the video and audio record that focus on the most significant aspects of the activity and can add time-coded annotations to explain the logic behind their choices and the significance of what is depicted, making DIVER a tool for reflection as well as capture. (See Figure 8.1.)

Activities in virtual environments can automatically produce records that may also prove useful in eportfolios. For example, in Taiwan researchers use the server logs produced when students use a Web-based learning management system to analyze the relationships of different components of the learning process (Liu, Chen, Wang, & Lu, 2002). The server logs record what actions are taken when and by whom in a format that is ideal for computational analysis. Portfolio authors, as well as instructors, could benefit from reflecting on patterns found in such records. Once a portfolio is composed and shared with others, such logs can also provide valuable information about audience behavior that might shape subsequent reflection and revision. Another type of automatically generated record is a record of changes to documents over time. Because eportfolios often are intended to make visible the process of creating something, as well as the final product, being able to point to successive versions can be very helpful in the processes of reflection and synthesis. Many applications, such as Microsoft Word, Google Docs, and most wikis, include such capabilities, which are crucial for explaining the evolution of collaboratively authored documents, providing a window into individual contributions and group dynamics.

FIGURE 8.1. A DIVER PATH

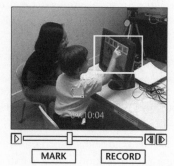

Welcome RM, Log-out

Dives | Movies | My Diver | Upload | Signup | Help | About

save as | paste | clipboard | remix

03:39:15 – 03:46:03   copy

 03:39:15 Good clip to illustrate the need for SLOW-MOTION controls: after observing her play by hitting the button, he is asked to start the video. It is barely perceptible since it happens so quickly that she reaches out to press the play button to illustrate, but before she reaches the screen, he has reached out before her to do it. This kind of observational learining and scaffolded near-completed action that a child then completes is often taken by parents as an indication of "understanding" (which she expresses too) when in fact it is highly scaffolded. But perhaps the next time the child will do it unassisted.

Posted Tue Oct 05 09:04:27 AM

▽ Add comment (3)

Posted Sun Oct 10 06:43:46 PM
This is definitely something to watch out for. It's really hard to tell sometimes if the child is really ascertaining the funtionality--especially when there is the tendency for them to just keep touching the screen to see what happens.

Posted Sun Oct 10 06:49:37 PM
Not sure I totally understand what you mean by 'slow motion controls.' Do you mean scaffold slower so that we can more easily detect understanding?

Posted Mon Oct 11 12:02:00 PM
I believe he's referring to literal slow-motion video controls. So we (the researchers analyzing the video) can easily slow down or speed up the action, so as to more precisely view the events taking place within the video document. This feature (the ability to elastically control the speed of playback) will add yet another dimension to DIVER guided noticing. We can already point in time, and in space, but now we'll also be able to emphasize a particular action by slowing down or speeding up the video. The goal is to "record" the analyst's speed control decisions, the same way we're recording their space/time choices.

Image courtesy of Stanford Center for Innovations in Learning.

Drawing on a number of technologies similar to those discussed so far in this section, several projects are attempting to capture a comprehensive record of an individual's life. The idea of what is now most commonly called lifelogging was introduced by the MIT Media Lab's Steven Mann, who continuously broadcast video of his life using a wearable webcam from 1994 to 1996 (Mann & Niedzviecki, 2001). The Microsoft Corporation's MyLifeBits project attempts to record "everything that [can] be captured" about engineer Gordon Bell's life into a database, including every document he creates or reads, audio recordings of his conversations, keystrokes and mouse clicks generated when he uses computers and other devices, recordings of TV programs he watches, and thousands of daily pictures taken by a specialized camera that are coded with GPS and environmental data (Gemmell, Bell, & Lueder, 2006). The project has produced both specialized hardware and software that are now being used by other researchers to investigate lifelogging.

The idea of digitally recording everything in one's life obviously raises a host of ethical and legal issues. Were such a practice to become common, new technical and legal means would be necessary to ensure that individuals retain control of their personal information and can reasonably respect the intellectual property rights of others (Cheng, Golubchik, & Kay, 2004). While authors have explored both utopian and dystopian visions of societies in which everything is recorded and available for analysis, capture of experience is likely to be a much more selective affair, at least for the foreseeable future (Gelernter, 1992; Orwell, 1983).

One context for capture possible through technology like MyLifeBits is intensive educational activities that are likely to become the focus of an eportfolio. A particularly generative example illustrates how technology can help eportfolio authors capture academic experience. At the University of North Carolina at Chapel Hill, researchers in the Memex Metadata for Student Portfolios project are investigating the use of MyLifeBits technology, along with tablet PCs, for documenting students' participation in field research activities in a biology course (Greenberg, 2006). The technology tracks students' use of documents in standard software packages, such as Microsoft Office, as well as what they experience through photos taken with a SenseCam that also captures GPS data and environmental data. The resulting record provides material on which students can reflect and incorporate as evidence in their eportfolios.

Key to making the resulting records usable and meaningful is the simultaneous capture of relevant metadata about the types of objects being used, their formats, and, most crucial, the contexts in which they are used. The researchers have developed what they term a context awareness framework with which to describe the activity being performed, with whom the students engage while performing it, and their cognitive state and personal behavioral characteristics at the time of performance (Crystal, 2006). The classification scheme for activities is designed to include information specific to an academic environment, such as the course and instructor for which the activity is being carried out.

While some metadata must be manually generated, as much as possible is derived, harvested, or automatically generated from what the hardware and software make available. Providing as much useful automated generation of metadata about context as possible is an objective of the MyLifeBits researchers as well. Because they envision documentation as a continuous process, they are wary of "asking the user to become a filing clerk—manually annotating every document, email, photo, or conversation" (Gemmell et al., 2006). Human annotation is more properly seen as a technique of reflection, of making sense of the records of activity, rather than capture.

A complete record of an individual's experience over, say, an eighty-three-year life span as envisioned by MyLifeBits would include over two hundred terabytes of data. Were the database to include a continuous video feed like the one Mann broadcast, the data would increase by several orders of magnitude. Although this is massive, the exponential decrease in the cost of storage makes such archiving practically conceivable. Because of this incredible volume, however, much of the MyLifeBits research has focused not on capture but on making it possible to manage and search the database. With the recent proliferation of capture technologies, a bigger challenge than recording one's activity may be deriving meaning from the resulting records. The first step toward this goal is personal information management.

Management

A collection of captured information is not yet an eportfolio. For information captured to be useful in an eportfolio, it has to be possible to locate items relevant to a particular task of reflection and synthesis. Because eportfolio authors have a limited amount of time and attention to devote to reviewing and reflecting, they need help to use them most effectively. Authors need to search through their personal information efficiently to find evidence on which to reflect and include in a lifelong learning eportfolio. Because the content that authors might wish to include is often collected over long periods of time and may be distributed across the Web, management tools need to ensure that information will be accessible as technology changes and regardless of where it is stored. Management technology also needs to help eportfolio authors connect their information to similarly distributed learning tools and services.

For text documents, full text search is a fairly mature technology. Many eportfolio systems, desktop operating systems, and general-purpose content management systems now include the ability to index and search documents in a wide variety of text-centered formats. Optical character recognition software, which has gone down in price and increased in accuracy in recent years, can be used to search text in many scanned documents as well.

Searching the content of images, audio, and video is more difficult. From a great deal of research under way in this area, however, results are already being incorporated into software targeted at the general public, such as facial recognition technology in Apple's iPhoto that allows users to search for photos of particular people. Lifelogging researchers have developed techniques for automatically segmenting streams of SenseCam photos by event through calculation of visual novelty, identifying landmark photos to represent each segment (Lee et al., 2008). Others have found ways to detect particularly significant portions of continuous audio recordings (Ellis & Lee, 2006).

In addition to searching the raw contents of items within a collection of eportfolio-related information, tools can also search and sort items based on metadata recorded about them. Many capture tools gather metadata about the context in which items are produced that could help an eportfolio author determine which items are appropriate for a given purpose. Some tools can also be used to annotate the contents of items more granularly, so that search tools can focus on specific sections or elements rather than entire documents. While annotation can later aid in the management of eportfolio collections, the process of annotating items is itself a type of reflection on them and is therefore examined in the next section.

Another issue in the management of collections of eportfolio-related information over extended periods of time, which is necessary for supporting genuinely lifelong learning, is the accessibility of the formats of digital documents over time. Most proprietary file formats popular twenty or thirty years ago, like Lotus 1-2-3 and WordStar, are not easily viewable using contemporary software. This same is likely to be true in the future. While many eportfolio systems, Web 2.0 tools, and general-purpose content management systems allow users to store virtually any kind of file, few offer the ability to convert those documents into formats that are more likely to be persistently usable. However, formats that have been formalized as international standards by such bodies at the International Organization for Standardization (ISO) and World Wide Web Consortium (W3C) and are popular enough that huge quantities of documents currently use them will likely be supported in the long term. For example, the PDF/A format is intended as an archival format for electronic documents. Based on the Adobe Portable Document Format (PDF), it was codified as an ISO standard in 2005. The standard also includes requirements for tools for viewing PDF/A files, ensuring that they are presented as originally intended. PDF/A is particularly appropriate for print-styled documents. While the standard included the ability to attach metadata, it does not allow for much of the internal structure of the document to be represented or annotated. In contrast, Extensible Markup Language (XML) makes it possible to represent both the structure and content of textual documents. Several formats, such as Open Document Format (ODF), which was approved as a standard by ISO/IEC in 2006, use XML to represent the structure of common types of documents, such as word processing documents, presentations, and spreadsheets. The widespread popularity of XHTML, another XML-based markup language codified as a W3C recommendation, for Web pages likely ensures its longevity, as does the popularity of common media formats such as JPEG and PNG for images, WAV and MP3 for audio, and MPEG-4 for video.

In addition, ensuring the ongoing accessibility of content, eportfolio authors also must cope with its distributed nature. The runaway popularity of Web 2.0 software and services has complicated the management of personal information. Rather than being stored on a personal computer or a single online system, many data and documents available for eportfolio use may already be stored and shared with others on a range of systems throughout the Web. For example, pictures might be stored on

Flikr or Picasa, video published on YouTube or Vimeo, presentations made viewable online using SlideShare, reflections on experiences made in a WordPress blog, and goals tracked using 43 Things. In addition, data and documents shared by other users of these systems, as well as their comments, may prove useful. Other data may be stored within institutional systems, such as learning management systems or talent management systems. It is inconvenient and inefficient for authors to copy all of these assets into a separate repository for the purpose of using them in an eportfolio. While it may be possible to link to or embed some items, this often requires making them publicly viewable, giving up the control over who gets to see them under what circumstances, which many Web 2.0 services offer. Individuals need a way to manage and repurpose the full range of information they have created and is available to them throughout the online "cloud."

A possible solution to the problem of distributed data and services is exemplified in Monica Lam's PrPl (PRivate-PubLic) project, which is part of the larger Programmable Open Mobile Internet 2020 project at Stanford University and might serve a key role in connecting multiple applications and data sources for use in the composition, publication, and analysis of eportfolios. PrPl centers on a "personal cloud butler," which manages the interaction between applications with which the user interacts directly and a variety of services and data sources distributed across the Web (Seong et al., 2009). Users register services with the butler, and it makes available to the data and documents the services control available to other applications and services according to finely grained access rules. Users can see what data are accessible to them and determine who can see them and use them, and under what circumstances. The butler maintains a semantic index of all the available data and metadata in Resource Description Format (RDF) and provides a semantic search function that retrieves results from across all of the registered services. The RDF format allows the representation of, and search across, complicated relationships among items, an important capability for applications to take advantage of the reflection and synthesis that are at the heart of eportfolios. The system also offers several types of user interface elements that applications that use data and services brokered by the butler can employ to present and allow readers to interact with them, such as a map, time line, and radial graph. As suggested in the section below focused on composition and analysis, an eportfolio itself can be thought of as an interface that conveys a message, so such user interface elements could serve as useful building blocks.

While PrPl is not specific to education, the PLEX personal learning tool developed at the University of Bolton in the United Kingdom operates on a similar principle (Liber, 2005). It provides a common interface to learning-related services and data distributed across multiple, distributed Web services, both general-purpose Web 2.0 tools, such as blogs and photo sharing sites, and enterprise institutional systems, such as course management systems like Moodle and Blackboard. The TENCompetence project's Personal Competence Manager also helps individuals choose from multiple learning services and manage data about their learning through creating profiles. These profiles represent the individual's competence in relationship to various contexts of learning that draw in distributed competency data and can be used to interact with both formal and informal learning resources (Berlanga, Sloep, Brouns, Bitter, & Koper, 2008; TENCompetence Foundation, 2008).

Both the PLEX and the Personal Competence Manager are examples of an effort to create software that helps individuals manage a personal learning environment. A recently introduced concept in learning technology, a personal learning environment (PLE) is the collection of tools that individual learners use to support their own learning (Attwell, 2006). Rather than trying to build a single tool to meet all the needs of learners, educational technologists interested in supporting lifelong and informal learning are increasingly working to make it easier for learners to use a wide range of existing general-purpose and fit-to-task tools together. This is the approach advanced in this chapter. The tools that support eportfolio practice can be seen as a subset of the technology that supports learning more generally. Determining what technology is useful for eportfolio composition and use means finding within the wide range of tools those that are relevant to the multiple dimensions of eportfolio practice: capture, management, reflection, synthesis, and analysis.

As supporting technological environments for eportfolio practice can be seen as a subset of support the cultivation of personal learning environments, so can managing eportfolio evidence and reflections be seen as a subset of personal information management (Beagrie, 2005; Jones, 2004). The content management challenges outlined in this section are certainly not specific to eportfolios, and many are addressed by general-purpose content management systems. However, it would be wrong to conclude that such general-purpose systems are sufficient to support the full eportfolio process and the eportfolio genre. Technology also can contribute to reflection, synthesis, and analysis, which are largely beyond the scope of management-focused applications but essential to optimal eportfolio practice.

Reflection

At the heart of the process of composing an eportfolio is reflection on evidence. Eportfolio authors need to move beyond simply aggregating and sorting evidence to reflect on what each piece means and how it relates to other items, the eportfolio as whole, and the author's identity and the institutional contexts in which he or she lives, works, and learns. Technology can support reflection in three ways: (1) enabling multimedia and hypertextual reflection, (2) scaffolding learning processes, and (3) facilitating interaction with audiences.

Previous chapters have demonstrated the importance of media other than linear text to the impact of eportfolios on learning and identity. The photos and videos in Samantha Slade's eportfolio in Chapter Two helped her make connections between her professional identity and her other roles in life. Sean Moore in Chapter One used the design of the interface of his eportfolio to visually reflect on his understanding of spiritual communities. The importance of visual design of the interface in reflecting on and articulating identity and capabilities is confirmed by the research on retention and student engagement at LaGuardia Community College and on motivation in eFolio Minnesota discussed in Chapter Six, as well as by the research on professional identity at Virginia Tech discussed in Chapter Four. Also examined in that chapter, research at Clemson shows how the sophistication of the way in which the different components of the portfolio are linked together mirrors the author's level of understanding of and engagement with his or her future profession. Because even static HTML websites can be used for linking to or embedding images and audio and video files and because they offer authors a great deal of control and flexibility in visual design and navigation, technology has supported multimedia and hypertextual reflection since early in the evolution of eportfolios (Rice, 2001).

More recently, interactive Web technologies have expanded on this base in five ways: enabling multimedia and hypertexual evidence and reflection, supporting annotation, enhancing visualization, scaffolding the learning process, and scaffolding deliberation. In addition, technically different approaches can be taken, for example, distributed scaffolding.

Enabling Multimedia and Hypertextual Evidence and Reflection First, as discussed in Chapter Six, interactive technologies make it possible for authors who have not yet developed significant Web development, graphic design, or visual and audio editing skills to incorporate multimedia evidence and reflect through the visual and hypertextual design process. While this ease of use makes such reflecting possible for a larger group of learners, it also can reduce expressive range. Authors do not have the level of control over how the eportfolio looks and the arrangement and presentation of its materials as they would with general-purpose Web design and media editing tools. While more research is needed to determine how much authorial control individuals need for the design experience to have an optimal impact on their learning and identity, the eFolio Minnesota research detailed in Chapter Six suggests that authors perceive even a relatively small degree of choice as meaningful for articulating the authenticity and integrity of their identities. Like other tools in a personal learning environment, those most appropriate for multimedia and hypertextual reflection are likely to vary from individual to individual. Those with little design expertise or technical prowess may benefit most from tools that are easy to use but limit choice, while those with more advanced skills may need more expressive technologies. LaGuardia Community College embraces this approach in support of their students' development of media rich eportfolios, helping beginning, intermediate, and advanced designers use sets of tools best suited to their needs (Clark & Eynon, 2009).

Supporting Annotation The second way that more recent Web technology is supporting multimedia and hypertextual reflection is through annotation. Reflection in eportfolios is different from other types of reflection supported by technology because it is reflection on evidence, as discussed in Chapter Five; therefore, having new ways to connect reflective commentary to the features of that evidence could prove powerful. The tagging and classification made possible by some capture and management technologies, the simplest form of annotation, is being used on a large scale in university settings. At Penn State University, students collect evidence and reflect on it using a customized version of the Movable Type blogging platform. Through tagging material using both institutional learning outcomes such as group facilitation and their own keywords, students reflect on the significance of their materials as they collect them (Johnson, 2009; Penn State University, 2009). Similarly, the Goal Aware Tools technology developed by Syracuse University for use within Sakai and with the Open Source Portfolio tools allows students to similarly make connections to a shared framework for examining learning (Cambridge, Fernandez, Kahn, Kirkpatrick, & Smith, 2008).

Annotations are more powerful when they can be made in relationship to specific contents of the documents serving as evidence. The DIVER system introduced earlier in this chapter includes such a capability. By creating a path through the audio and video evidence, DIVER authors can direct the viewer's attention to what they believe is most significant. Along the way, they can record notes linked to specific places in the path, explaining the logic behind the choice of focus and reflecting on the meaning of what the audio and video record captures. The Project Pad software developed at Northwestern University offers a similar capability to add time-coded annotations to audio and video files, as well as to textual transcripts that are synched with them (Smith, 2005). In addition, Project Pad allows the annotation of images. Authors can zoom in to the desired level of detail, making it possible to precisely specify minute details of complex images. The process of annotation in Project Pad can be collaborative. Because multiple authors can annotate a single media file, the process of reflection can become a conversation. A career counselor, for example, might use such a tool to offer feedback on a video of a group of eportfolio authors giving a presentation, and each of those authors could make his or her own reflective annotations on his or her contributions to and experience of the presentation, yielding a richly dialogical account. VoiceThread, a commercial Web application, offers some analogous, albeit less sophisticated, collaborative annotation capabilities.

Annotation of specific sections of a document is also possible with print. Common tools such as Microsoft Word and Adobe Acrobat allow comments linked to particular passages and locations on the page. The limitation of these capabilities is that they require readers to open the documents in the original applications in order to see the annotations. More promising are tools that can be used for creating and viewing annotations with a Web interface or producing annotation in an open format easily viewable and analyzable using a wide range of technologies. Among many tools for annotating Web pages that have been developed over the past ten years, a simple but capable one is Commentpress, an extension to the WordPress blogging platform developed by the Institute for the Future of the Book so that multiple readers can comment on specific pages and paragraphs of an extended text rather than simply on a single post (Institute for the Future of the Book, 2008). At the University of Michigan, the master's in social work program has used XML features in recent versions of Microsoft Word to ask students to indicate which paragraphs or sections of their written work demonstrate their proficiency in one or more of the program's learning outcomes (Fitch, Gibbs, Peet, Reed, & Tolman, 2007). The machine-readable XML data can then be extracted from the human-readable Word document for analysis. Rather than introducing a wholly new technology to learners, the researchers at Michigan built on tools that learners already were using to help them examine their learning and make the results of that self-assessment available for use in other tools. This approach too holds promise.

Enhancing Visualization   The digital medium can also support reflection through visualization. Visualization is particularly powerful as a tool for synthesis—for integrating multiple items of evidence and multiple reflections, articulating the relationships between them visually in order to produce a symphonic representation, a key component of eportfolio composition. Concept mapping tools, in particular, are being used successfully to support eportfolio development. At George Mason University, for example, students in some classes create concept map eportfolios that show the relationships of course concepts, general education learning outcomes, and examples of students' work. Students then annotate the arrows on the map that indicate the connections of the concepts, outcomes, and works, explaining their significance to the author's learning. These annotations are viewable when a reader rolls over the arrow (See Figure 8.2.)

FIGURE 8.2. A CONCEPT MAP EPORTFOLIO FROM GEORGE MASON UNIVERSITY

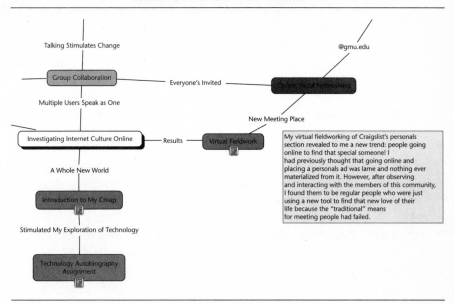

Cerpus, a Norwegian company, has developed BrainBank Learning, a concept-mapping tool designed to help school-aged students create eportfolios (Lavik & Nordeng, 2004; Nordeng, Dicheva, Garchol, Ronningsbakk, & Meloy, 2005). As at George Mason, teachers using BrainBank focus on helping eportfolio authors articulate the relationships between the parts and the whole of the eportfolio in order to help readers know where they are in the "world" of the student's learning as they examine a particular item. The developers of BrainBank Learning call this capacity "polyscopic structuring of information" (Nordeng, Guescini, & Karabeg, 2006). Beyond offering a visual representation of the relationships among items for readers, BrainBank Learning also represents the relationships as a Topic Map, using the Semantic Web language of the same name. The Confolio system, developed at the Royal Institute of Technology in Sweden, enables authors to create concept map eportfolios using a unified language modeling technique, which allows a structured representation of context (Naeve, Nilsson, Palmér, & Paulson, 2005; Naeve, 2005). As in Brainbank, the visual relationships among items are represented in a Semantic Web format—in this case, using RDF. The semantic representation of eportfolio maps in both systems enables computers to analyze the relationships among items and the overall structure of an eportfolio or set of eportfolios. This capability could prove of great importance, as explored in the section on composition and analysis later in this chapter.

The Visual Understanding Environment (VUE), another concept mapping tool, this one developed at Tufts University with support from the Mellon Foundation, can also work with information in Semantic Web formats—in this case, RDF and OWL (Tufts Academic Technology Services, 2008). Connectivity matrices can be exported for statistical analysis of the structure of a map. In addition, VUE can automatically generate maps that visualize the relationships within semantic data imported in a range of formats. A visualization in the form of a concept map also could be used as a heuristic to help learners generate reflections. For example, a visual representation of the links in a collection of eportfolio-related information or the connections among one's friends on a social network site might clarify the ways that positions within social contexts and networks affect learning. VUE adds to its semantic functionality the native ability to connect concepts within a map to online repositories and the ability to specify multiple pathways that guide viewers through sequences of nodes.

Scaffolding the Learning Process In addition to enabling multimedia and hypertextual reflection, technology can support the process of reflection and synthesis through scaffolding reflective learning. Scaffolding involves providing an appropriate amount of structure to help a learner think as experts do. Chapter Six explained how research at Kapi'olani Community College, George Mason University, and IUPUI showed that the Open Source Portfolio Matrix helped students reflect on their work and experiences in relationship to multiple dimensions of a shared conceptual framework—a kind of advanced reflection termed *matrix thinking*. The matrix tool offers an organizing framework for students' evidence and reflection, providing prompts for reflection at each intersection between two dimensions. For example, IUPUI's English capstone matrix asks students to select and reflect on work related to the intersection of IUPUI's principles of undergraduate learning and three contexts for learning, while Kapi'olani's matrix invites students to think through the intersection of six native Hawaiian values and the stages of the journey of an outrigger canoe, a culture metaphor for development over time (Cambridge et al., 2008). The matrix tool also scaffolds the process of sharing evidence and reflection with an audience and receiving a response. The tool notifies readers of completed cells so that they can provide feedback and assess the development of evidence and reflection, prompting authors to revise if necessary.

The remainder of this section introduces additional technological means for scaffolding: ePEARL, the Learning Record Online, Web Services for Reflective Learning, Careers Wales Online, CopperCore, LAMS, and VIP. Each example illustrates an emerging way in which technology can guide eportfolio authors reflecting on their learning and performance in dialogue with others.

Perhaps the most fully realized example of eportfolio software that scaffolds the process of learning at a granular level is the ePEARL (Portfolio Électronique Réflexif pour L'apprentissage des Éléves, which translates as reflexive electronic portfolio for student learning) project at Concordia University in Montreal, Canada. ePEARL is software designed to promote self-regulated learning. It is used by primary and secondary students in schools throughout Quebec, as well as elsewhere in Canada. Research on its use in French immersion schools for grades 5 and 6 shows that it contributes to gains in self-regulated learning attitudes and behaviors (Abrami et al., 2007).

The design of ePEARL is grounded in research on self-regulated learning, which has three phases: forethought, which includes goal setting and self-efficacy; performance, which includes self-recording; and self-reflection, which includes self-judgment and self-reaction. Features of the software support each of these phases. Goal-setting tools ask students to define general goals for their learning, goals specific to particular tasks, and strategies they plan to use to achieve them. For each task, they indicate how well they think they will do it, how hard it will be, and how much they want to do it, helping them gauge and track their level of self-efficacy. (See Figure 8.3.) When recording the completion of a learning activity, in addition to uploading files of various types, students can create audio recordings of their immediate reflections. As they reflect orally and in writing, the system reminds them of their goals, intended strategies, and feelings about the task before it began. Once students have reflected, they can receive feedback from teachers, peers, and parents. Selecting evidence and reflections for their eportfolios that ePEARL has helped them generate also helps them to consider

FIGURE 8.3. EPEARL MOTIVATION SCAFFOLDING

Motivation

Image courtesy of the Centre for the Study of Learning and Performance.

the reasoning behind their choices. ePEARL guides young students through a process of self-regulation that experts in a domain engage in, explicitly or implicitly, without the need for such structure. As students gain experience and confidence in higher grades, another version of the software offers them more flexibility and less scaffolding.

Appropriate to students in higher education, the Learning Record Online (LRO), a course-based Web application for reflective assessment, provides less structure than ePEARL at the level of individual activity while still guiding students through a structured process of documenting and self-assessing their learning (Martin, 2002). Developed at the University of Texas at Austin, the LRO has been used by dozens of universities in at least ten U.S. states. Over the course of the semester, students upload samples of their work, formal and informal, and write short accounts of critical incidents or insights in their learning that pertain to the course learning outcomes and their general development in five dimensions of learning: confidence and independence, skills and strategies, knowledge and understanding, use of prior and emerging experience, and reflection (Syverson, 2000). At the middle of the term, students analyze the collected evidence and reflections in terms of the course goals and the five dimensions of learning and then make a grade recommendation by applying a set of grading criteria set by the instructor to their interpretation. The Learning Record then goes through a process of moderation in which two or more other students and the instructor individually read it and recommend a grade based on the strength of the record. This moderation process it itself a dialogical form of reflection. During the second half of the semester, students continue to gather evidence and self-observation and again interpret the collection and suggest a grade at the end, which, most of the time, the instructor is able to confirm due to the midterm calibration.

The LRO guides students through an iterative process of networked and symphonic reflection on their course-related learning. The practice of making self-observations over time generates new connections between concepts and experiences that accumulate over the course of the semester. The interpretation of observations and samples of work and the middle and end synthesize this evidence to present an integrated representation of learning. The LRO Web application builds on the Online Learning Record, which embraced the same process but asked students to publish their learning records as static Web pages. Because the software handled the logistics of moderations and helped students more easily record observations and samples of work consistently, the Web application provided the opportunity to offer targeted feedback earlier in the semester. Because reflecting well is a learned skill many students have not developed prior to the course, instructors who see self-observations early in the semester can offer more timely suggestions on writing effective reflections, leading to stronger learning records at the midterm and end of course.

Beyond a single application, scaffolding can be offered as a Web service within a range of systems. For example, Web Services for Reflective Learning (WS4RL) guides individuals through structured processes of setting goals, reflecting on their learning, and documenting their competencies (Marshall, Grant, & Strivens, 2005). These services can be accessed within an eportfolio system, within a course management system, or from a personal learning environment management system such as PLEX or the OutilVIF system discussed later in this section.

Beyond the academy, projects are also using technology to scaffold the process of documenting and reflecting on learning and professional capability. For example, Career Wales Online, available to all citizens of Wales, offers guided processes for exploring learning opportunities, documenting educational progress, and building a curriculum vitae, as well as games that help individuals reflect on career goals and work experience and prepare for college and job interviews. Recently eFolio Minnesota has added interviews and "toolkits" that guide authors through a set of questions as a starting point for composing eportfolios (Olsen, Schroeder, & Wasko, 2009).

Learning design standards and tools are being developed to generalize such processes of providing sequenced guidance for learning. Because learning is likely to involve both documents and other people, learning design needs to describe interactions between people and both software and each other. The focus therefore should be on activity rather than content. The IMS Learning Design Specification, which builds on the Educational Modeling Language developed at the Open University of the Netherlands, provides such a grammar (Koper, Olivier, Anderson, Barritt, & Campbell, 2003; Koper & Tattersall, 2005). The CopperCore run-time engine makes it possible to support IMS Learning Design in a variety of applications, including learning management systems and eportfolio systems.

While not compliant with IMS Learning Design in a technical sense, the Learning Activity Management System (LAMS), developed at Macquarie University in Australia, embraces a similar approach to supporting learning activities, allowing educators to specify sequences of interactions between people in different roles and a set of tools that guide a learning experience (Dalziel, 2004). For example, students preparing to reflect on their critical thinking ability might be guided through a series of tasks: reading an article on the topic using a resources tool, writing about it individually in response to a set of prompts, discussing the article and their responses with a preselected group of other students using a chat tool, and uploading and submitting for review by their instructor selected documents they created that illustrate their development as critical thinkers. Finally, after they receive feedback from the instructor, they use another tool to write a reflective interpretation of their evidence. In a face-to-face classroom, such sequencing is often performed by the instructor. LAMS allows the technology to play this mediating role.

Systems like LAMS and CopperCore make it easier to provide this structure online and possible to share such learning designs with others. Their limitations, and those of other current implementations of learning design, are that they are application-centric rather than person-centric. Unlike with a personal learning environment, all of the tools and people who together will play a part in a learning activity have to be part of the same system. This cuts against the grain of the movement toward supporting learning with more widely distributed tools and through multiple social networks, a topic that will be taken up in the section after next and for the remainder of the chapter.

Scaffolding Deliberation   As technology can be used to scaffold the process of composing and responding to an eportfolio, so it can also be used to aid groups of readers in deliberating about its quality and about institutional decisions informed by its content. Technology has been developed specifically to advance online deliberative democracy, while other systems are designed to provide support for collaborative argument and decision making in a wider range of contexts.

Online deliberation technology is still in the early stages of its development (Davies, 2009). It has generally been targeted at increasing civic participation over the Internet in the public sphere, where it has met with only limited success. Most online deliberation tools encourage rule-based discussion in line with the principles of deliberative democracy theory, but these restrictions raise the barrier to entry, working against the goal of inclusivity and widespread participation (Lim & Kahn, 2008). Within institutions, however, where discussion and decision making tend to be more formalized, these tools may prove more productive.

Most online deliberation tools seek to scaffold the process and norms of discussion to ensure that participants are informed and all voices are heard and given appropriate weight in the decision-making process. For example, UnChat, developed in collaboration with participatory democracy scholar Benjamin Barber, distributes the role of moderator among all participants, who take turns enforcing the norms of discussion (Bodies Electric LLC, 2002). E-Liberate, developed at Evergreen State University under the direction of community networking pioneer Doug Shuler, automates Robert's Rules of Order (Shuler, 2009). Perhaps the most successful example of this category is the software developed to bring online the deliberative polling process developed by James Fishkin at the University of Texas at Austin. This process guides participants through multiple rounds of information sharing, discussion, and polling to yield a measure of informed group opinion (Fishkin, 2009).

Collaborative argumentation and decision support systems focus on another principle of deliberative democracy: reasonableness. They help discussants visualize arguments as they unfold, recording the process, analyzing quality, and recommending solutions (Kirschner, Buckinham Shum, & Carr, 2003). For example, QuestMap is an "issue based information system" that allows participants to capture the structure and dynamics of an argument as it occurs, producing a visual representation similar to the concept maps discussed in an earlier section, using a visual grammar that identifies problems, claims, warrants, backing, and data and the relationships among all of these elements (Conklin, 1997; Carr, 2001). HERMES, a system developed in Greece and Hong Kong, computationally tracks reasoning in online discussion with the goal of moving the group toward consensus (Karacapilidis & Papadias, 2001). Using algorithms derived from a range of information and decision science theories, HERMES tracks positions, constraints, issues, and alternatives as it looks for connections and inconsistencies in order to recommend the conclusions that are best supported at any given point in a deliberation.

While online deliberation and collaborative argumentation support systems have the potential to enhance group decision making about and informed by eportfolios, they share the same limitation of the other scaffolding mechanisms examined so far: all of the activity has to occur within a single system rather than through the multiple, distributed tools and services that are increasingly involved in online learning and conversation.

Distributed Scaffolding The VIF eportfolio project takes a different approach from the systems and standards for scaffolding the learning process and deliberation so far. The project focuses on supporting the successful and harmonious integration of new immigrants into the society of the Quebec region (Slade, 2008b). (The letters VIF in the project's title stand for Valorisation Intégration Francisation, which translates roughly to Enrichment, Integration, and Francization—the process of developing an identity grounded in French language and culture.) A collaboration of several provincial government agencies and Percolab, an educational services company based in Montreal, the project recognizes that there are already rich and diverse resources and services available to immigrants. These resources can help immigrants with the basics of integration, such as developing and documenting language proficiency and vocational competences; support workplace integration through searching for jobs or learning about workplace culture; and help ease transition into daily life in Quebecois society through learning about health services, leisure activities, and paths toward citizenship. Many of these resources provide structured guidance that scaffolds for immigrants the complex processes of learning the language, culture, and policies of their new home, and participating in these activities often leads to powerful articulations of their changing identities as new members of the community. However, these activities are often difficult to access because they are widely distributed, poorly publicized, and fragmented. The project is cataloguing the services already available online and bringing online those that are not yet available digitally.

Even more significant, the project is creating a modular, widget-based environment within which immigrants can link interfaces to the services themselves and representations of results of their use. Widgets are small, downloadable applications that can run within a Web browser that supports open Web standards and can be embedded within Web pages and other Web applications (Caceres, 2009). The services offered to immigrants are packaged as widgets and made accessible through a customized version of an open source portal system, Portaneo. (See Figure 8.4.) Through the portal, immigrants can add services useful to them and delete ones that are not, controlling on which pages of their eportfolio they

FIGURE 8.4. OUTILVIF EPORTFOLIO FOR IMMIGRANTS

Image courtesy of Percolab.

appear, where they are placed on the screen, how much space they are allotted, and what they are called.

While some widgets primarily help the eportfolio authors access information and reflect on their skills and goals, many also produce representations of authors' knowledge, skills, and priorities and could make possible for audiences, as well as authors, richer interaction than would be possible in a static Web page. The portal thus serves two purposes. First, it allows eportfolio authors to compose an interface that connects them to multiple and distributed services and social networks useful in documenting and reflecting on their learning and identities. In this way, it is similar to the tools for managing personal learning environments discussed earlier in this chapter. Second, it allows authors to compose an interface for their audiences. Not simply a container for services, this interface is a way to meaningfully arrange them and use them to communicate meaning. The services can work together with text and other media included within an eportfolio to invite readers to interact with the author's self-representation in ways not possible through a static Web page.

This kind of composition is similar to that observed by Perkle (2006) in his research on MySpace discussed in Chapter Seven. Just as the teenagers Perkle studied used snippets of code hosted elsewhere to embed media and interactive functionality into their profiles, so eportfolio authors using systems like those in the OutilVIF eportfolio project can incorporate widgets into their eportfolios to embed personal information and enable their audiences to interact with it in new ways. For example, a widget might include a list of people with expertise in a particular area who agree through the service to be listed, as they might agree to be listed as friends in a social network site, offering a kind of social validation of the author's claims about his or her capabilities. Alternatively, a service might translate an eportfolio author's narrative self-assessment of language ability in a standardized format readable by computers, such as that defined for the European Language Passport, or it might assert of a professional certification by a university of professional association so that a reader could have increased confidence in its validity. Because these widgets rely on content or functionality distributed across the network, as the MySpace profiles do, the OutilVIF eportfolios are materially connected to the network. Their meaning depends on their participation in the network of content and services.

My own website illustrates this pattern of material participation. Into the interface of my website page that lists presentations at conferences, I have incorporated code that enables readers to interact with slides from the presentation posted on SlideShare, a Web 2.0 tool. While simply posting the PowerPoint files for my presentations on my own site would have been easier, using SlideShare gives my readers additional options. They can view the slides directly in their Web browsers rather than having to download them and open them in PowerPoint. They can post comments on them; see related presentations that other SlideShare users and I have posted; see how many people have read them; easily post a reference to them through other services such as Twitter, Del.icio.us, or Facebook; and, in some cases, listen to audio recordings of me speaking that are synched with the slides.

While these capabilities help make the documentation of my professional life more compelling and communicative for my audience, it would be difficult and time-consuming for me to replicate this functionality on my own site, and there is likely no single online tool that offers such extensive services for all the types of professional information I might wish to include. It would not be sufficient, however, to use SlideShare in place of the presentation page on my site because I wish to create an interface to the presentations that allows them to be sorted and filtered in a wide range of ways and to visualize the presentations on a map, capabilities SlideShare does not offer. To integrate these additional features, I incorporate code that draws on an additional service: the remotely hosted Semantic Interoperability of Metadata and Information in unLike Environments (SIMILE) Exhibit library developed at MIT, which pulls data about my presentations from a Google Docs spreadsheet. Using SlideShare and SIMILE helps me communicate some of what I want to say about myself. I believe it is important to make my work public in a variety of formats and easily searchable so that it reaches a wide audience, and I believe that its situation within social networks in which it is shared and discussed helps to demonstrate and multiply its value. My site would lose meaning if it were divorced from the network.

Composition and Analysis: Facilitating Interactions with Audiences Through Expressive Interfaces

Along with capture, management, and reflection, composition and analysis are essential eportfolio processes. The example of my website illustrates two features of synthesis and analysis. First, tools for management and reflection can often also be used for composition and analysis. Because some kinds of reflection in eportfolios are integrative through articulating how connections among elements add up to a whole in order to communicate with an audience, some reflection *is* composition. Visualization, in particular, can powerfully represent identity, development, and achievement holistically. Providing my readers with the ability to see my presentations on a world map conveys the global scope of my work. Similarly, management tools that allow portfolio information to be searched and indexed can be incorporated into the interface of an eportfolio to influence how the audience analyzes it. By establishing a set of categories on which readers of my website can filter presentations, I suggest which aspects of those presentations are most worthy of attention. The tools an author offers to readers through the eportfolio's interface are parts of the eportfolio's message, not just a way to make use of it. Choosing and integrating the tools is therefore an act of composition.

Second, in addition to the tools themselves, the results of using these tools may become part of the eportfolio's message. Tools for interaction, such as those that scaffold reflection and deliberation discussed earlier, allow authors to make their readers' activity part of the text of the eportfolio through linking the portfolio into online social networks. In the simplest instance, the comments readers leave about my presentations in SlideShare become part of what my website communicates. Connecting my website to the network I have established through the social media functionality of SlideShare is a form of synthesis. The comments of the members of that network, which may constitute analysis of my work, both add meaning and validate that integration. Composition and analysis become complexly intertwined and fundamentally collaborative processes.

The ability of technology to connect authors and audiences using online social networks has been a recurring theme throughout this chapter and was treated at greater length earlier in the book. Collaborative annotation tools, for example, allow structured conversations grounded in close attention to eportfolio evidence, and the tools for guiding reflective processes manage the interactions between authors and their audiences. Chapter Seven examines the potential of using features of blogs and SNS to support eportfolio composition and use in dialogue with other learners and teachers, facilitating an ongoing process of networked reflection that informs periodic symphonic synthesis. Chapters Four and Six demonstrate the importance of supporting standardized representations of eportfolio information that link back to personalized ones so that institutional readers can select eportfolios that warrant the investment of time to read in their fuller, more complex form.

Earlier chapters also show the importance of visual and hypertextual design in articulating authenticity and integrity. Through choices about the look and feel, arrangement of information on the screen, and paths for navigating through the eportfolio, authors create an expressive interface to selected evidence and reflections collected over time. The emerging technologies for supporting learning and self-representation discussed in this chapter suggest that the expressiveness of such interfaces is augmented by integrating services and formats that support interaction with computer, as well as human, readers. As the example of the OutilVIF eportfolio suggests, services that enable new kinds of interaction within a larger narrative structure can be considered part of the composition process of an eportfolio. An eportfolio that capitalizes on these capabilities can no longer be seen as a text that could be isolated from its participation within social and computational networks. Rather, the choices the author makes about such participation are those about the story the eportfolio tells, to whom such a story is directed, and what kinds of relationships it invites with them.

The Processed Portfolio The challenge of imagining how the incorporation of distributed, modular, and computational information and services into eportfolios can transform the genre is similar to that of envisioning how electronic books might be more than just digitized versions of their print predecessors. In exploring the future of electronic books, the publisher Joseph Esposito (2003) contrasts the "primal" and the "processed" book. The primal book is entirely under the control of its creator, self-enclosed and unchanging. A processed book, in contrast, mediates a network of activities of readers, both human and computer. A processed book is "equal to the sum of things that can be linked to it and through it." Its meaning and value are a product of this activity. Many literary theorists would argue that the meaning of primal texts has always also been determined by the ways in which readers make sense of them within discourse communities. What is new about a processed book is the ability to make this activity visible and to shape it through the capabilities incorporated into the book itself. Such capabilities should not be seen as technological enhancements to the primal book. Rather, integrating them in a way that shapes how meaning is made of the book is part of the process of composition, a new dimension of authorship. The shift from the primal to processed book constitutes "a modification of the act of creation" (Esposito, 2003). People write books to try to influence how others make sense of the world through directing their attention to particular images, ideas, and ways of thinking. The new technology enables authors to compete for that attention in a broader set of ways, using not just language and media but also computation. While it is possible to search or analyze the contents of digitized primal books, such capabilities are integral parts of processed books. They actively facilitate computational "processing." Analysis is not something done to a processed book, as it is a primal one, but something that it participates in.

The emerging technologies that can support eportfolio practice make possible a similar transition from the primal to the processed eportfolio. As eportfolio authors control how services and information formats that support interaction and computational analysis are integrated into their eportfolio compositions, they can use these capabilities to address their audiences. Four of Esposito's five metaphors for the processed book help chart the possibilities of the processed portfolio: network node, portal, self-referencing text, and machine component (Esposito, 2003).

The first two of these are already familiar. Thinking of an eportfolio as a network node means that its value is determined in part by its connectivity to the network. The connections help express the meaning of the eportfolio, enhancing its credibility and making it accessible to a broader audience. The eportfolio is materially connected to the network. An eportfolio as portal connects its audience not just with information but also with services that allow them to interact with that information in new ways and make the products of that interaction visible within the eportfolio itself. These interactive capabilities become part of the eportfolio's message.

Eportfolio as Self-Referencing Text Thinking about an eportfolio as a self-referencing text suggests an important kind of service that might be integrated into it: a service that analyzes its contents. An eportfolio as a self-referencing text, for example, might use a tool like VUE to create a visual representation of how the evidence and reflections it includes are linked together. Given that research suggests that the complexity of such hypertextual organization parallels the sophistication of its author's professional knowledge and self-understanding, such a visualization could be used to demonstrate the maturity of the author's professional identity (Stephens, 2009). An even simpler example might be using a tool such as Wordle.net to incorporate a visualization of the frequency of word use for a given item within the eportfolio or for the eportfolio as a whole, helping the reader understand key concepts that recur throughout a work or body of work. (See Figure 8.5.) A wide range of additional tools, long in use in computational

FIGURE 8.5. WORDLE WORD FREQUENCY DIAGRAM OF THIS CHAPTER

linguistics and gaining prominence in the digital humanities, can be used for more sophisticated statistical analysis of the contents of texts or collections of texts. The Software Environment for the Advancement of Scholarly Research (SEASR) provides a framework through which analysis and visualization tools similar to those discussed in this section can be linked together, working in a manner analogous to that of the personal learning environment management tools discussed earlier in this chapter (University of Illinois Urbana–Champaign, 2009).

An example of a text analysis tool is the Leximancer system, developed at the University of Queensland in Australia, which analyzes the contents of text in order to identify concepts and the relationships between them (Smith, 2003). A machine-learning algorithm is used to group similar words together into concepts, and passages in the text are then tagged with the concepts to which they relate most strongly. This identification of concepts provides the reader with an alternative means for navigating the document, useful in a very large eportfolio. In addition, readers can see which concepts frequently co-occur with others and which have the highest degree of connectedness and centrality within the semantic map of the text the analysis generates. Congruence between the identified concepts is central to an eportfolio: those the author explicitly embraces would add to the persuasiveness of the author's reflective argument.

Rather than concepts emergent within the text, the DocuScope tool, developed at Carnegie Mellon University, looks for instances of a large set of micro-rhetorical features of a text, drawing on the representation theory of composition developed by David Kaufer and Brain Butler (Kaufer & Butler, 2000; Kaufer, Geisler, Vlachos, & Ishizaki, 2006). Kaufer and Butler believe that the meaning and persuasiveness of texts depend on skillful use of representational effects—slight alterations to the structure and contents of sentences that fit them to the rhetorical context. For example, passages within texts differ in whether they take a first-person or third-person perspective, appeal to personal or shared authority, directly address the reader, and focus on the past, present, or future. Any given genre combines these elements on recognizable patterns. DocuScope identifies uses of language that reflect choices that authors make throughout a text and statistically analyzes the patterns in their choices. DocuScope is designed to help writers compare their own works in progress with exemplary texts written for a similar purpose for a similar audience. Through considering how the texts differ, students can think through strategies for revision. Eportfolio authors might employ a similar strategy, comparing micro-rhetorical patterns in the reflective narratives of their eportfolios with those in other eportfolios that they admire. Thus, DocuScope illustrates how analysis services can support the process of composition of an eportfolio as well as become part of the eportfolio message itself.

Eportfolio as Machine Component While eportfolios as self-referencing texts provide the ability to analyze the content part of their messages, eportfolios as machine components acknowledge the role of analysis in the larger systems of which they are, or could be, a part. Eportfolios as machine components are designed in a way that allows their contents and how they are used to be analyzed more effectively through making that content and activity more easily analyzable by computers. This is particularly important for supporting interaction with institutional audiences that need to make sense of large collections of eportfolios, making comparisons and reading in a way that best takes advantage of the available time and attention of human readers.

A first way that an eportfolio can serve as a machine component is by making records of how it is composed and used available to services that analyze the portfolio for patterns in its evolution and reception. For example, as discussed in the capture section earlier in this chapter, eportfolios can include logs of actions undertaken during the process of their composition, such as how often the author engaged in online discussion with peers or how frequently and extensively the eportfolio was revised. Machine learning techniques can help authors and educators see relationships between certain patterns of activity and the qualities of the resulting eportfolios. For example, researchers in Taiwan have used Bayesian network software to help teachers infer causality (Liu et al., 2002). The software develops "belief" networks that show possible causal relationships among the activities, indicating, for example, that students whose eportfolios claim that they have a high level of competence in a skill are often those most likely to be willing to read and respond to others' eportfolios.

Software can also be used to discover patterns in the online conversations that eportfolios mediate. The Distributed Innovation and Scalable Collaboration in Uncertain Settings (DISCUS) project sees computers as mediators of collaborative creativity. Using genetic algorithms, it combines content analysis, social network analysis, and visualization tools to analyze the content and dynamics of online conversation. It can produce visual representations of how concepts connect and overlap and how they are used across networks of interconnected people and documents. The Collecció system focuses on analyzing patterns of annotation across collections of documents and groups of people, producing what the developers call "domain interactivity diagrams" to understand how meaning is made through dialogue around the documents (Rodriguez & Eklundh, 2006). These kinds of visualizations, produced dynamically as people and systems interact around eportfolios, could help authors understand if and how audiences are making sense of their eportfolios and how they relate to the eportfolios of others within their institutions and social networks. Institutional audiences could use such systems to examine the degree to which eportfolios are successfully shaping how people interact within their memberships and to compare general patterns of composition and use with those of particular eportfolio authors and readers.

Designing eportfolios as machine components also means making it easier for services to analyze the intended meaning of their content and connect it to shared conceptual frameworks. Institutional audiences often need to select from and make comparisons among large collections of eportfolios. While standardization simplifies analysis because it makes explicit the structure of eportfolios and the purpose of their content so that software can more easily understand them, eportfolios that embrace the cultural ideal of lifelong learning and are designed for human readers rarely have a standardized structure. While the tools and techniques for analyzing unstructured content discussed so far in this section are promising, making structure that is implicit in a human-readable format explicit for computational services is likely to lead to more efficient and accurate analysis. If the eportfolio is to remain true to the genre, which is key to achieving authenticity and integrity and mediating deliberation, such explication must not impose an institutionally defined structure on the human-readable form of the eportfolio.

This challenge can be addressed through semantic annotation. Eportfolio authors annotate their eportfolios, showing which items, pages, or passages relate to which categories from a shared conceptual framework. For example, an individual seeking professional certification might compose an eportfolio that articulates the symphonic integrity of her career identity in relationship to this person's full sense of identity as enacted across multiple spheres of life, as advocated in Chapter Two. In its basic form, such a self-representation would be difficult for a university, professional association, or governmental body to deal with in the face of many such eportfolios to review, as demonstrated by the research presented in Chapter Six. However, the eportfolio author might also tag certain elements of the eportfolio as showing that she possesses specific professional competencies as defined by the institution. This would allow the certifying agency to more easily identify the evidence and reflective interactions most relevant to making a judgment about a particular competency. It would also allow a potential employer to identify eportfolios that contain evidence related to a particular desired competency or set of competencies. Because that evidence is embedded in computer-readable form within the more complex, human-readable eportfolio, once the pool of potential employees is narrowed down, the employer would be able to take into account the richer representation of professional identity and capability it presents. Similarly, an accrediting body could choose a selection of eportfolios to review in full as part of the deliberative process of revising their standards. Readers too could annotate the eportfolios to record their own interpretations and judgments in terms of the standards, and their annotations could be compared with those of the author.

In addition to annotating items, or parts of items, within an eportfolio, authors and readers can annotate the connections among them. A characteristic that distinguishes a genuine eportfolio from a simple collection of eportfolio-related information is that a genuine eportfolio explains how the different items relate to one another and to the whole. These relationships too can be annotated to show their function. RDF, the Semantic Web language used by the PrPl system discussed earlier in this chapter, is particularly powerful for semantic annotation of eportfolios in part because it elegantly and flexibly represents such relationships. The LEAP 2.0 project, sponsored by the Centre for Educational Technology and Interoperability Standards (CETIS) in the United Kingdom, is developing standardized ways to describe relationships between elements in eportfolios using RDF. It includes an improved version of a classification scheme for relationships developed for the original U.K. Learning Information Profile (LEAP) candidate standard and further developed in the IMS ePortfolio Specification. The PIOP project, a collaboration between several U.K. developers funded by Joint Information Systems Committee (JISC), is using a similar relationships classification to describe connections between eportfolio elements that are shared serially between systems using the Atom standard, which is similar to RSS and is often used to publish feeds of items from social software, such as blog posts and photos.

As the annotation section earlier in this chapter made clear, computer-readable annotations can be stored within a number of file formats designed to produce documents for human readers. For example, the University of Michigan embedded annotations that map passages within student essays to programmatic learning outcomes using the XML capabilities within Microsoft Word. Early formats for representing eportfolios in a standardized format, such as the IMS ePortfolio Specification, also use XML, as do some currently under development, such as the Postsecondary Education Standards Council academic eportfolio (Cambridge, Smythe, & Heath, et al., 2005). For eportfolios, RDF has an advantage over XML not only because of the ease of representing relationships but also because RDF does not require a predefined classification scheme. The structure of a valid XML document must conform to a predefined schema that specifies the elements of which a conforming document can be made up and how they can be nested hierarchically. While RDF supports the use of ontologies, which serve a similar function, it does not require them. Because the type of information an eportfolio might contain will change over time and because it may be addressed to multiple audiences in multiple social and institutional contexts over time, such flexibility is important. Within institutions, too, structured representations need to account for varied conceptual frameworks across organizational units. In a university, for example, each department may have slightly different aspects of writing that it values in accordance with the conventions of its specific discipline or profession.

Making comparisons of learning outcomes across higher education institutions, too, has proved to be difficult in part because each institution has distinctive goals for its graduates, a problem compounded by the internal diversity of departmental priorities. In the United States, far from being a problem, such diversity has been a historical strength of higher education, suggesting that it ought to be further cultivated even in the face of a need to look at outcomes more systematically. While the Association of American Colleges and Universities' VALUE project, discussed in Chapters Four and Five, made some progress toward defining general ways to talk about what is valuable in student learning that might be used on a national level, the project's leaders acknowledge that the rubrics they have developed will need to be modified at the institutional and departmental levels to be usable. Another strength of RDF and other Semantic Web technologies is the ability to combine multiple classification schemes and represent the relationships among them. Just as the meaning of the relationships among items within an eportfolio can be represented, so can the relationships between, say, "critical thinking" as defined by one university and "analytical problem solving" as defined by another.

Such mapping is also necessary at the transition from education to the workforce and back again. Mapping competencies defined and tracked by educational institutions to those defined by employers and professional bodies and vice versa is necessary. In the next phase of their work on eportfolio and competencies, the IMS Global Learning Consortium is working with HR-XML, the key standards body for the human resource industry, to develop a process for exchanging competency information and for developing such mappings. The TAS[3] project, a multi-institutional, public-private initiative in Europe discussed in Chapter Six, is building an infrastructure for managing the sharing of eportfolio information across institutions and formats, mapping the categories and vocabularies of all the systems, domains, and institutions they support to a very granular, universal set of information types in order to allow mappings among all of them (Vervenne, 2008).

Such efforts will likely benefit from some standardization. Formally defining ontologies that describe the general structure of an eportfolio, the relationships among its parts, and the competencies valued in particular institutions or domains can make the use of eportfolios to represent ability more feasible and efficient. Researchers and developers are exploring several means for defining and managing such specifications. A team at Simon Fraser University has developed a high-level ontology for RDF eportfolios, and Austrian researchers have explored adapting general-purpose global ontologies for use with eportfolios and the process of alignment that such use would entail (Brokenshire, Bogyo, & Kumar, 2004; Hilzensauer, Hornung-Prahauser, & Schaffert, 2005; Hornung-Prahauser,

Behrendt, & Benari, 2005). LEAP 2.0 is defining the types of items that are often included in an eportfolio and the relationships they can have with each other.

Because most eportfolios are designed to be viewed with a Web browser, a promising approach to annotation is to embed semantic annotations directly within the XHTML code that the browsers render. RDFa is being developed by the W3C as a means to embed RDF data within XHTML. The LEAP 2.0 project has begun exploring the use of RDFa for semantically annotated eportfolios. Such an approach is particularly promising because it supports drilling back down from the Semantic Web representation of the eportfolio into the human-readable one, a move that Chapter Four demonstrates is key to connecting eportfolios to institutional decision-making processes in a way that embraces what is distinctive and powerful about the genre.

Semantic annotation using Semantic Web technologies, combined with tools for connecting up and analyzing the resulting information about learning, performance, and capability, has the potential to help eportfolio practitioners address the split between personalized and standardized eportfolios with which this book opened. Through embedding structured information with personalized eportfolios, allowing for drilling down and scaling up, and providing the means to chart the relationships among individual, group, institutional, national, and international semantic networks, Semantic Web technology looks to be key to the next generation of eportfolio practice. As we move from the primal to the processed portfolio through semantic annotation, individuals and institutions can interact in new ways that best take advantage of the time and attention of both.

Questions for Practice

Combined with other systems similar to those described throughout this chapter, Semantic Web technology promises to support eportfolio composition and use in a way that raises questions that can inform the selection of tools now and in the future:

- What kind of evidence of learning and performance does the technology help eportfolio authors capture? Does it help them create multimedia records of ephemeral activities? Can it take advantage of the capture capabilities of mobile technologies, such as cell phones?
- What kind of metadata does the technology enable authors to add to items they might include in their eportfolios? What metadata are automatically generated? Do they support tagging? Can you give eportfolio authors access to controlled vocabularies that correspond with institutional conceptual

frameworks, such as programmatic learning outcomes or professional competencies?

- How does the technology support searching and organizing eportfolio items? Can it search the contents of file formats that eportfolio authors are likely to use, or is it limited to text entered directly into the system?
- How well can it integrate or be integrated with other tools that you might wish to use to support eportfolio authors? How modular is it? Does it enable them to access data and services from Web 2.0 tools or from institutional enterprise systems, such as course management systems? Does it offer an application programming interface (API) to enable other systems to use its data and services? Can it create and use RSS and Atom feeds?
- How well does it support meaningful visual design and hyperlinking? Does it balance expressive range and ease of use in a way that matches the needs of eportfolio authors with different levels of technical expertise?
- Does the technology support annotation of eportfolio items and their contents? Can eportfolio authors annotate audio and video as well as textual evidence? Are the annotations represented in a language that other systems could analyze?
- How does the technology scaffold the process of reflection? Does it allow you to offer eportfolio authors sequenced prompts? Does it allow you to guide the workflow of interactions among authors, readers, and evaluators? Does the technology implement a particular pedagogy or theoretical understanding of learning and professional competence, or does it offer you the ability to customize it to fit your own?
- What capabilities does the technology offer to support social interaction? Does it allow comments from audiences such as colleagues and teachers? Does it enable students to link their portfolios to social networks of which they are a part and incorporate information about and from others into their eportfolios?
- In what ways does the technology allow authors and audiences to analyze the contents of an eportfolio? How does it support analysis of how the eportfolio is used? Can authors incorporate analysis and visualization capabilities as part of the message their eportfolios convey to their audiences? Can eportfolios be exported in formats that allow them to be used in other systems?
- Does the technology support comparisons between large numbers of eportfolios? Do these analysis tools facilitate drilling back down into the full eportfolios to help you interpret the results of the comparisons?
- Given that no single system or tool is likely to address all of these dimensions of technology support for eportfolios in a way that fits the needs of any individual or institution perfectly, how might you combine technologies to support the complete process?

CONCLUSION

This book envisions the role that eportfolios can play in supporting lifelong learning, defined as the process of articulating a distinctive, integrated identity grounded in evidence of learning and performance and using that self-representation to participate in institutions and social networks. Analyzing what I believe exemplifies the best of current practice, many of the projects and eportfolios I have examined both illuminate this potential and make concrete steps toward realizing it. As a member of the faculty of New Century College of George Mason University, I have been privileged to teach in a community that was invested in the cultural and educational ideals that underlie the conception of lifelong learning that I have developed here. Through such organizations at the Inter/National Coalition for Electronic Portfolio Research, EPAC, Sakai, and the IMS Global Learning Consortium, I have had the pleasure of working with many of the leaders of promising projects from around the world.

I am keenly aware that significant obstacles must be overcome for the practices I have highlighted to become more widely accepted, as the chapters on assessment, eportfolios beyond the academy, and technology that can support eportfolios make clear. Fully supporting individuals in articulating their authenticity and integrity with eportfolios and ensuring that their eportfolios play a genuine role in institutional decision making require cooperative work by technology developers, professional associations and unions, governmental agencies, schools, businesses, nongovernmental organizations, and innovative individuals worldwide. Charting future directions for each of these sectors would be a book in itself.

Much of this book has focused on higher education institutions, which are part of this larger system. Because I, and probably most of you, engage with eportfolios most extensively through higher education, I close by briefly considering some of the changes needed in higher education for it to embrace lifelong learning with eportfolios and to point to some allied movements for change. One of the reasons implementing eportfolio programs is so challenging is that they touch everything: virtually every obstacle to improving teaching and learning in higher education is also an obstacle to using eportfolios well. However, the fact that the effective support of eportfolio composition is so closely related to larger challenges is also a strength in that it allies eportfolio educators with other reformers across higher education. While vital and growing, the eportfolio movement is dwarfed by the scale of the transformations for which it calls. I believe that only when the eportfolio movement takes its place as part of a larger constellation of initiatives pushing for innovation will its goals be achievable.

Four changes seem necessary if higher education is to play the role I hope for it in supporting lifelong learning. Higher education needs to take responsibility for supporting learning across each student's life that is grounded in a distinctive identity; it needs to commit to inclusive dialogue as the foundation for making decisions about teaching and learning; it needs to dedicate itself to supporting the use of multiple, distributed technologies in concert, customized to the needs of individual teachers and learners; and it needs to take responsibility for cultivating learning throughout the society of which it is a part.

Even in most universities that see supporting student learning as central to their missions, the student learning that matters most is often limited to academic knowledge and skills acquired in individual classrooms. While institutions often seek to support students through educationally purposeful cocurricular activities, many faculty members and administrators see the learning that participation in these programs encourages as peripheral to their responsibilities. They also see the informal learning that students do in their larger lives as beyond their purview. Even in the case of learning that originates in the classroom, colleges and universities do not frequently support students' making connections across courses and over time in relationship to their distinctive understanding of themselves and the professional and civic communities in which they are preparing to play leadership roles. Valuing and supporting lifelong learning, in contrast, requires more holistic thinking about students' learning careers. Supporting student learning must mean cultivating students' development both within and beyond the classroom and supporting them in synthesizing that knowledge across formal and informal experiences through the lens of their distinctive relationships and commitments. The impact of eportfolios will be stronger as support expands for taking responsibility to support students' learning as a whole.

Multiple sectors in higher education are taking up this challenge. The more expansive understanding of supporting student learning is being advanced through partnerships between student affairs and academic affairs educators and through integrative learning initiatives. In 1998, the American Association for Higher Education, the American College Personnel Association, and NASPA issued a joint report arguing that supporting student learning is a responsibility shared by faculty and staff in both academic and student affairs (American Association for Higher Education, American College Personnel Association, & NASPA: Student Affairs Administrators in Higher Education, 1998). Over the next decade, the number of efforts to promote learning through coordination of the curriculum and cocurriculum grew significantly, and their significant impact on student learning is beginning to be documented (Nesheim et al., 2007). Faculty members and student affairs staff working on these projects have come to share a common identity as educators responsible for student learning both within and beyond the classroom. The third cohort of the Inter/National Coalition for Electronic Portfolio Research was composed of teams of educators from both student and academic affairs working together to support students' learning throughout their undergraduate learning careers using eportfolios. This work has been possible, and its impact has been multiplied, by the culture of broadened and shared responsibility that the movement toward partnership has begun to establish.

The past decade has also seen a push toward more intentional support for integrative learning. Through initiatives such as the Association of American Colleges and Universities and the Carnegie Foundation for the Advancement of Teaching's Integrative Learning Project, campuses have begun to support students in making connections across classes, disciplines, and contexts and to create opportunities for students to synthesize their learning and connect it to their identity and future aspirations (Huber et al., 2007; Huber & Hutchings, 2004). Here too the composition and use of eportfolios have played a central role in many of these innovations in curriculum, pedagogy, and assessment (DeZure, Babb, & Waldmann, 2005).

In addition to confining the learning they value to that which occurs within the classroom, colleges and universities also have often considered that classroom to be the sole domain of an individual faculty member. While an individual class may play a loosely defined role within the curriculum of a larger course of study or the general education requirements of the university as a whole, the teaching and learning that goes on within the class is often treated as a private matter between the instructor and his or her students. Some faculty perceive any effort by others who hold a stake in the institution's work to document the results of that activity or to influence its form or content as a dangerous intrusion that devalues their scholarly expertise and threatens their academic freedom. In contrast, the deliberative ideal advanced in this book suggests that decisions about curricular design and pedagogy ought to be informed by inclusive dialogue that takes into account distinctive interests and perspectives through looking carefully at students' work and their reflective interpretations of it.

Here too eportfolio educators can build on and work in concert with other change movements within higher education, particularly the scholarship of teaching and learning. Ernest Boyer (1990), the late president of the Carnegie Foundation for the Advancement of Teaching, coined the term *scholarship of teaching* in 1990 as part of his effort to reframe the full range of important professorial activities as elements of scholarship. Like traditional research, which Boyer called the *scholarship of discovery,* teaching can also be a form of scholarship when faculty make their teaching public, open it to peer critique, and make it available for reuse (Shulman, 1998). Because a scholarly account of effective teaching requires systematic inquiry into the impact of pedagogical practices on student learning, the "scholarship of teaching" soon became the "scholarship of teaching and learning." As privileged informants on their own learning, students became essential collaborators in such scholarship (Yancey, 1998).

Supported by the Carnegie Academy for the Scholarship of Teaching and Learning Campus Program, which was led by the American Association for Higher Education, faculty and administrators at hundreds of colleges and universities in the United States and Canada worked together to support the scholarship of teaching and learning on their campuses, helping faculty investigate and make public the ways in which their work in the classroom supports student learning so that teaching and learning can become community property (Cambridge, 2004). Later configurations of campuses in leadership clusters and groups furthered the advances in practice and policy at colleges and universities in multiple countries. The movement has become global, as evidenced by the national diversity of active participants in the International Society for the Scholarship of Teaching and Learning, whose conferences have grown each year. In putting student learning at the center of the process of making decisions about pedagogical and programmatic design and making the improvement of teaching and learning a collaborative endeavor, the scholarship of teaching and learning sets the groundwork for deliberative assessment with eportfolios. As a means for presenting the results of the scholarship of teaching and learning, the eportfolio genre itself has proved effective in creating a shared culture of responsibility for learning. Faculty members have created course and teaching eportfolios that connect pedagogical materials and evidence of student learning with teachers' reflective interpretations to share their professional identities and accomplishments with other members of their institutions and fields (Cambridge, 2001).

Through faculty eportfolios and other means, the scholarship of teaching and learning makes the work of the university in supporting student learning more open, inviting a broader cross-section of the campus community into the discussion of how to strengthen that support.

Support for the use of technology in higher education needs to become more open. Academic technology units of colleges and universities take on the responsibility to develop, implement, and support technology in teaching and learning in a way that maximizes use across campus. Given this priority, technologists often choose to support technologies that are likely to meet needs common to the broadest possible group of faculty and students. They also favor technology over which they have the most control so that disruptions in service are less likely and support is easier to offer. Because of these preferences, much of the focus of academic technology work tends to be general-purpose enterprise systems that are standardized for use across campus, such as course management systems or assessment databases, meeting primarily least-common-denominator needs. However, taking advantage of the potential of the emerging technologies and social software and services discussed throughout this book requires a different model. Students and educators need to use multiple, distributed services in concert, and the particular set of these optimal to supporting learning may vary considerably from learner to learner and context to context.

The open education movement is helping higher education institutions reenvision how to support the use of technology in teaching and learning to embrace this new reality. A recent book edited by Toru Iiyoshi and Vijay Kumar (2008) chronicles the movement's efforts toward openness in technology, content, and knowledge. Rather than searching for monolithic systems that can meet everyone's needs, institutions are developing new models that allow institutional systems to work with distributed services and sources of data from across the Web, chosen by those most directly involved in the processes of learning. New technology is being designed to be interoperable with other systems and to allow customization and extension, not just by programmers but by teachers and learners as well. Rather than training educators and learners in the mechanics of using tools, academic technologists are beginning to see their role as guiding individuals in the process of choosing and learning to use technologies independently. Academic content— lectures, data sets, assignments, textbooks, research articles—is also increasingly being made publicly available for use by anyone, within or beyond the university. Open technology and open content help to build a culture of open knowledge, in which the process of creating, teaching, and learning in the disciplines and professions becomes a cooperative endeavor that can embrace the distinctive contributions and serve the unique needs of individual students and educators while also advancing the collective enterprise of creating an educated public.

Through articulating individual identity and capability in connection with social networks and institutional decision-making processes, eportfolios can contribute to this culture, which makes such articulation and participation more accessible and powerful.

The push to make academic content universally accessible suggests another shift needed for higher education to fully support lifelong learning. Most institutions of higher education embrace their responsibility to support the learning of the students enrolled in their courses and programs. Far fewer, however, see that responsibility extending to others beyond their campus communities. Some institutions seek to keep their distance from the larger society of which they are a part in order to cultivate knowledge, inspire learning, and stimulate critique untainted by the immediate demands of politics and commerce. Recently, however, other institutions have begun to define themselves as engaged universities (Holland, 2001; Hollander & Saltmarsh, 2000). Engaged campuses construct knowledge and work for change through direct participation in civic life, putting the resources of the academic community to work in addressing the problems of the cities, regions, and nations of which they are a part. Through service-learning, students develop and put into use their knowledge of the disciplines and professions they study in a way that benefits the public good (Jacoby & Associates, 1996). Through conducting and applying their research where there is a concrete social need for it, faculty members contribute to the public good through their practice of the scholarship of engagement (Boyer, 1996).

While engagement can work in service of a wide range of admirable goals, I suggest that colleges and universities have a special responsibility to support learning throughout the societies of which they play a part. Learning is at the heart of the mission of higher education, and research on the demands for learning throughout life suggests that that mission cannot be accomplished solely through attention to those members of society who happen to be enrolled in a college or university at a given time. Rather than simply supporting their students' learning, colleges and universities should put their expertise and infrastructures to work in partnership with other institutions—schools, employers, government agencies, community service organizations—to improve the quality of learning in the many distributed contexts in which it must occur for individuals to prosper in our rapidly changing world. Through helping individuals articulate their distinctive identities in order to chart the paths of their learning and influence the shape of the institutions in which they learn, eportfolios have a central role to play in the learning society that higher education can help bring into being.

REFERENCES

Abrami, P. C., Wade, C. A., Pillay, V., Aslan, O., Bures, E. M., & Bentley, C. (2007, October). *Encouraging self-regulated learning through electronic portfolios*. Paper presented at the World Conference on E-Learning in Corporate, Government, Healthcare, and Higher Education, Quebec City, Canada.

Ainley, P., & Rainbird, H. (Eds.). (1999). *Apprenticeship: Toward a new paradigm for learning*. London: Kogan Page.

Alheit, P. (1992). The biographical approach to adult education. In W. Mader (Ed.), *Adult education in the Federal Republic of Germany: Scholarly approaches and professional practice* (pp. 186–224). Vancouver: University of British Columbia.

Allen, M., Condon, W., Dickson, M., Forbes, C., Meese, G., & Yancey, K. B. (1997). Portfolios, WAC, email, and assessment: An inquiry on Portnet. In K. B. Yancey & I. Weiser (Eds.), *Situating portfolios: Four perspectives* (pp. 370–384). Logan: Utah State University Press.

American Association for Higher Education. (2003). *Electronic portfolio clearinghouse*. Washington, DC: Author.

American Association for Higher Education, American College Personnel Association, & NASPA: Student Affairs Administrators in Higher Education. (1998). *Power partnerships: A shared responsibility for learning*. Washington, DC: Authors.

American Association of Colleges and Universities. (2002). *Greater expectations: A new vision for learning as a nation goes to college*. Washington, DC: Author.

American Council on Education. (2006). *Assessing international learning outcomes*. Retrieved from www.acenet.edu/Content/NavigationMenu/ProgramsServices/cii/res/assess/

Arendt, H. (1958). *The human condition*. Chicago: University of Chicago Press.

Arthur, M. B., & Rousseau, D. M. (Eds.). (1996). *The boundaryless career: A new employment princple for a new organizational era*. New York: Oxford University Press.

Association of American Colleges and Universities. (2007). *College learning for the new global century*. Washington, DC: Author.

Association of American Colleges and Universities. (2009a). *VALUE-Plus: Rising to the challenge*. Retrieved from www.aacu.org/Rising_Challenge/index.cfm

Association of American Colleges and Universities. (2009b). *VALUE: Valid assessment of learning in undergraduate education*. Retrieved from www.aacu.org/value/index.cfm

Attwell, G. (2006, November). *Personal learning environments*. Paper presented at the Centre for Educational Technology and Interoperability Standards Conference, Manchester, England.

Bakhtin, M. M. (1982). *The dialogic imagination: Four essays*. Austin: University of Texas Press.

Bandura, A. (1997). *Self-efficacy: The exercise of control*. New York: Worth.

Banta, T. (2010, January). *The role of e-portfolios in guiding improvement and demonstrating accountability*. Paper presented at the annual meeting of the Asssociation of American Colleges and Universities, Washington, DC.

Barr, M. A. (1995). Who's going to interpret performance standards? A case for teacher judgment. In P. H. Dryer (Ed.), *The Claremont Reading Conference 59th yearbook*. Claremont, CA: Institute for Developmental Studies.

Barr, M. A., & Cheong, J. (1995). Achieving equity: Counting on the classroom. In M. T. Nettles & A. L. Nettles (Eds.), *Equity and excellence in educational testing and assessment* (pp. 161–184). Norwell, MA: Kluwer.

Barrett, H. (2008, March). *Online personal learning environments: Structuring electronic portfolios to support lifelong and life wide learning*. Paper presented at the Conference of the Society for Information Technology and Teacher Education, Las Vegas, NV.

Barrett, H., & Carney, J. (2005). *Conflicting paradigms and competing purposes in electronic portfolio development*. Retrieved from http://electronicportfolios.com/portfolios/LEAJournal-BarrettCarney.pdf

Barrett, H., & Wilkerson, J. (2004). *Conflicting paradigms in electronic portfolio approaches: Choosing an electronic portfolio strategy that matches your conceptual framework*. Retrieved from www.electronic-portfolios.com/systems/paradigms.html

Bass, R., & Linkon, S. L. (2008). On the evidence of theory: Close reading as a disciplinary model for writing about teaching and learning. *Arts and Humanities in Higher Education, 7*(3), 245–261.

Bateson, M. C. (1989). *Composing a life*. New York: Grove Press.

Batson, T. (2007, December 12). The ePortfolio hijacked. *Campus Technology*. Retrieved from http://campustechnology.com/Articles/2007/12/The-ePortfolio-Hijacked.aspx?p=1

Baxter Magdola, M. B. (2001). *Making their own way: Narratives for transforming higher education to promote self-development*. Sterling, VA: Stylus.

Beagrie, N. (2005). Plenty of room at the bottom? Personal digital libraries and collections. *D-Lib Magazine, 11*(6). Retrieved from www.dlib.org/dlib/june05/beagrie/06beagrie.html

Beaufort, A. (2007). *College writing and beyond: A new framework for university writing instruction*. Logan: Utah State University Press.

Beetham, H. (2006). *E-portfolios in post-16 learning in the UK: Developments, issues and opportunities*. Bristol, England: Joint Information Systems Committee.

Belenky, M. F., Clinchy, B., Goldberger, N., & Tarule, J. (1988). *Women's ways of knowing: The development of self, voice, and mind*. New York: Basic Books.

Bellah, R. N., Madsen, R., Sullivan, W. M., Swindler, A., & Tipton, S. M. (1996). *Habits and the heart: Individualism and commitment in American life* (2nd ed.). Berkeley: University of California Press.

Benjamin, J. (1988). *The bond of love: Psychoanalysis, feminism, and the problem of domination.* New York: Pantheon.

Berlanga, A. J., Sloep, P. B., Brouns, F., Bitter, M., & Koper, R. (2008). Towards a TENCompetence eportfolio. *International Journal of Emerging Technologies in Learning, 3,* 24–28.

Bird, A. (1996). Careers as repositories of knowledge: Considerations for boundaryless careers. In M. B. Arthur & D. M. Rousseau (Eds.), *The boundaryless career: A new employment principle for a new organizational era* (pp. 150–168). New York: Oxford University Press.

Bloom, A. (1987). *The closing of the American mind.* New York: Simon & Schuster.

Bodies Electric LLC. (2002). *Unchat.* Retrieved from http://web.archive.org/web/20070726075430/http://www.unchat.com/unchat.html

Boud, D., Keogh, R., & Walker, D. (Eds.). (1985). *Reflection: Turning experience into learning.* London: Routledge.

boyd, d. (2004, April). *Friendster and publicly articulated social networking.* Paper presented at the Conference on Human Factors and Computing Systems, Vienna, Austria.

boyd, d. (2007). None of this is real: Identity and participation in Friendster. In J. Karaganis (Ed.), *Structures of participation in digital culture* (pp. 132–157). New York: Social Science Research Council.

boyd, d. m., & Ellison, N. B. (2007). Social network sites: Definition, history, and scholarship. *Journal of Computer-Mediated Communication, 13*(1), article 11. Retrieved from http://jcmc.indiana.edu/vol13/issue1/boyd.ellison.html

Boyer, E. L. (1990). *Scholarship reconsidered: Priorities of the professoriate.* Princeton, NJ: Carngie Foundation for the Advancement of Teaching.

Boyer, E. L. (1996). The scholarship of engagement. *Bulletin of the American Academy of Arts and Sciences, 49*(7), 18–33.

Bridges, W. (1994). *Jobshift: How to prosper in a workplace without jobs.* Cambridge, MA: Perseus.

Broad, B. (2003). *What we really value: Beyond rubrics in teaching and assessing writing.* Logan: Utah State University Press.

Brokenshire, D., Bogyo, B., & Kumar, V. (2004, October). *Towards an upper-level ontology for information exchange in eportfolios.* Paper presented at the second International ePortfolio Conference, La Rochelle, France.

Brookfield, S. D. (1986). *Understanding and facilitating adult learning.* San Francisco: Jossey-Bass.

Bureau of Labor Statistics. (2008). *Number of jobs held, labor market activity, and earnings growth among the youngest baby boomers: Results from a longitudinal survey* [Press release]. Retrieved from www.bls.gov/news.release/pdf/nlsoy.pdf

Burnett, M. N., & Williams, J. M. (2009). Institutional uses of rubrics and e-portfolios: Spellman College and Rose-Hulman Institute. *Peer Review, 11*(1), 24–27.

Cable, S. (2003, October). *Implementing the eportfolio in the corporate sector: Strategy and practice.* Paper presented at the First International ePortfolio Conference, Portiers, France.

Cable, S. (2007, October). *Eportfolio for the largest professional body in Europe: Successes and challenges.* Paper presented at the Fifth International ePortfolio Conference, Maastricht, The Netherlands.

Caceres, M. (2009). *Widgets 1.0: Requirements* (Working draft). W3C.

Calhoun, C. (1995). Standing for something. *Journal of Philosophy, 92*(5), 235–260.

Cambridge, B. (Ed.). (2001). *Electronic portfolios: Emerging practices in student, faculty, and institutional learning.* Washington, DC: American Association for Higher Education.

Cambridge, B. (2004). *Campus progress: Supporting the scholarship of teaching and learning.* Sterling, VA: Stylus.

Cambridge, D. (2006a). Integral eportfolio interoperability with the IMS ePortfolio Specification. In A. Jafari & C. Kaufman (Eds.), *Handbook of research on ePortfolios* (pp. 234–347). Hershey, PA: Idea Group.

Cambridge, D. (2006b). Personally engaged information literacy in general education through information ecology and fieldwork. In C. Gibson (Ed.), *Student engagement and information literacy* (pp. 143–168). Chicago: Association of College and Research Libraries.

Cambridge, D. (2008a). Audience, integrity, and the living document: Efolio Minnesota and lifelong and lifewide learning with eportfolios. *Computers and Education, 51*(3), 1227–1246.

Cambridge, D. (2008b). Layering networked and symphonic selves: A critical role for eportfolios in employability through integrative learning. *Campus-Wide Information Systems, 25*(4), 244–262.

Cambridge, D. (2008c). Universities as responsive learning organizations through competency-based assessment with electronic portfolios. *Journal of General Education, 57*(1), 51–64.

Cambridge, D. (2009). Two faces of integrative learning online. In D. Cambridge, B. Cambridge, & K. B. Yancey (Eds.), *Electronic portfolios 2.0: Emergent research on implementation and impact* (pp. 41–50). Sterling, VA: Stylus.

Cambridge, D. (in press-a). From metaphor to analogy: How the National Museum of the American Indian can inform the Augusta Community Portfolio. In R. Rice & K. Wills (Eds.), *ePortfolio performance support systems*. West Lafayette, IN: Parlor Press.

Cambridge, D. (in press-b). Reflective assessment with portfolios in New Century College: Students as authoritative informants and competencies as boundary objects. In J. O'Connor & L. Smith (Eds.), *Connecting the classroom to the world*. Sterling, VA: Stylus.

Cambridge, D., & Cambridge, B. (2003, October). *The future of eportfolio technology: Supporting what we know about learning.* Paper presented at the first International ePortfolio Conference, Portiers, France.

Cambridge, D., Cambridge, B., & Yancey, K. B. (Eds.). (2009). *Electronic portfolios 2.0: Emergent research on implementation and impact.* Sterling, VA: Stylus.

Cambridge, D., Fernandez, L., Kahn, S., Kirkpatrick, J., & Smith, J. (2008). The impact of the Open Source Portfolio on learning and assessment. *Journal of Online Learning and Teaching, 4*(4), 490–502.

Cambridge, D., Kirkpatrick, J., Peet, M., & Rickards, W. (2009, October). *Sharing the future of what we VALUE: Faculty deliberations about assessment rubrics for and as SoTL.* Paper presented at the International Society for the Scholarship of Teaching and Learning Conference, Bloomington, IN.

Cambridge, D., Owen, J., Smith, L., Blank-Godlove, J., Danner, K., Eby, K., et al. (2009). *INCEPR final report.* Inter/National Coalition for Electronic Portfolio Research. Retrieved from http://ncepr.org/finalreports/cohort3/George%20Mason%20Final%20Report.pdf

Cambridge, D., Smythe, C., & Heath, A. (2005). *IMS ePortfolio Specification v1.0* (Final Specification Version 1.0). Burlington, MA: IMS Global Learning Consortium.

Carr, C. S. (2001, March). *Computer-supported collaborative argumentation: Supporting problem-based learning in legal education.* Paper presented at the Computer Support for Collaborative Learning Conference, Maastricht, The Netherlands.

Chen, H. L., Cannon, D., Gabrio, J., Leifer, L., Toye, G., & Bailey, T. (2005, June). *Using wikis and weblogs to support reflective learning in an introductory engineering design course.* Paper presented at the American Association for Engineering Education Annual Conference and Exposition, Portland, OR.

Cheng, W. C., Golubchik, L., & Kay, D. G. (2004). Total recall: Are privacy challenges inevitable? *Proceedings of the 1st ACM Workshop on Continuous Archival and Retrieval of Personal Experiences* (pp. 86–92). New York: ACM.

Chickering, A. W., Dalton, J. C., & Stamm, L. (2006). *Encouraging authenticity and spirituality in higher education.* San Francisco: Jossey-Bass.

Chickering, A. W., & Mentkowski, M. (2005). Assessing ineffable outcomes. In A. W. Chickering, J. C. Dalton, & L. Stamm (Eds.), *Encouraging authenticity and spirituality in higher education* (pp. 220–242). San Francisco: Jossey-Bass.

Ciccone, A. A., Myers, R. A., & Waldmann, S. (2008). What's so funny? Moving students toward complex thinking in a course on comedy and laughter. *Arts and Humanities in Higher Education, 7*(3), 308–322.

Clark, J. E., & Eynon, B. (2009). E-portfolios at 2.0—Surveying the field. *Peer Review, 11*(1), 18–23.

Clarke, R. C., & Mayer, R. E. (2002). *E-learning and the science of instruction: Proven guidelines for consumers and designers of multimedia learning.* San Francisco: Pfeiffer.

Claus, G. (2008, May). *Eportfolio for the employability of all.* Paper presented at the Conversations on Competencies: Eight ePortfolio Projects for Lifelong Learning, Employability and Learning Organizations, Montreal.

Cohn, E. R., & Hibbits, B. J. (2004). Beyond the electronic portfolio: A lifetime personal web space. *EDUCAUSE Quarterly, 27*(4), 8–10.

Collins, A. (1992). Portfolios for science education: Issues in purpose, structure, and authenticity. *Science Education, 76*(4), 451–463.

Commission of the European Communities. (2000). *A memorandum on lifelong learning.* Brussels: Author.

Conference on College Composition and Communication. (2008). *Writing assessment: A position statement.* Champaign, IL: Author.

Conklin, E. J. (1997). *Designing organizational memory: Preserving intellectual assests in a knowledge economy.* Retrieved from http://cognexus.org/dom.pdf

Cotterill, S., Angarita, M., Horner, P., Teasdale, D., Moss, J., Jones, S., et al. (2007, October). *Toward the m-portfolio.* Paper presented at the Fifth International ePortfolio Conference, Maastricht, The Netherlands.

Cotterill, S., Jones, S., Walters, R., Horner, P., Moss, J., & McDonald, A. (2006, September). *Evaluating the use of hand-held computers to access electronic portfolios and clinical guidelines in a wireless environment for undergraduate medical education.* Paper presented at the Assocation for the Study of Medical Education, Aberdeen, Scotland.

Crystal, A. (2006, June). *Design research for a context-aware capture system to support biology education.* Paper presented at the Conference on Designing Interactive Systems, University Park, PA.

Cummings, R. E., & Barton, M. (Eds.). (2008). *Wiki writing: Collaborative learning in the college classroom.* Ann Arbor, MI: Digital Culture Books.

Dalziel, J. (2004, December). *Implementing learning design: The learning activity management system (LAMS).* Paper presented at the ASCILITE Conference, Perth, Western Australia.

Davies, T. (2009). Introduction: The blossoming field of online deliberation. In P. Davies & S. P. Gangadharan (Eds.), *Online deliberation: Design, research, and practice* (pp. 1–19). Stanford, CA: Center for the Study of Language and Information.

de Groot, R. (2007, October). *Eportfolio for a 21st century public employment service.* Paper presented at the fifth International ePortfolio Conference, Maastricht, The Netherlands.

DeFillipi, R. J., & Arthur, M. B. (1996). Boundaryless contexts and careers: A competency-based perspective. In M. B. Arthur & D. M. Rousseau (Eds.), *The boundaryless career: A new employment principle for a new organizational era* (pp. 116–131). New York: Oxford University Press.

Delandshere, G., & Arens, S. A. (2003). Examining the quality of the evidence in preservice teacher portfolios. *Journal of Teaching Education, 54*(1), 57–73.

Department for Education and Skills. (2005). *Harnessing technology: Transforming learning and children's services.* London: Author.

Derrida, J. (1980). *Writing and difference.* Chicago: University of Chicago Press.

Desmet, C., Griffin, J., Miller, D. C., Balthazor, R., & Cummings, R. (2009). Re-visioning revision with eportfolios in the University of Georgia first-year composition program. In D. Cambridge, B. Cambridge, & K. B. Yancey (Eds.), *Electronic portfolios 2.0: Emergent research on implementation and impact* (pp. 155–164). Sterling, VA: Stylus.

DeZure, D., Babb, M., & Waldmann, S. (2005). Integrative learning nationwide: Emerging trends and practices. *Peer Review, 7*(4), 24–28.

Donath, J., & boyd, d. (2004). Public displays for connection. *BT Technology Journal, 22*(4), 71–82.

Downes, S. (2007). *Learning networks in practice.* Coventry, England: British Educational Communications and Technology Agency.

Driessen, E. W., Overeen, K., van Tartwijk, J., van der Vleuten, C. P., & Muijtjens, A. M. (2006). Validity of portfolio assessment: Which qualities determine ratings? *Medical Education, 39*, 862–866.

Eakin, P. J. (1999). *How our lives becomes stories: Making selves.* Ithaca, NY: Cornell University Press.

Efimova, L., Hendrick, S., & Anjewierden, A. (2005, October). *Finding "the life between buildings": An approach for defining a weblog community.* Paper presented at the Internet Research 6.0: Internet Generations Conference, Chicago.

Ellis, D.P.W., & Lee, K. (2006). Accessing minimal-impact personal audio archives. *IEEE Multimedia, 13*(4), 30–38.

Ellison, N. B., Steinfield, C., & Lampe, C. (2007). The benefits of Facebook "friends": Social capital and college students' use of online social network sites. *Journal of Computer-Mediated Communication, 12*(4), article 1. Retrieved from http://jcmc.indiana.edu/vol12/issue4/ellison.html

Elmholdt, C., & Brinkmann, S. (2006). Discursive practices at work: Constituting the reflective learner. In D. Boud, P. Cressey, & P. Docherty (Eds.), *Productive reflection at work: Learning for changing organizations* (pp. 170–180). London: Routledge.

EPAC. (2009). *Eportfolio-related tools and technologies.* Retrieved from http://epac.pbworks.com/Evolving+List%C2%A0of%C2%A0ePortfolio-related%C2%A0Tools

Esposito, J. J. (2003). The processed book. *First Monday, 8*(3). Retrieved from http://firstmonday.org/htbin/cgiwrap/bin/ojs/index.php/fm/article/view/1038/959

Eynon, B. (2009). Making connections: The LaGuardia ePortfolio. In D. Cambridge, B. Cambridge, & K. B. Yancey (Eds.), *Electronic portfolios 2.0: Emergent research on implementation and impact* (pp. 59–68). Sterling, VA: Stylus.

Facebook. (2009). *Statistics.* Retrieved from www.facebook.com/press/info.php?statistics

Firssova, O. (2007, October). *E-portfolio as a coaching support tool for workplace learning of teachers.* Paper presented at the Fifth International ePortfolio Conference, Maastricht, The Netherlands.

Fishkin, J. (2009). Virtual public consultation: Prospects for Internet deliberative democracy. In P. Davies & S. P. Gangadharan (Eds.), *Online deliberation: Design, research, and practice* (pp. 23–36). Stanford, CA: Center for the Study of Language and Information.

Fitch, D., Gibbs, T., Peet, M., Reed, B. G., & Tolman, R. (2007). XML and eportfolios. *Journal of Educational Technology Systems, 26*(3), 319–333.

Foucault, M. (1984). The ethics of care of the self as a practice of freedom. In J. Bernauer & D. Rasmussen (Eds.), *The final Foucault* (pp. 2–3). Cambridge, MA: MIT Press.

Fournier, J., Lane, C., & Corbett, S. (2007, June). *The journey to best practices: Results of a two-year study of e-portfolio implementation in beginning composition courses.* Paper presented at the World Conference on Educational Multimedia, Hypermedia, and Telecommunications, Vancouver, Canada.

Franklin, B. (1985). *Benjamin Franklin's autobiography.* New York: Norton.

Freidman, T. (2006). *The world is flat: A brief history of the twenty-first century.* New York: Farrar, Straus, & Giroux.

Fugate, M., Kinicki, A. J., & Ashforth, B. E. (2004). Employability: A psycho-social construct, its dimensions, and applications. *Journal of Vocational Behavior, 65*(1), 14–38.

Gallie, W. B. (1956). Essentially contested concepts. *Proceedings of the Aristotelian Society, 56,* 167–198.

Gardner, H., Csikszentmihalyi, M., & Damon, W. (2001). *Good work: When excellence and ethics meet.* New York: Basic Books.

Garrett, B., & Jackson, C. (2008). A mobile clinical e-portfolio for nursing and medical students, using wireless personal digital assistants (PDAs). *Nurse Education in Practice, 6*(6), 339–346.

Gawande, A. (2002). *Complications: A surgeon's notes on an imperfect science.* New York: Picador.

Gelernter, D. (1992). *Mirror worlds: Or the day software puts the universe in a shoebox . . . how it will happen and what it will mean.* New York: Oxford University Press.

Gemmell, J., Bell, G., & Lueder, R. (2006). MyLifeBits: A personal database for everything. *Communications of the ACM, 49*(1), 88–95.

Gilligan, C. (1982). *In a different voice: Psychological theory and women's development.* Cambridge, MA: Harvard University Press.

Goodson, I. F. (2005). *Learning, curriculum, and life politics.* London: Routledge.

Granovetter, M. (1973). The strength in weak ties. *American Journal of Sociology, 78*(6), 1360–1380.

Gray, P. J. (2002). The roots of assessment: Tensions, solutions, and research directions. In T. Banta & Associates (Eds.), *Building a scholarship of assessment* (pp. 49–66). San Francisco: Jossey-Bass.

Greenberg, J. (2006, July). *Memex Metadata (m2) for personal educational portfolio.* Paper presented at the Microsoft Research Faculty Summit, Redmond, WA.

Groth, G. A. (2001). Dialogue in corporations. In D. Schoem & S. Hurtado (Eds.), *Intergroup dialogue: Deliberative democracy in school, college, community, and workplace* (pp. 194–209). Ann Arbor: University of Michigan Press.

Guignon, C. (2004). *On being authentic.* New York: Routledge.

Gutmann, A., & Thompson, D. (1996). *Democracy and disagreement.* Cambridge, MA: Belknap Press.

Gutmann, A., & Thompson, D. (2004). *Why deliberative democracy?* Princeton, NJ: Princeton University Press.

Hall, S. (1999). Encoding, decoding. In S. During (Ed.), *The cultural studies reader* (2nd ed., pp. 507–517). London: Routledge.

Hallam, P. J. (2000). *Reliability and validity of teacher-based reading assessment: Application of "quality assurance for teacher-based assessment" (QATA) to California Learning Record moderations* (Unpublished doctoral dissertation). University of California, Berkeley.

Hamilton, S. (2006). A principle-based eport goes public (and almost loses its principles!). In A. Jafari & C. Kaufman (Eds.), *Handbook of research on ePortfolios* (pp. 434–446). Hershey, PA: Idea Group.

Hamp-Lyons, L., & Condon, W. (2000). *Assessing the portfolio: Principles for practice, theory and research.* Cresskill, NJ: Hampton Press.

Handa, C. (Ed.). (2004). *Visual rhetoric in a digital world: A critical sourcebook.* New York: Bedford/St. Martin's Press.

Hardiman, R., & Jackson, B. W. (2001). Cultural study groups: Creating dialogue in a corporate setting. In D. Schoem & S. Hurtado (Eds.), *Intergroup dialogue: Deliberative democracy in school, college, community, and workplace* (pp. 181–193). Ann Arbor: University of Michigan Press.

Harding, S. (1991). *Whose science? Whose knowledge? Thinking from women's lives.* Ithaca, NY: Cornell University Press.

Harley, P., & Smallwood, A. (2005, October). *Eportfolios for transition and integration: Collaborative work in progress in Nottingham's schools, colleges, and universities.* Paper presented at the Third International ePortfolio Conference, Cambridge, England.

Harley, P., & Smallwood, A. (2006). *Implementing an institution-free model of eportfolio practice across educational sectors: The Nottingham experience.* Paper presented at the Fourth International ePortfolio Conference, Oxford, England.

Hartnell-Young, E., Harrison, C., Crook, C., Pemberton, R., Joyes, G., Fisher, T., et al. (2007). *The impact of e-portfolios on learning.* Coventry, England: Becta.

Hartnell-Young, E., Smallwood, A., Kingston, S., & Harley, P. (2006). Joining up the episodes of lifelong learning: A regional transition project. *British Journal of Educational Technology, 37*(6), 853–866.

Hartnell-Young, E., & Vetere, F. (2007). Eportfolios capturing learning on the move. In M. Kankaanranta, A. Grant, & P. Linnakylä (Eds.), *E-portfolio: Adding value to lifelong learning* (pp. 155–175). Jyväskylä, Finland: University of Jyväskylä Institute for Educational Research.

Haswell, R. (Ed.). (2001). *Beyond outcomes: Assessment and instruction within a university writing program.* Westport, CT: Ablex.

Hayles, N. K. (2007). Narrative and database: Natural symbionts. *PMLA, 122*(5), 1603–1608.

Henscheid, J. M. (2000). *Professing the disciplines: An analysis of senior seminar capstone courses.* Columbia, SC: National Resource Center for the First-Year Experience and Students in Transition.

Herring, S. C., Scheidt, L. A., Bonus, S., & Wright, E. (2004, January). *Bridging the gap: A genre analysis of weblogs.* Paper presented at the 37th Annual Hawaii International Conference on System Sciences, Honolulu.

Hilzensauer, W., Hornung-Prahauser, V., & Schaffert, S. (2005). *Requirements for personal development planning in eportfolios supported by Semantic Web technology.* Salzburg, Austria: Salzburg Research.

Himmelfarb, G. (1996). *The de-moralization of society: From Victorian virtues to modern values.* New York: Vintage.

Hirsch, P. M., & Shanley, M. (1996). The rhetoric of boundaryless—Or, how the newly empowered managerial class bought into its own marginalization. In M. B. Arthur & D. M. Rousseau (Eds.), *The boundaryless career: A new employment principle for a new organizational era* (pp. 218–234). New York: Oxford University Press.

Hoffmann, T. A. (2004). Delineations on the Web: Computer-mediated portfolio development at the University of Maryland University College. In E. Michelson & A. Mandell (Eds.), *Portfolio development and the assessment of prior learning: Perspectives, models, and practices* (pp. 216–231). Sterling, VA: Stylus.

Holland, B. A. (2001). Toward a definition and characterization of the engaged university. *Metropolitan Universities, 2*(3), 20–29.

Hollander, E. L., & Saltmarsh, J. (2000). The engaged university. *Academe, 86*(4), 29–32.

Hornung-Prahauser, V., Behrendt, W., & Benari, M. (2005, September). *Developing further the concept of eportfolio with the use of Semantic Web technologies.* Paper presented at the Eighth International Conference on Interactive Computer Aided Learning, Villach, Austria.

Huba, M. E., & Freed, J. E. (2000). *Learner-centered assessment on college campuses: Shifting the focus from teaching to learning.* Needham Heights, MA: Allyn & Bacon.

Huber, M. T., Brown, C., Hutchings, P., Gale, R., Miller, R., & Breen, M. (2007). *Integrative learning: Opportunities to connect.* Stanford, CA: Carnegie Foundation for the Advancement of Teaching and Association of American Colleges and Universities.

Huber, M. T., & Hutchings, P. (2004). *Integrative learning: Mapping the terrain.* Washington, DC: Association of American Colleges and Universities.

Hughes, J. (2009). Becoming eportfolio learners and teachers. In D. Cambridge, B. Cambridge, & K. B. Yancey (Eds.), *Electronic portfolios 2.0: Emergent research on implementation and impact* (pp. 51–58). Sterling, VA: Stylus.

Hull, G. A., & Katz, M. L. (2006). Crafting an agentive self: Case studies of digital storytelling. *Research in the Teaching of English, 41*(1), 43–81.

Iiyoshi, T., & Kumar, M.S.V. (Eds.). (2008). *Opening up education: The collective advancement of education through open technology, open content, and open knowledge.* Cambridge, MA: MIT Press.

Institute for the Future of the Book. (2008). *Commentpress.* Retrieved from www .futureofthebook.org/commentpress/

Ittelson, J. (2001). Building an e-dentity for each student. *EDUCUASE Quarterly, 24*(4), 43–45.

Jacoby, B., & Associates. (1996). *Service-learning in higher education: Concepts and practices.* San Francisco: Jossey-Bass.

Jarrett, K. (2004). Battlecat then, battlecat now: Temporal shifts, hyperlinking and database subjectivities. In L. Gurak, S. Antonijevic, L. Johnson, C. Ratliff, & J. Reyman (Eds.), *Into the blogosphere: Rhetoric, community, and culture of weblogs.* Minneapolis: University of Minnesota Press.

Johnson, D. (2006, October). *Omnipresent eportfolio activity enabled by mobile technology.* Paper presented at the Fourth International ePortfolio Conference, Oxford, England.

Johnson, G. (2009). *Inter/National Coalition for Electronic Portfolio Research: Final report, Penn State University.* Retrieved from http://ncepr.org/finalreports/cohort3/Penn%20State%20Fina l%20Report.pdf

Joint Information Systems Committee. (2007). *Regional interoperability project on progression for lifelong learning: Use cases.* Retrieved from www.nottingham.ac.uk/rippll/keydocuments.htm

Jones, P. R. (2007, October). *Breaking out of the box: Demand led e-portfolio for employability.* Paper presented at the Fifth International ePortfolio Conference, Maastricht, The Netherlands.

Jones, W. (2004). Finders, keepers? The present and future perfect in support of personal information managment. *First Monday, 9*(3). Retrieved from http://131.193.153.231/ www/issues/issue9_3/jones/index.html

Kahn, S. (2001). Linking learning, improvement, and accountability: An introduction to electronic institutional portfolios. In B. Cambridge (Ed.), *Electronic portfolios: Emerging practices in student, faculty, and institutional learning* (pp. 135–158). Washington, DC: American Association for Higher Education.

Karacapilidis, N., & Papadias, D. (2001). Computer supported argumentation and collaborative decision making: The HERMES system. *Information Systems, 26*(4), 259–277.

Kaufer, D., & Butler, B. S. (2000). *Designing interactive worlds with words: Principles of writing as representational composition.* New York: Routledge.

Kaufer, D., Geisler, C., Vlachos, P., & Ishizaki, S. (2006). Mining textual knowledge for writing education and research: The Docuscope project. In L. Waes, M. Leitjen, & C. Neuwirth (Eds.), *Writing and digital media* (pp. 115–129). New York: Elsevier.

Kegan, R. (1982). *The evolving self: Problem and process in human development.* Cambridge, MA: Harvard University Press.

Kegan, R. (1994). *In over our heads: The mental demands of modern life.* Cambridge, MA: Harvard University Press.

Ketcheson, K. (2001). Portland State University's electronic institutional portfolio: Strategy, planning, and assessment. In B. Cambridge (Ed.), *Electronic portfolios: Emerging practices in student, faculty, and institutional learning* (pp. 178–191). Washington, DC: American Association for Higher Education.

Ketcheson, K. (2009). Sustaining change through student, departmental, and institutional portfolios. In D. Cambridge, B. Cambridge, & K. B. Yancey (Eds.), *Electronic portfolios 2.0: Emergent findings and shared questions* (pp. 137–144). Sterling, VA: Stylus.

Kimball, M. (2005). Database e-portfolio systems: A critical appraisal. *Computers and Composition, 22*(4), 434–458.

King, P. M., & Kitchener, K. S. (1994). *Developing reflective judgment.* San Francisco: Jossey-Bass.

Kirkpatrick, J., Renner, T., Kanae, L., & Goya, K. (2009). A values-driven eportfolio journey: Nā wa•a. In D. Cambridge, B. Cambridge, & K. B. Yancey (Eds.), *Electronic portfolios 2.0: Emergent findings and shared questions* (pp. 97–102). Sterling, VA: Stylus.

Kirschner, P. A., Buckingham Shum, S. J., & Carr, C. S. (Eds.). (2003). *Visualizing argumentation: Software tools for collaborative and educational sense-making.* New York: Springer-Verlag.

Kolb, D. A. (1983). *Experiential learning: Experience as the source of learning and development.* Upper Saddle River, NJ: Prentice Hall.

Koper, R., Olivier, B., Anderson, T., Barritt, C., & Campbell, K. (2003). *IMS learning design specification* (Final specification). Lake Mary, FL: IMS Global Learning Consortium.

Koper, R., & Specht, M. (2007). TENCompetence: Life-long competence development and learning. In M. A. Sicilia (Ed.), *Competencies in organizational e-learning: Concepts and tools* (pp. 234–252). Hershey, PA: IGI Global.

Koper, R., & Tattersall, C. (2004). New directions for lifelong learning using network technologies. *British Journal of Educational Technology, 35*(6), 689–700.

Koper, R., & Tattersall, C. (2005). *Learning design: A handbook on modelling and delivering networked education and training.* New York: Springer.

Kuhn, T. (1970). *The structure of scientific revolutions* (2nd ed.). Chicago: University of Chicago Press.

Lahiri, J. (2004). *The namesake: A novel.* Boston: Mariner Books.

Lampe, C., Ellison, N., & Steinfield, C. (2007, April–May). *A familier Face(book): Profile elements as signals in an online social network.* Paper presented at the Computer/Human Interaction Conference, San Jose, CA.

Lasch, C. (1991). *Culture of narcissism: American life in an age of diminishing expectations* (Rev. ed.). New York: Norton.

Latour, B. (1991). *We have never been modern.* Cambridge, MA: Harvard University Press.

Lave, J., & Wenger, E. (1991). *Situated learning: Legitimating peripheral participation.* New York: Cambridge University Press.

Lavik, S., & Nordeng, T. W. (2004, September). *Brainbank learning—Building topic-map based e-portfolios.* Paper presented at the First International Conference on Concept Mapping, Pamplona, Spain.

Lee, H., Smeaton, A. F., O'Connor, N. E., Jones, G., Blighe, M., Byrne, D., et al. (2008). Constructing a sensecam visual diary as a media process. *Multimedia Systems, 14*(6), 341–349.

Lenhart, A. (2009). *Adults and social network websites.* Retrieved from www.pewinternet.org/PPF/r/272/report_display.asp

Lenhart, A., & Fox, S. (2006). *Bloggers.* Retrieved from www.pewinternet.org/Reports/2006/Bloggers.aspx

Lenhart, A., & Madden, M. (2007). *Teens, privacy and online social networks: How teens manage their online identities and personal information in the age of MySpace.* New York: Pew Internet and American Life Project.

Levy, D. M. (2001). *Scrolling forward: Making sense of documents in the digital age.* New York: Arcade.

Liber, O. (2005). *PLE project summary.* Retrieved from http://zope.cetis.ac.uk/members/ple/resources/ple_summary

Lim, M., & Kahn, M. E. (2008). Politics: Deliberation, mobilization, and networked practices of agitation. In K. Varnelis (Ed.), *Networked publics* (pp. 77–108). Cambridge, MA: MIT Press.

Liu, C.-C., Chen, G.-D., Wang, C.-Y., & Lu, C.-F. (2002). Student performance assessment using Bayesian network and Web portfolios. *Journal of Educational Computing Research, 27*(4), 437–469.

Lorenzo, G., & Ittelson, J. (2005). *Demonstrating and assessing student learning with eportfolios.* Boulder, CO: EDUCAUSE Learning Initiative.

MacAlpine, M. (2005). E-portfolios and digital identity: Some issues for discussion. *E-Learning, 2*(4), 378–387.

MacIntyre, A. (2007). *After virtue: A study in moral theory.* South Bend, IN: University of Notre Dame Press.

Maki, P. (2003). *Assessing for learning: Building sustainable commitment across the institution.* Sterling, VA: Stylus.

Mann, S., & Niedzviecki, H. (2001). *Cyborg: Digital destiny and human possibility in the age of the wearable computer.* Scarborough, Ontario: Doubleday Canada.

Manovich, L. (2001). *The language of new media.* Cambrige, MA: MIT Press.

Marshall, A., Grant, S., & Strivens, J. (2005). *Web services for reflective learning.* Bristol, England: Joint Information Systems Committee.

Martin, K. (2002). Portfolio assessment and the Learning Record Online. *Kairos, 7*(3). Retrieved from http://english.ttu.edu/KAIROS/7.3/binder2.html?coverweb/LRO/index.htm

Mason, M. (1980). The other voice: Autobiographies of women writers. In J. Olney (Ed.), *Autobiography: Essays theoretical and critical* (pp. 207–235). Princeton, NJ: Princeton University Press.

McPherson, P., & Shulenburger, D. (2006). *Toward a voluntary system of accountability program (VSA) for public universities and colleges*. Washington, DC: National Association of State Universities and Land-Grant Colleges.

Meeus, W., Petegem, P. V., & Looy, L. V. (2006). Portfolio for higher education: Time for a clarificatory framework. *International Journal of Teaching and Learning in Higher Education, 17*(2), 127–135.

Meijers, F. (1998). The development of a career identity. *International Journal for the Advancement of Counseling, 20*(3), 191–207.

Melman, S. (2001). *After capitalism: From managerialism to workplace democracy*. New York: Knopf.

Mentkowski, M., & Associates. (1999). *Learning that lasts: Integrating learning, development, and performance in college and beyond*. San Francisco: Jossey-Bass.

Miller, C. R. (1984). Genre as social action. *Quarterly Journal of Speech, 70*(2), 151–167.

Miller, C. R., & Shepherd, D. (2004). Blogging as social action: A genre analysis of the weblog. In L. Gurak, S. Antonijevic, L. Johnson, C. Ratliff, & J. Reyman (Eds.), *Into the blogosphere: Rhetoric, community, and culture of weblogs*. Minneapolis: University of Minnesota Press.

Mirvis, P. H., & Hall, D. T. (1994). Psychological success and the boundaryless career. *Journal of Organizational Behavior, 15*(4), 365–380.

Moon, J. (2004). *A handbook of reflective and experiential learning: Theory and practice*. London: RoutledgeFalmer.

Moore, S. (2007). *Spiritual communities—Electronic portfolio*. Retrieved from www.livemoore.com/india/portfolio.html [retrieved March 1, 2008; link no longer active as of 2010].

Moss, P. A. (1994). Can there be validity without reliability? *Educational Researcher, 23*(2), 5–12.

Moss, P. A. (2004). The meaning and consequences of "reliability." *Journal of Educational and Behavioral Statistics, 29*(2), 245–249.

Naeve, A. (2005). The Human Semantic Web: Shifting from knowledge push to knowledge pull. *International Journal of Semantic Web and Information Systems, 1*(3), 1–30.

Naeve, A., Nilsson, M., Palmér, M., & Paulsson, F. (2005). Contributions to a public e-learning platform: Infrastructure, architecture, frameworks and tools. *International Journal of Learning Technology, 1*(3), 352–381.

Nardi, B., Schiano, D. J., Gumbrecht, M., & Swartz, L. (2004). Why we blog. *Communications of the ACM, 47*(2), 41–46.

National Committee of Inquiry into Higher Education. (1997). *Higher education in a learning society*. London: Author.

National Council for Accreditation of Teacher Education. (2001). *Professional standards for accreditation of schools, colleges, and departments of education*. Washington, DC: Author.

National Council of Teachers of English & Council of Writing Program Administrators. (2008). *NCTE-WPA white paper on writing assessment in colleges and universities*. Champaign, IL: Authors.

Nesheim, B. E., Guentzel, M. J., Kellogg, A. H., McDonald, W. M., Wells, C. A., & Whitt, E. J. (2007). Outcomes for students of student affairs–academic affairs partnership programs. *Journal of College Student Development, 48*(4), 435–454.

Nordeng, T. W., Dicheva, D., Garchol, L. M., Ronningsbakk, L., & Meloy, J. R. (2005, October). *Topic maps for integrating eportfolio with ecurriculum*. Paper presented at the Third International ePortfolio Conference, Cambridge, England.

Nordeng, T. W., Guescini, R., & Karabeg, D. (2006). Topic maps for polyscopic structuring of information. *International Journal of Continuing Engineering Education and Life-Long Learning, 16*(1/2), 35–49.

Northouse, P. G. (2007). *Leadership: Theory and practice* (4th ed.). Thousand Oaks, CA: Sage.

Nussbaum, M. C. (1997). *Cultivating humanity: A classical defense of reform in liberal education.* Cambridge, MA: Harvard University Press.

Nyham, B. (2006). Collective reflection for excellence in work organizations: An ethical "community of practice" perspective on reflection. In D. Boud, P. Cressey, & P. Docherty (Eds.), *Productive reflection at work: Learning for change organizations* (pp. 133–145). London: Routledge.

Olsen, L., Schroeder, L., & Wasko, P. (2009). Moving eFolio Minnesota to the next generation: From individual portfolios to an integrated institutional model. In D. Cambridge, B. Cambridge, & K. B. Yancey (Eds.), *Electronic portfolios 2.0: Emergent findings and shared questions* (pp. 165–174). Sterling, VA: Stylus.

Orwell, G. (1983). *1984.* New York: Plume.

Palen, L., & Dourish, P. (2003, April). *Unpacking "privacy" for a networked world.* Paper presented at the SIGCHI Conference on Human Factors in Computing Systems, Fort Lauderdale, FL.

Palmer, P. (2000). *Let your life speak: Listening for the voice of vocation.* San Francisco: Jossey-Bass.

Pea, R. (2006). Video-as-data and digital video manipulation techniques for transforming learning sciences research, education and other cultural practices. In J. Weiss, J. Nolan, & P. Trifonas (Eds.), *International handbook of virtual learning environments* (pp. 1321–1393). Norwell, MA: Kluwer.

Pea, R., Mills, M., Rosen, J., Dauber, K., Effelsberg, W., & Hoffert, E. (2004). Project interactive: Digital video repurposing. *IEEE Multimedia, 11*(1), 54–61.

Peet, M. (2005). *We make the road by walking it: Critical consciousness, structuration, and social change school.* Ann Arbor: Unversity of Michigan.

Penn State University. (2009). *Blogs as portfolio.* Retrieved from http://ets.tlt.psu.edu/wiki/Blogs_as_Portfolio

Perkle, D. (2006). *Copy and paste literacy: Literacy practices in the production of a MySpace profile.* Retrieved from http://people.ischool.berkeley.edu/~dperkel/media/dperkel_literacymyspace.pdf

Perry, W. G. (1998). *Forms of ethical and intellectual development in the college years: A scheme.* San Francisco: Jossey-Bass.

Pink, D. H. (2005). *A whole new mind: Moving from the information age to the conceptual age.* New York: Riverhead Books.

Plater, W. M. (2006). The promise of the student electronic portfolio: A provost's perspective. In A. Jarafi & C. Kaufman (Eds.), *Handbook of research on ePortfolios* (pp. 62–73). Hershey, PA: Idea Group.

Poster, M. (1990). *The mode of information: Poststructuralism and social context.* Cambridge: Polity Press.

Poster, M. (1995). *The second media age.* Cambridge: Polity Press.

Putnam, R. (2000). *Bowling alone: The collapse and revival of American community.* New York: Simon & Schuster.

Ramos, M. C., & Mitchell, C. (2001). Dialogue throughout an organization. In D. Schoem & S. Hurtado (Eds.), *Intergroup dialogue: Deliberative democracy in school, college, community, and workplace* (pp. 210–224). Ann Arbor: University of Michigan Press.

Ravet, S. (2005, May). *Eportfolio for a learning society.* Paper presented at the eLearning Conference, Brussels, Belgium.

Ravet, S. (2006, October). *Estrategies for empowering individuals.* Paper presented at the Fourth International ePortfolio Conference, Oxford, England.

Reich, R. B. (2000). *The future of success: Working and living in the new economy*. New York: Vintage.

Reid, A. (2008). *The two virtuals: New media and composition*. West Lafayette, IN: Parlor Press.

Rhodes, T. L. (2009). The VALUE project overview. *Peer Review, 11*(1), 4–7.

Rhodes, T. L. (Ed.). (2010). *Assessing outcomes and improving achievement: Tips and tools for using rubrics*. Washington, DC: Association of American Colleges and Universities.

Rice, J. E. (2008). Rhetoric's mechanics: Retooling the equipment of writing production. *College Composition and Communication, 60*(2), 366–387.

Rice, R. (2001). Composing the intranet-based electronic portfolio using "common" tools. In B. Cambridge (Ed.), *Electronic portfolios: Emerging practices in student, faculty, and institutional learning* (pp. 37–43). Washington, DC: American Association for Higher Education.

Rickards, W. H., Diez, M. E., Ehley, L., Guilbault, L. F., Loacker, G., Reisetter Hart, J., et al. (2008). Learning, reflection, and electronic portfolios: Stepping toward an assessment practice. *Journal of General Education, 57*(1), 31–50.

Rickards, W. H., & Guilbault, L. (2009). Studying student reflection in an electronic portfolio environment: An inquiry in the context of practice. In D. Cambridge, B. Cambridge, & K. B. Yancey (Eds.), *Electronic portfolios 2.0: Emergent research in implementation and impact* (pp. 17–28). Sterling, VA: Stylus.

Rodriguez, H., & Eklundh, K. S. (2006). Visualizing patterns of annotation in document-centered collaboration on the Web. In L. Waes, M. Leitjen, & C. N. Neuwirth (Eds.), *Writing and digital media* (pp. 131–143). New York: Elsevier.

Rorty, R. (1982). Method, social science, and social hope. In R. Rorty, *Consequences of pragmatism: Essays, 1972–1980* (pp. 191–210). Minneapolis: University of Minnesota Press.

Rose, M. (2004). *The mind at work: Valuing the intelligence of the American worker*. New York: Viking.

Rose, N. (1999). *Powers of freedom: Reframing political thought*. New York: Cambridge University Press.

Rosenfield, I. (1988). *The invention of memory: A new view of the brain*. New York: Basic Books.

Ross, J. A. (2006). The reliability, validity, and utility of self-assessment. *Practical Assessment, Research and Evaluation, 11*(10), 1–13.

Rost, J. C. (1993). *Leadership for the twenty-first century*. Westport, CT: Praeger.

Rousseau, D. M. (1990). New-hire perceptions of their own and their employer's obligations: A study of psychological concepts. *Journal of Organizational Behavior, 11*(5), 389–400.

Russell, R. (1998). Workplace democracy and organizational communication. *Electronic Journal of Communication, 8*(1). Retrieved from www.cios.org/EJCPUBLIC/008/1/00811.HTML

Sandal, M. (1984). The procedural republic and the unencumbered self. *Political Theory, 12*(1), 81–96.

Saunders, L. (1997). Against deliberation. *Political Theory, 25*(3), 347–377.

Schärer, R., Little, D., & Goullier, F. (2004). *A European language portfolio: From piloting to implementation (2001–2004)*. Strasbourg: Council of Europe Language Policy Division.

Schön, D. (1983). *The reflective practitioner: How professionals think in action*. New York: Basic Books.

Seimens, G. (2005). Connectivism: Learning as network creation. *ASTD Learning News, 10*(1). Retrieved from www.elearnspace.org/Articles/networks.htm

Sennett, R. (1998). *The corrosion of character: The personal concequences of work in the new capitalism*. New York: Norton.

Sennett, R. (2006). *The culture of the new capitalism*. New Haven, CT: Yale University Press.

Seong, S.-W., Hangel, S., Brigham, C., Sengupta, D., Bayer, G., Seo, J., et al. (2009, April). *A distributed social-networking infrastructure with personal-cloud butlers.* Paper presented at the World Wide Web Conference, Madrid, Spain.

Shavelson, R. J., Klein, S., & Benjamin, R. (2009). The limitations of portfolios. *Insider Higher Ed.* Retrieved from www.insidehighered.com/views/2009/10/16/shavelson

Shuler, D. (2009). Online civic deliberation with e-liberate. In P. Davies & S. P. Gangadharan (Eds.), *Online deliberation: Design, research, and practice* (pp. 293–302). Stanford, CA: Center for the Study of Language and Information.

Shulman, L. S. (1998). Course anatomy: The dissection and analysis of knowledge through teaching. In P. Hutchings (Ed.), *The course portfolio: How faculty can examine their teaching to advance practice and improve student learning* (pp. 5–12). Washington, DC: American Association for Higher Education.

Sill, D. J. (2001). Integrative thinking, synthesis, and creativity in interdisciplinary studies. *Journal of General Education, 50*(4), 288–311.

Slade, S. (2008a, May). *Close up of two professional eportfolios.* Paper presented at the Conversations on Competence Conference, Montreal, Canada.

Slade, S. (2008b, October). *Eportfolio for immigrants: Modular personal portal supporting lifelong learning.* Paper presented at the ePortfolio and Digital Identity Conference, Maastricht, The Netherlands.

Slade, S., & Otis, Y. (2007, October). *The competence portfolio: Reflection for organizational renewal.* Paper presented at the Fifth International ePortfolio Conference, Maastricht, The Netherlands.

Smallwood, A., & Kingston, S. (2006). *Regional interoperability project on progression for lifelong learning: Final report.* Bristol, England: Joint Information Systems Committee.

Smallwood, A., & Kingston, S. (2007, October). *New vocational pathways and workforce development.* Paper presented at the Fifth International ePortfolio Conference, Maastricht, The Netherlands.

Smith, A. E. (2003, May). *Automatic extraction of semantic networks from text using Leximancer.* Paper presented at the Human Language Technology Conference, Edmonton, Alberta.

Smith, B. L. (1997). Curricular structures for cumulative learning. In J. N. Gardner, G. Van der Veer, & Associates, *The senior year experience: Facilitating integration, reflection, closure, and transition* (pp. 81–94). San Franscico: Jossey-Bass.

Smith, F. (1990). *To think.* New York: Teachers College Press.

Smith, J. (2005). *Project Pad.* Retrieved from http://projectpad.northwestern.edu/ppad2/

Smith, P. (2004). *The quiet crisis: How higher education is failing America.* San Francisco: Jossey-Bass/Anker.

Smith, S. (1993). *Subjectivity, identity, and the body: Women's autobiographical practices in the twentieth century.* Bloomington: Indiana University Press.

Smith, S., & Watson, J. (Eds.). (1996). *Getting a life: Everyday uses of autobiography.* Minneapolis: University of Minnesota Press.

Somerville, M. M., Smith, G., & Macklin, A. S. (2008). The ETS iSkills assessment: A digital age tool. *Electronic Library, 26*(2), 158–171.

Star, S. L., & Griesemer, J. R. (1989). Institutional ecology, "translations" and boundary objects: Amateurs and professionals in Berkeley's Museum of Vertebrate Zoology, 1907–39. *Social Studies of Science, 19*(3), 387–420.

Stefanakis, E. H. (2002). *Multiple intelligences and portfolios: A window into the learner's mind.* Portsmouth, NH: Heinemann.

Stefani, L., Mason, R., & Pegler, C. (2007). *The educational potential of e-portfolios: Supporting personal development and reflective learning.* London: Routledge.

Stephens, B. (2009). E-portfolios in an undergraduate research experiences program. In D. Cambridge, B. Cambridge, & K. B. Yancey (Eds.), *Electronic portfolios 2.0: Emergent research in implementation and impact* (pp. 103–108). Sterling, VA: Stylus.

Stevens, H. (2008). The impact of e-portfolio development on the employability of adults aged 45 and over. *Campus-Wide Information Systems, 25*(4), 209–218.

Stone, D., Patton, B., & Heen, S. (1999). *Difficult conversations: How to discuss what matters most.* New York: Penguin.

Strauss, A., & Corbin, J. (1990). *Basics of qualitative research: Grounded theory procedures and techniques.* Thousand Oaks, CA: Sage.

Sullivan, W. M. (2005). *Work and integrity: The crisis and promise of professionalism in America* (2nd ed.). San Francisco: Jossey-Bass.

Sunstein, C. R. (2006). *Infotopia: How many minds produce knowledge.* New York: Oxford University Press.

Syverson, M. A. (2000). *The learning record.* Retrieved from www.cwrl.utexas.edu/~syverson/olr/

Taylor, C. (1989). *Sources of the self: The making of modern identity.* Cambridge, MA: Harvard University Press.

Taylor, C. (1991). *The ethics of authenticity.* Cambridge, MA: Harvard University Press.

Taylor, C. (1995). The politics of recognition. In A. Gutmann (Ed.), *Multiculturalism: Examining the politics of recognition* (pp. 25–74). Princeton, NJ: Princeton University Press.

Taylor, I., & Burgess, H. (1995). Orientation to self-directed learning: Paradox nor paradigm? *Studies in Higher Education, 20*(1), 87–99.

TENCompetence Foundation. (2008). *Personal competence manager.* Retrieved from www .tencompetence.org/web/guest/overview;jsessionid=7402A322653B01B95C4EDEEB5F D4687F

Thaiss, C., & Zawacki, T. M. (2006). *Engaged writers and dynamic disciplines: Research on the academic writing life.* Portsmouth, NH: Boynton/Cook.

Tosh, D., Werdmuller, B., Chen, H. L., Light, T. P., & Haywood, J. (2006). The learning landscape: A conceptual framework for eportfolios. In A. Jafari & C. Kaufman (Eds.), *Handbook of research on ePortfolios* (pp. 24–32). Hershey, PA: Idea Group.

Treuer, P., & Jenson, J. D. (2003). Electronic portfolios need standards to thrive. *EDUCAUSE Quarterly, 26*(2), 34–42.

Tufts Academic Technology Services. (2008). *Virtual understanding environment.* Retrieved from http://vue.tccs.tufts.edu/

Ulmer, G. (1989). *Teletheory.* New York: Routledge.

Ulmer, G. (2003). *Internet invention: From literacy to electracy.* New York: Longman.

University of Illinois Urbana–Champaign. (2009). *Software environment for the advancement of scholarly research.* Retrieved from http://seasr.org/documentation/

U.S. Department of Education. (2006). *A test of leadership: Charting the future of U.S. higher education.* Washington, DC: Author.

Vervenne, L. (2007, October). *Competency workgroup.* Paper presented at the HR-XML Consortium Europe Conference, Maastricht, The Netherlands.

Vervenne, L. (2008, October). *Towards a crossroads bank for employability data exchange: The digital repository approach.* Paper presented at the ePortfolio and Digital Identity Conference, Maastricht, The Netherlands.

Vervenne, L., & Mensen, T. (2006, October). *3portfolio: The Nedcar/MCA employability challenge.* Paper presented at the Fourth International ePortfolio Conference, Oxford, England.

Waldron, J. (2002). Is the rule of law an essentially contested concept (in Florida)? *Law and Philosophy, 21*(2), 137–164.

Wei, C. (2004). Formation of norms in a blog community. In L. Gurak, S. Antonijevic, L. Johnson, C. Ratliff, & J. Reyman (Eds.), *Into the blogosphere: Rhetoric, community, and culture of weblogs*. Minneapolis: University of Minnesota Press.

Weigel, V. (2001). *Deep learning for a digital age: Technology's untapped potential to enrich higher education*. San Francisco: Jossey-Bass.

Wenger, E. (1998). *Communities of practice: Learning, meaning, and identity*. New York: Cambridge University Press.

Wertsch, J. (1985). *Vygotsky and the social formation of mind*. Cambridge, MA: Harvard University Press.

Wexler, J. G. (2001). The role of institutional portfolios in the revised WASC accreditation process. In B. Cambridge (Ed.), *Electronic portfolios: Emerging practices in student, faculty, and institutional learning* (pp. 209–216). Washington, DC: American Association for Higher Education.

Wiggins, G., & McTiche, J. (1998). *Understanding by design*. Alexandria, VA: Association for Supervision and Curriculum Development.

Wilcock, A. A. (1999). Reflections on doing, being and becoming. *Australian Occupational Therapy Journal, 46*(1), 1–11.

Wilkerson, J. R., & Lang, W. S. (2003). Portfolios, the Pied Piper of teacher certification assessments: Legal and psychometric issues. *Education Policy Analysis Archives, 11*(45). Retrieved from http://epaa.asu.edu/ojs/article/viewFile/273/399

Williams, B. (2004). *Truth and truthfulness: An essay in genealogy*. Princeton, NJ: Princeton University Press.

Williams, J. (2002). The engineering portfolio: Communication, reflection, and student learning outcomes assessment. *International Journal of Engineering Education, 18*(2), 199–207.

Wills, S. (2008, February). *Eportfolio practice: Current issues and future needs*. Paper presented at the Australian ePortfolio Symposium, Brisbane.

Wilson, S. (2005). *PowerPoint [and Flickr] slides on eportfolios*. Retrieved from http://zope.cetis.ac.uk/members/scott/blogview?entry=20050523083528

Yancey, K. B. (1998). *Reflection in the writing classroom*. Logan: Utah State University Press.

Yancey, K. B. (2004a). Postmodernism, palimpest, and portfolios: Theoretical issues in the representation of student work. *College Composition and Communication, 55*(4), 731–767.

Yancey, K. B. (2004b). *Teaching literature as reflective practice*. Champaign, IL: National Council of Teachers of English.

Yancey, K. B., & Weiser, I. (1997). Situating portfolios: An introduction. In K. B. Yancey & I. Weiser (Eds.), *Situating portfolios: Four perspectives* (pp. 1–20). Logan: Utah State University Press.

Yerxa, E. J. (1994). Dreams, dilemmas, and decisions for occupational therapy practice in a new millennium: An American perspective. *American Journal of Occupational Therapy, 48*(7), 586–589.

Young, C. (2009). The MAED English education electronic portfolio experience: What pre-service English teachers have to teach us about EP's and reflection. In D. Cambridge, B. Cambridge, & K. B. Yancey (Eds.), *Electronic portfolios 2.0: Emergent research in implementation and impact* (pp. 181–192). Sterling, VA: Stylus.

Young, I. M. (1996). Communication and the other: Beyond deliberative democracy. In S. Benhabib (Ed.), *Democracy and difference: Contesting the boundaries of the political* (pp. 67–94). Princeton, NJ: Princeton University Press.

Young, I. M. (2002). *Inclusion and democracy*. New York: Oxford University Press.

INDEX